Violence against Women in Families and Relationships

Violence against Women in Families and Relationships

Volume 3
Criminal Justice and the Law

Edited by
Evan Stark and Eve S. Buzawa

Praeger Perspectives

Praeger

An Imprint of ABC-CLIO, LLC

A B C CLIO

Santa Barbara, California • Denver, Colorado • Oxford, England

Library of Congress Cataloging-in-Publication Data
Violence against women in families and relationships /
edited by Evan Stark and Eve S. Buzawa.
    v. ; cm.
  Includes index.
  Contents: vol. 1. Victimization and the community response —
vol. 2. The family context — vol. 3. Criminal justice and the law —
vol. 4. The media and cultural attitudes.
    ISBN 978-0-275-99846-2 (set : alk. paper) — ISBN 978-0-275-99848-6
(vol. 1) — ISBN 978-0-275-99850-9 (vol. 2) — ISBN 978-0-275-99852-3
(vol. 3) — ISBN 978-0-275-99854-7 (vol. 4) — ISBN 978-0-275-99847-9 (ebook)
    1. Abused women. 2. Family violence. I. Stark, Evan.
II. Buzawa, Eva Schlesinger.
  HV6626.V56 2009
  362.82'92—dc22   2009006262

13 12 11 10 9   1 2 3 4 5

This book is also available on the World Wide Web as an eBook.
Visit www.abc-clio.com for details.

ABC-CLIO, LLC
130 Cremona Drive, P.O. Box 1911
Santa Barbara, California 93116-1911

This book is printed on acid-free paper ∞

Manufactured in the United States of America

Contents

Set Introduction
Evan Stark and Eve S. Buzawa   vii

Introduction to Volume 3
Eve S. Buzawa   xix

Chapter 1: The Real Crime of Domestic Violence
               Deborah Tuerkheimer   1

Chapter 2: Battered Women Who Fight Back against
               Their Abusers
               Leigh Goodmark   23

Chapter 3: Women's Use of Violence with Male
               Intimate Partners
               Suzanne C. Swan, Jennifer E. Caldwell, Tami P. Sullivan,
               and David L. Snow   47

Chapter 4: Evolution of the Police Response to Domestic Violence
               Eve S. Buzawa and David Hirschel   69

Chapter 5: The Prosecution of Domestic Violence
               across Time
               Christopher D. Maxwell, Amanda L. Robinson,
               and Andrew R. Klein   91

Chapter 6: Offenders and the Criminal Justice System
               Andrew Klein   115

Chapter 7: Abusers' Narratives Following Arrest and Prosecution
               for Domestic Violence
               Keith Guzik   137

Chapter 8:   Programs for Men Who Batter
                Daniel G. Saunders   161

Chapter 9:   Batterer Programs and Beyond
                Michael Rempel   179

Chapter 10: Why Sex and Gender Matter in Domestic
                Violence Research and Advocacy
                Molly Dragiewicz   201

Index   217

About the Editors and Contributors   225

Set Introduction

Evan Stark and Eve S. Buzawa

The first call for shelter in the United States was made to Women's Advocates in St. Paul, Minnesota one afternoon in May 1972. The story of this group of courageous women opens *Violence against Women in Families and Relationships*. As recalled by Sharon Vaughan, a founder of the program and a pioneer in the battered-women's movement:

> The call was ... from Emergency Social Services. A worker said a woman was at the St. Paul Greyhound bus station with a two-year-old child. To get a job, she had traveled 150 miles from Superior, Wisconsin, with two dollars in her pocket. What were we expected to do? Where would they stay after two days at the Grand Hotel? One of the advocates borrowed a high chair and stroller and we took them to the apartment that was our office. These were the first residents we sheltered. The two-year-old destroyed the office in one night because all the papers were stacked on low shelves held up by bricks. His mother didn't talk about being battered; she said she wanted to go to secretarial school to make a life for her and her son. She tried to get a place to live, but no one would rent to her without a deposit, which she didn't have.... After a couple of weeks, she went back to Superior, and every Christmas for several years sent a card thanking Women's Advocates for being there and enclosed $2.00, the amount she had when she came to town.

This recollection captures several major themes highlighted in volume 1: the importance of women reaching out to other women, the reinforcing effects of poverty and domestic violence, and the extent to which those who escape abuse are intent on reconnecting with their hopes and dreams for a better life.

The shelter started in St. Paul was one stimulus for a domestic violence revolution that quickly circled the globe, stirring women from all walks of life, of all races, religions, and ages, and in thousands of neighborhoods, to challenge men's age-old prerogative to do with them as they willed. Even as these grassroots movements offered victims options for safety and empowerment that were never before available, they called on their governments to do the same. Importantly, these calls elicited an unprecedented response, almost certainly because women had become a formidable political and economic force. In its scope and significance, the domestic violence revolution is a watershed event in our lifetime.

On the ground, the domestic violence revolution consists of four critical components: the proliferation of community-based services for battered women; a growing sensitivity to how domestic violence affects families and particularly the children who are exposed to this violence; the criminalization of domestic violence and the corresponding mobilization of a range of state resources to protect abused women and their children and to arrest, sanction, or counsel perpetrators; and challenges to the normative values that have allowed men to exercise illegitimate forms of power and control in relationships and families. Although huge obstacles remain to changing cultural mores, these challenges now extend to the popular media, which shape how tens of millions of children and adults interpret the world around them.

Violence against Women in Families and Relationships takes stock of the seismic changes instigated by the domestic violence revolution, devoting separate volumes to its major components: community-based services (Volume 1), the family (Volume 2), the criminal justice response (Volume 3), and popular culture and the media (Volume 4). In addition to describing what happened, two overriding questions link these volumes. How is our world different today than when the domestic violence revolution began? Are abused women and their children better off because of these changes? We also identify the remaining obstacles to eliminating sexual injustice in relationships and families, ask what can be done to remove these obstacles, and identify a host of innovative programs designed to do this. The major conceptual contribution of these volumes is to provide an understanding of abuse that extends far beyond physical violence to the broad range of tactics actually used to coerce and control women and children in relationships.

THE DOMESTIC VIOLENCE REVOLUTION

Our goal is to provide a map of the scope and significance of the domestic violence revolution.

Since the opening and diffusion of shelters, the policies and the legal landscape affecting victims of partner abuse have changed dramatically. Reforms include billions of dollars in federal support for intervention, removing discretion in deciding whether to arrest those who assault their partners, a range of new protections for victims, the burgeoning of a vast network of researchers, specialized and integrated domestic violence courts and prosecutorial approaches (called "dedi-cated" or "evidence based"), one-stop justice centers, and putting part-ner abuse center stage in decisions about custody and visitation. In the past, battered women who retaliated against abusive partners hid their abuse, fearing it would provide a motive for their crimes. Today, women accused of crimes against abusive partners can use a "battered woman's defense" and call on a new class of experts to support their claims of victimization. The constitutional rationale for these reforms in the United States is straightforward: under the Equal Protection Clause of the Fourteenth Amendment, women assaulted by present or former partners are entitled to the same rights and protections as those who are assaulted by strangers. In other countries, domestic violence has been identified as violation of basic human rights.

The helping professions have also undergone radical changes in response to the domestic violence revolution. Medicine, nursing, public health, psychology, psychiatry, social work, and child welfare have intro-duced a range of innovative programs to identify and respond more appropriately to the adult and child victims of abuse. Forty years ago, when Anne Flitcraft asked the director of the emergency medical services at Yale–New Haven Hospital if she could study "battered women" for her medical school thesis, he was puzzled. "What's a battered woman?" he asked. Today, in part as a result of pioneering research by Dr. Flitcraft and hundreds of other scholars, training in the health, mental health, legal, and social service professions would be remiss if it did not include specialized units on domestic violence. Every major health care organization has made domestic violence a priority. Hundreds of hospitals in the United States have protocols requiring that medical personnel identify and refer victims of abuse. In hundreds of communities, once perpetrators are arrested, they are offered counseling as an alternative to jail through "batterer interven-tion programs." Moreover, several thousand localities now host collabora-tive efforts to reduce or prevent abuse in which community-based services such as shelters join with courts, law enforcement, local businesses, child protection agencies, and a range of health, education, and service organi-zations. In dozens of communities, small and large businesses alike have taken initiatives to extend protections from abusive partners to employees or supported broader community-based initiatives.

Never before has such an array of resources and interventions been brought to bear on abuse or oppression in relationships and families. By any conventional standard, the domestic violence revolution has been an incredible success. Politicians across a broad spectrum have embraced its core imagery of male violence and female victimization. As telling is an increasing sensitivity to the portrayal of abused women by the mass media and a growing awareness of how mainstream mes-sages conveyed by sports, popular music, and other cultural media con-tribute to abusive behavior by males.

Hundreds of thousands of men, women, and children owe the fact that they are alive to the availability of shelters, to criminal justice and legal reforms, and to equally important shifts in research, health services, and popular culture. Just recently, historically speaking, a man's use of coercion to chastise or discipline his female partner or his children was widely considered a right inherited with his sex. This is no longer so.

In 1977, during one of the many incidents when Mickey Hughes assaulted his wife Francine, their 12-year-old daughter Christy called police. He threatened to kill Francine with police present. This seemed like "idle talk," an officer testified at Francine's trial for murder. "He hadn't killed her before; he wouldn't do so now." A few hours after they left, Francine set fire to the bed in which her husband was sleeping and he was fatally burned.

Things have changed dramatically since 1977. Mickey was never arrested, though he had raped Francine on several occasions and assaulted her dozens of times. Not until 1979, as the result of lawsuits in Oakland, California, and New York, were police required to replace their "arrest-avoidance" strategy, respond quickly to domestic violence calls, and presumptively arrest whenever they had probable cause to believe a felonious assault had occurred or when a misdemeanor assault was committed in their presence. Marital rape was still not a crime in 1977, and in New York and a number of other states was not even considered grounds for divorce. In several states, Francine could have gotten an injunction, though police had no role in enforcing these orders, and only if she was married, and only pursuant to a divorce.

Farrah Fawcett portrayed Francine in a TV film version of this story, *The Burning Bed*. In the mid-1990s, when her boyfriend slammed Fawcett to the ground and choked her after an argument at a restaurant, he was arrested, tried, and convicted. By this time, the marriage-rape exemption was largely abolished, police in most areas were mandated to arrest perpetrators whom they believed had committed a domestic violence crime, and courts in most countries were routinely providing a range of protections for abuse victims. On the two occasions that Francine left Mickey to return to her parents, he stalked and harassed her without consequence. Today, stalking is a crime and harassment is widely recognized as a facet of abuse. Aside from her family, Francine had no recourse, no shelter to enter, and no support services. A woman faced with a burning-bed situation today would mount a "battered woman's defense" rather than plead "temporary insanity," as Francine did. The forces of law and order that protected a man's right to "physically correct" his wife in 1977 now target this bastion of male authority for destruction.

Perhaps the most significant change that resulted from the domestic violence revolution involves the portrayal of male violence against women in the media, particularly in film and on TV, the ultimate family medium. As women made unprecedented gains in economic, political, and cultural status after 1960, the hazards that men pose to their wives and girlfriends became a moral compass for the integrity of relationships generally. From Johannesburg to Caracas, from Jerusalem to Dayton, Ohio, young girls understand that no male has the right to lay his hands on them if they do not want him to do so. Well into the 1980s, violence continued to be glamorized as the penultimate test of manhood (the ultimate test remains sexual conquest), as illustrated by the popularity of gangsta rap and *James Bond* and *Rambo* films. But male violence has increasingly been forced to share the stage with images of women as equally capable of using force and of abusive men as purposeful, obsessive, and cruel rather than romantic. Julia Roberts' portrayal of a housewife who kills an abusive husband who is stalking her in *Sleeping with the Enemy* (1991) contrasts sharply with Eleanor Parker's role in the 1955 film *The Man with the Golden Arm* as a wife who sets out to heal her husband (played by Frank Sinatra) while enduring his physical abuse, betrayal, heroin addiction, and mental torment.

Partner violence against women is no longer "just life." And yet, anyone with reasonable sympathies and a passing acquaintance with abuse or current interventions will have a range of questions about the impact of even the most dramatic reforms.

VICTIMIZATION AND THE COMMUNITY RESPONSE

Volume 1 reviews the development, operations, and effectiveness of battered women's programs; the progress of intervention in health; and the interplay of domestic violence with race, poverty, sexual identity, and the changing economic landscape of communities caused by globalization. The core questions addressed in this volume are as follows: what do battered women's programs actually do? Has the "success" of the shelter movement led it to compromise its original ideals? Is the support that advocates provide sufficient to help victims regain their footing? To what extent does help "help"? Or does it actually make things worse by blaming victims for their abuse? Does the medical system need to look beyond physical violence to improve its response? What special problems face lesbian victims of abuse? What unique dynamics are put into play in the experience of abuse by the disadvantages associated with poverty, racism, or deindustrialization? How must intervention change to accommodate these dynamics? Where do we go from here?

THE FAMILY CONTEXT

Volume 2 looks at the ways in which domestic violence shapes family dynamics in general and affects children in particular and at the two major systems responsible for managing these effects: the child welfare system and the family court. How are children threatened by domestic violence and coercive control? Domestic violence is the most common background factor for child abuse and neglect, and it is typically the same man who is abusing the mother who is the source of harm to children. After much prodding, the child welfare system began to address domestic violence. But its first steps were missteps. Instead of protecting mothers and their children, the child welfare system punished them for being beaten. Why did this happen, and what can be done to correct this problem? Family courts have also been pressured to consider domestic violence in custody and divorce cases. But are they doing so? How can the family court reconcile concerns for the safety of women and their children in abusive relationships with the widespread belief that children must have access to both parents after divorce? To what extent are each of the systems confronted by victims of battering and their children sending contradictory messages that do as much to confuse and further entrap them as to provide for their safety? What reforms are needed to set child welfare and family court systems on the right track? And what about the offending fathers? How do they extend their abusive strategies during custody disputes? And what about the movement for "father's rights"? Is it a positive or negative force in this process? Can offending men learn to father more appropriately? How does working with them on fathering affect how they understand and treat the women in their lives? What is at the root of the problems with these systems? Are we dealing primarily with individual bias or something more systemic? How would broadening our understanding of abuse to include the multiple ways in which men subjugate their partners enhance the child welfare or family court response?

CRIMINAL JUSTICE AND THE LAW

From the start, the domestic violence revolution in the United States called on the state to mobilize its justice resources to protect victims and hold offenders accountable for their acts, usually through some combination of arrest, incarceration, and/or reeducation. Volume 3 reviews the revolutionary changes in policy, criminal law, and policing affected by the domestic violence revolution. Severe violence against wives had been against the law for centuries. But it was only in the 1980s, as states passed domestic violence laws and made arrest mandatory in abuse cases, that police, prosecutors, and the criminal courts treated it as a crime. How are these reforms working? Has the domestic violence revolution relied too heavily on criminal justice? Have the changes in policing, prosecution, and criminal law gone too far or not far enough? Are abusive men changed by arrest? Does counseling for batterers work, and, if so, with what kinds of men? How should we understand and respond to partner violence by women or to families in which both partners are abusive?

THE MEDIA AND CULTURAL ATTITUDES

However much the domestic violence revolution may have reformed the helping and justice professions, these changes are unlikely to endure unless the underlying cultural supports for domestic violence are displaced. Prevailing cultural norms reproduce the sex stereotypes that underlie sexual inequality even as women win formal legal equality and make unprecedented gains in education, income, and political participation. Volume 4 maps how these stereotypes are represented and challenged in a range of cultural media, including newspapers, film, women's magazines, video games, and rap. After explaining how the core narratives in a culture shape experience, the chapters in this volume consider what the stories told about sexual violence in these media suggest about how and why violence against women happens; who or what causes it; whether it is the by-product of specific social factors, malevolence, or just "bad luck" for instance; and how it can be ended. How these stories are constructed is as important as what they say. This volume considers the transformative potential of the media, including theater, as well as the role they play in reinforcing the status quo. The closing chapter considers whether community values have, in fact, changed over the course of the domestic violence revolution.

WHAT YOU'LL FIND HERE

An estimated 13,000 books and monographs about domestic violence have appeared since the early 1970s. Digesting and translating this published material are obviously beyond our capacity. Nevertheless, we started this project by scouring this literature for the major trends and cutting-edge ideas about abuse. Next, we reached out to both established scholars as well as to younger researchers doing cutting-edge work. We asked these writers to do three things: tell us *what* has changed; tell us *how* these changes have affected families, particularly the women, children, and men most immediately involved; and speculate about *what is next*. Where are we likely to go, and where *should* we go from here? We welcomed criticism of existing approaches. We are not pushing a particular cause. But if there are new approaches, innovative practices, or changes in policy that would help set things right, we wanted readers to know about them. And we insisted they write for educated readers who have little or no prior knowledge of the subject, not always an easy thing for scholars whose main audiences tend to consist of academics like themselves. The model we suggested was a feature article for the Sunday newspaper. Think of yourself as the expert you are, we told them. This meant limiting notes to direct quotations and controversial statistics. We gave the contributors the option of directing readers to further information likely to be available on the Web or at a public library. Frankly, this charge posed an editorial challenge we had not anticipated.

One might think that summarizing the wealth of research on violence in families would be sufficient. Not so. One of the most insidious characteristics of the type of oppression we address in personal life is that it typically occurs "behind closed doors" and proceeds in ways that are often hidden from outsiders, often including close friends, neighbors, coworkers, and helping professionals. Researchers too have little direct access to victims or offenders and typically meet them or hear their stories only after they call police, come to court, or enter a shelter. Since whether victims report what is happening to them is largely a function of the opportunity to do so as well as the fear of possible consequences, millions of battered women and their children have no contact with police, shelters, courts, hospitals, or child welfare and so never appear in the public spaces where data are collected. Telephone surveys pick up some of this hidden abuse. But the questions asked on surveys are too broad to capture its meaning, contexts, dynamics, or far-reaching consequences. We were less interested in generalities about abuse than in the nuances, the particulars. We are not after sensationalism. But we wanted readers to know battered women as people, to walk in their shoes to some extent, as well as read *about* them. Another problem is that researchers can ask questions only about things they already know are present. A key theme in these volumes is that the images of violence and physical injury that have dominated our understanding of abuse miss an underlying reality of coercion and control in these relationships that can be as devastating as assault and is almost always more salient for victims. The harms caused by these coercive and controlling tactics are rarely recognized, let alone documented, even among those who are able to get help. The fact that so many of those affected are poor or from disadvantaged groups also contributes to their invisibility.

To unlock the knowledge contained in what Yale University political scientist James Scott calls the "hidden transcripts" of these lives, it is necessary to listen directly to the voices of women and children who experience battering as well as to their abusive partners. This means allowing them to tell their stories as they were lived rather than as filtered through the preconceptions we all bring to the field, ourselves included. In addition to chapters that summarize what is known about particular aspects of interpersonal violence, therefore, we have called on practitioners who work or have worked directly with victims, perpetrators, and their children in a variety of settings. A number of the practitioners herein have helped to design or implement imaginative programs. We include authors who have started or worked in shelters, facilitated batterer intervention programs, trained child welfare workers, and directed a state coalition for battered women. We have several chapters by lawyers who have represented battered women and their children in family and criminal courts and other chapters by forensic psychologists and social workers. Several of our authors have translated their research into practice. In a chapter in volume 4, anthropology professor Elaine J. Lawless describes a theater project she started with a colleague and some students at the University of Missouri. Professor Lawless had conducted fieldwork for a book at a battered women's shelter in her community. Feeling dissatisfied with a purely academic presentation of her "findings," she helped students perform the stories she had collected as monologues to stimulate a broad, community-wide discussion about abuse. The presentations not only gave audiences a picture of the abuse going on around them but also opened up a space in which student actors and audience members could tell their own stories about abuse, some of which became part of subsequent "performances," creating a community of witnesses that enhanced the overall safety of women and children in that neighborhood.

A basic premise of the shelter movement is that those who are battered by their partners are the only real "experts" on their experience and that their expertise is the centerpiece of any real knowledge about how abuse unfolds. We have tried to respect this view by interspersing the informational chapters with chapters that rely heavily on women's stories or explain why "storying" domestic violence is so important. If we have succeeded, the topical chapters should dovetail with lived experiences of abuse. Like the Missouri theater project, we hope these volumes help stimulate a broad-ranging conversation and new ways of seeing, listening to, and interpreting what is happening in our midst.

These volumes also have an international dimension, though it is unfortunately limited to English-speaking countries. We include writers from England, Canada, Scotland, and Australia. The authors of these chapters have done groundbreaking work in their particular areas for which there was often no parallel in the United States. For example, the report on child homicides prepared by Hilary Saunders on behalf of Women's Aid Federation England (WAFE) is a stunning model of advocacy that has elicited family court reforms that are long overdue in the United States. But the international focus also reflects the fact that both the grassroots women's movements in these countries and the systemic changes they elicited have grown from a continuing interchange between researchers and practitioners in these nations.

In each of the respects outlined above, this set of volumes is unique—in its breadth, its mix of researchers and practitioners, the emphasis on victim voices, the attempt to weigh changes in popular culture, its international scope, and its focus on what lies ahead.

But our approach will not satisfy everyone.

Most of us initially got involved in the domestic violence field because we hoped to call attention to and ameliorate the injustices suffered by millions of women and children who were being subjugated in their relationships, mainly (but not only) by male partners, and because we found the response to this suffering by the courts, police, hospitals, and other institutions woefully inadequate. From this vantage, behavior is seen as abusive and as meriting public concern if it involves coercive and/or controlling behavior whose primary intent and/or consequence is to hurt, threaten, frighten, or control a partner. Notice the broad understanding of abuse.

From the day we welcomed the first victims to our shelters, our strongest feelings of sympathy and anger were elicited by the physical scars caused by their partner's violence. Even though many women insisted that the "violence wasn't the worst part," hinting at a yet-to-be-identified range of tactics used by their partners that they found even more hurtful than physical abuse, it was the woman's bruised face or broken bones that held our attention as well as the media's.

We now know that abuse is limited to physical and psychological abuse in only a minority of cases, somewhere between 20 and 40 percent. In the rest, the vast majority, forms of coercion such as violence, threats, or stalking are combined with a pattern of control that can include tactics to isolate victims; restrict their access to money, food, transportation, medical care, or other basic necessities; and microregulate their everyday activities, such as how they dress, cook, clean, talk on the phone or relate to their children. This pattern, known as coercive control, is referred to repeatedly throughout the volumes and is the major focus of chapters by Stark (volume 2), Lischick (volume 2), and Turkheimer (volume 3). Because the aim of coercive control is to limit a victim's resources as well as their opportunities to escape, it greatly heightens women's risk of being seriously injured or killed as well as of developing a range of medical, behavioral, and mental health problems. But the major consequence of being subjected to this strategy over time is that victims become entrapped. Their autonomy is compromised, and their basic liberties protected by the U.S. Constitution are abrogated, such as the right to free speech, their freedom of movement, and their right to make decisions about their bodies. Many of the rights that are violated by coercive control are so tightly woven into the fabric of everyday life that they are rarely protected explicitly (such as the right to cook, clean, dress, or toilet as they wish) and have to be inferred as rights by our general right to pursue our lives as we please. While women frequently assault male and female partners, coercive control appears to be largely committed by men against female partners. Of the estimated 15 million U.S. women who are battered, somewhere between 8 and 12 million are victims of coercive control.

If our major focus is on the use of violence in these relationships despite our broad definition and on the provision of safety, this is because of the appalling consequence of violence for the women who seek help and because most research and almost all interventions are designed in response to domestic violence, not coercive control. But even here, it is not violence per se that concerns us, but coercion used in the context of inequality, coercion that exploits and strengthens existing disadvantages.

Our framework will make at least two groups unhappy. A significant minority of researchers in the domestic violence field morally opposes the use of violence in any form in families or relationships and believe that trying to distinguish the use of force by its motive, context, or consequence or by the relative standing of its victims expresses a personal bias. To this group, couples who use force during fights among relative equals are as wrong to do so as is the man whose violence is unilaterally designed to quash his partner's autonomy. So committed are many in this group to a vision of families and intimate relationships as nonviolent spaces of cooperation that they oppose a vigorous police response in any but the most extreme cases, favoring couples counseling and other forms of conflict resolution instead. This group also holds that women's use of force with their partners is as significant a matter of public concern as men's use of force, even though the probability of injury is far greater to victimized women in these situations; women are far more likely to report being threatened or controlled by abuse than men and they are far more likely to seek or require outside help. Another group will also be unhappy with us. This group opposes vigorous state intervention in abuse less because of its devotion to the family than because they worry that inviting the state into people's personal lives will ultimately do more harm than good, no matter the rationale. This group is willing to accept a wide range of controlling and physically hurtful behavior in relationships to preserve privacy.

We are concerned with preserving and protecting physical integrity at all levels of relationships. But we hope this set helps shift attention from the sheer physical violations caused by abuse to the ways in which coercion and control are used to deny persons their rights and liberties in personal life. However imperfectly they may do so, we believe that governments have an obligation to address these harms and with the same commitment they bring to stemming harms in public life.

Many of those who pick up these volumes will undoubtedly do so because they have experienced abuse in their own lives or known someone who has. As several of the authors eloquently report, the forms of violence, intimidation, isolation, humiliation, and "control" that excite much of the help sought by women who have been battered by partners are closer in their dynamic to hostage taking than to what we normally think of as assault. Except, of course, these victims are "hostages at home"; they have been prisoners in their personal lives. It is easy to be depressed by the statistics and descriptions presented in these pages or to become cynical about the willingness of humans to inflict cruelty even on those they supposedly care for.

But we ask readers to also consider this: that the women who populate these pages have survived to tell their own stories. And many women and children subjected to abuse have done more than merely survive, as Hilary Abrahams illustrates in volume 1 in her record of women who have left shelter: "I sometimes feel like a spring flower." Some elements of women's stories may elicit pity; other details we provide about abuse may provoke anger, even outrage, as they should. Clearly, no community can be truly whole or free so long as one group is allowed to use the means of coercion and control to subjugate others, whether sex or some other factor is the basis for this practice. Once we know such crimes are occurring in our midst, we cannot turn away. But in addition to our protection and concern, the women in these volumes deserve our respect and admiration because of the courage, strength of character, and resolve required to survive the forms of oppression they faced.

We have recently completed a presidential race in which one of the candidates was justly celebrated for his ordeal as a POW (prisoner of war) during the Vietnam War. To those of us who have worked in this field, it is absolutely clear that resisting, standing up to, or even just surviving coercive control is often comparable to the heroism exhibited by returning POWs. If only as a token, we offer these volumes in lieu of a public monument to those who have survived the horrors of personal life. And there is a larger lesson too. Once we appreciate what the women here have accomplished, we see that each of us may be capable of remaking the world we are given, even against what may seem at first impossible odds.

The final justification for this set is that our society has invested billions of dollars and hundreds of millions of human service hours in managing the domestic violence in our midst. Apart from the unprecedented commitment of resources to protect women and children and hold perpetrators accountable are the enormous costs of not effectively addressing abuse in families and relationships. We have made a huge investment in ending an age-old form of injustice. Readers deserve an accounting.

Introduction to Volume 3

Eve S. Buzawa

Volume 3 in *Violence against Women in Families and Relationships* examines the background, current status, and potential for change of the criminal justice system's response to crimes involving domestic violence. Written from a variety of disciplinary perspectives and by practitioners as well as academics, these chapters place the criminalization of domestic violence in its historical context and assess the strengths and limitations of an approach dominated by the requirements of the criminal justice system. Topics considered include landmark domestic violence legislation, how the police response is influenced by the organization and culture of policing, the dimensions and dilemmas created by women's violence, the prosecutorial and court response, how programs for offenders operate and whether they succeed, and what research on offenders implies for reforming the legal and criminal justice response.

Violence against women has been socially sanctioned since ancient times. While there are significant variations in how societies have responded to domestic violence over time, the right of the male patriarch to use violence to enforce his will on the women and children under his control has gone largely unchallenged by government, law, and the major religions.

This historical precedent points to the two realities that underlie the chapters in this volume: that modern society could rely on neither inherited legal nor cultural norms to combat abuse and that addressing abuse as criminal conduct required shifting the normative basis for the societal response as well as changing the substance of the legal and criminal justice response. It was the notion that persons who use force to control family members should be excluded from their society that was culturally "deviant." Some of the problems that authors identify with the current response to domestic violence reflect the constraints inherent in any attempt to manage social problems through law and criminal justice. But affecting change in behavior widely viewed as a natural birthright poses unique challenges that would limit the efficacy of even the best-designed interventions and policies.

The domestic violence revolution that incited this set is approaching its fourth decade. Yet, despite these decades of research, public discussion, and an active legislative effort to develop explicit statutory definitions, fundamental controversies continue regarding the definition of domestic violence. There are societal definitions, legal definitions, and research definitions—all of which differ.

It is in the face of these continuing controversies that the criminal justice system has undergone dramatic change from its traditional response of benign neglect. In fact, the criminal justice system has altered its response more dramatically to this offense than it has to any other single crime. The growing recognition that domestic violence is a crime, not just a "personal" or family problem, has set in motion a number of innovations designed to radically alter how law, criminal justice, and related agencies respond to domestic violence.

Unfortunately, these changes were preceded by decades of acknowledged neglect. Pressures from battered women's advocates and their feminist allies, highly publicized research, lawsuits holding police liable for failing to protect victims of domestic violence, and financial incentives linked to domestic violence legislation combined to support the criminalization of domestic violence. With the emergence of a new pro-arrest consensus, the traditional policy of nonintervention lost credibility, at least officially.

The first chapter in this volume discusses how the ambiguities that surround how we understand domestic violence have hindered the efficacy of new legislation. People are generally aware of the unprecedented wave of domestic violence statutes implemented in all 50 states as well as of supporting federal legislation. However, as law professor Deborah Tuerkheimer argues, there is a huge gap between the specific violent acts the new laws define as criminal and their implicit acceptance of a range of behaviors that comprise the complex totality of domestic violence as it is known and experienced by victims. She argues that while reforms in the criminal justice system focus on improved enforcement of existing statutes, it is the laws themselves that are fatally flawed and in need of major reform. She identifies a range of offenses that constitute "domestic violence" but that fall outside the purview of most new criminal statutes. Professor Tuerkheimer highlights the disparity between the view of domestic violence as an ongoing pattern of behavior held by most social scientists in the field and the focus of police, prosecutors, and the courts on sporadic violence and discrete illegal acts viewed in isolation. Because of its narrow purview, the legal system often fails to recognize, let alone appreciate, the significance of the typical pattern of repeated, if relatively minor, violence and so cannot address coercive control and other nonphysical acts of abuse.

A more comprehensive view of domestic violence would extend to controlling behaviors and encompass psychological, verbal, and economic abuse. One reason these behaviors are often not included in statutory restrictions is that they are alternately seen as ambiguous and difficult to identify and not worthy of a criminal sanction. Including these acts in a statutory definition of domestic violence is not intended to minimize the trauma of direct physical abuse. Rather, Tuerkheimer would have us focus on the law's response on the variety of techniques used to impose domination and control on an autonomous person, not merely on physical violence or threats.

The legal reforms Tuerkheimer favors may be warranted. But it is also possible that other social mechanisms, such as civil restraining orders, might supplement the admittedly restrictive criminal statutes by addressing some of the elements of domestic violence she identifies. Similarly, effective relief might be provided by expanding the application of other statutes not expressly linked to domestic violence at the moment, including harassment or stalking laws.

A second issue is the extent to which domestic violence should be seen primarily as a crime against women or whether there is a sufficient degree of gender symmetry in the commission of such acts to justify committing substantial research dollars and justice resources to partner violence committed by women. This is critically important. If domestic violence is conceptualized as a crime against women primarily, the view implied by entitling the primary federal statute the Violence Against Women Act, then it is hardly surprising that gender-neutral state statutes lack a sufficient focus on transcendent aspects of gender and control in relationships. Conversely, if the crime of domestic violence is truly gender neutral, we would have to rethink the orientation of batterer treatment programs (which are designed for male offenders almost exclusively) or develop a parallel track for female offenders. Similarly, assistance for the victims of battering is presently geared almost exclusively to the needs of women victims of heterosexual violence, leaving both male victims of female violence and victims of same-sex violence without much support, let alone "shelter."

The argument that domestic violence is gender neutral relies heavily on statistical reports of male and female violence. These originated with the National Family Violence Survey (NFVS), designed by family violence researchers Murray Straus and Richard Gelles. Based on self-reports of violent behavior and victimization from women as well as men, such studies consistently show relatively similar rates committed and initiated by women and men. While studies emphasize that females are far more likely than males to be injured by their intimate partner, many proponents of gender neutrality believe that all acts of intimate violence should be addressed in a nonpreferential manner. The argument has also been made that, while men's rate of partner violence has declined, women are becoming more violent in relationships. Finally, we know there are high rates of same-sex intimate partner violence.

When we consider the broad range of evidence, the extent and nature of female violence appear more complicated than the proponents of gender neutrality suggest. For one thing, some population surveys report rates of female violence against partners that are considerably lower than those for male partners. For example, based on a representative survey of 8,000 men and women, the National Violence Against Women Survey (NVAWS) reported that nearly 25 percent of surveyed women but only 8 percent of surveyed men said that they were raped or physically assaulted (or both) by a current or former spouse, a cohabitating partner, or a date at some point in their lifetime.[1] While some might be surprised that the rate of violence against men is even as high as this study suggests, it is clearly lower than the rate suffered by women.

For another thing, while it is true that arrests of women for domestic violence have increased in recent years far more rapidly than arrests of men, the National Crime Victimization Survey (NCVS), which provides data directly from victims, reports that male victimization rates have remained stable in recent years. What has apparently changed is the willingness of police to arrest women either independently as perpetrators or as part of a dual arrest of both partners.

Debate continues about the relative numbers of men and women who are violent with their partners. There is fairly universal agreement that male assaults against females are far more likely to be serious assaults and that females are considerably more likely to be seriously injured by their partners than men. Women are also at greater risk for the multiple types of victimization described by Tuerkheimer, as well as recurrent violent victimization within relationships. From this perspective, it is inadequate to simply count violent acts without studying the context, frequency, and outcomes of these acts.

Several chapters explore the dichotomy of male versus female violence, whether such incidents should be treated as analogous to violence by males, and the need to examine women's use of violence in the context in which it is used.

Molly Dragiewicz explores a key source of confusion in gender-neutral approaches, the conflation of sex and gender in discussions of partner violence. She distinguishes sex, the biological fact, from the sociological construct of gender. While biology may contribute to a propensity or capacity for certain types of violence, it does not cause intimate partner violence. By contrast, she argues that gender-based violence is an integral part of society based on inequality of power, whether of strength, in its crudest form, or economics or social prestige. One implication of the Dragiewicz chapter is that it is appropriate to examine the influence of gender on the dynamics of partner violence (i.e. of socially constructed roles associated with biological males and females), even in cases of female violence. But it is in the distinction between coercive control and simple domestic violence that the failure of gender-neutral laws becomes most apparent. Not only are many of the tactics evident in coercive control directly linked to gender inequalities (such as denied access to money or paid employment), but also their specific aim is to enforce traditional gender stereotypes by regulating how they dress, clean, cook, or perform sexually. She argues that in failing to distinguish between those (primarily men) who exercise "coercive control" by many means and those (primarily women) who merely react to pervasive cultural norms that disempowered them, gender-neutral laws fail battered women.

Suzanne Swan, Jennifer Caldwell, Tami Sullivan, and David Snow also address the debate about whether women are as violent as men in intimate relationships and whether women's violence resembles men's violence. They summarize the vast differences in the outcomes for women versus men. Drawing on the NFVS, for instance, they report that women were six times more likely to be injured by partner assaults than men (3.0 and 0.5 percent, respectively). They describe the distinctive set of motivations and behaviors that typify women's violence and argue that they require different intervention approaches than violence by male offenders.

Other controversies have arisen about the extent to which institutions have effectively responded to domestic violence, and whether unintended consequences have occurred as a result of statutory implementation. The next several chapters of the volume focus on the evolution of the criminal justice system's response to domestic violence.

In their chapter, Buzawa and Hirschel describe the evolution of the police response to domestic violence in the context of a more general societal shift toward the increased use of formal social controls. This shift was reflected both by the passage of federal statutes, the Violence Against Women Act of 1994 as amended, for instance, and perhaps even more dramatically by state legislation, where specific attention was given to the police role when intervening to stop abuse. They emphasize that proponents of more aggressive intervention may not have totally understood the impact of laws or policies that mandate a particular response, especially in those states or police departments that *require* officers to make an arrest in cases of intimate partner violence. They review a considerable body of research delineating potentially undesirable consequences for victims and how many victims feel disempowered by their inability to control the outcome of a call for police assistance. For example, some victims prefer an intervention to not involve arrest because of the potential financial impact on the offender if he is unable to work, or if she is unable to work due to required court appearances. In addition, victims who choose to remain with offenders may find their relationship harmed, while those leaving may find themselves in greater danger from the offender. As a result, victim reporting may diminish, and in such jurisdictions, a smaller population of victims may actually be served. Finally, they note that mandatory arrest requirements have brought about an unexpected increase in the arrest of women, as well as an increase in dual arrests (i.e., the arrest of both parties).

Unfortunately, as Buzawa and Hirschel note, the dramatic increase in arrest rates and the increased responsiveness of police do not appear to deter many offenders. The publication of evidence questioning the efficacy of arrest has caused the focus of research to shift to what happens to offenders and victims after an arrest is made. After all, if police are viewed as the "gatekeepers" to the criminal justice system, then it may be unrealistic to expect that an arrest by itself would be sufficient to deter offenders.

The focus on prosecution has been growing as practitioners and policy makers have begun to realize that the mere arrest of an offender is not sufficient to deter reoffending and/or protect victims. Following an examination of the police role, questions have been raised about the practices and efficacy of prosecutors once these cases were turned over to their offices. In their chapter, Christopher Maxwell, Amanda Robinson, and Andrew Klein discuss how the role of prosecution in cases of domestic violence has changed as the result of increased mandates and expectations for aggressive case prosecution. While mandating prosecution in cases of domestic assault is more problematic for legislatures than mandating arrest, there has nonetheless been a massive increase in the proportion of cases prosecuted. However, victim cooperation continues to be a key factor in determining whether cases are successfully prosecuted.

Maxwell et al. discuss how prosecutors also have the capability to perform key services for victims other than merely prosecuting cases. Specifically, they can help reduce victim fear, provide a degree of ongoing protection, facilitate access to needed services, and offer victim advocacy services. The authors also report that the establishment of specialized prosecution programs and specialized domestic violence courts has resulted in a higher proportion of successfully prosecuted cases. But they caution that successful prosecution does not necessarily produce a satisfactory outcome for victims. While some victims may be safer as the result of prosecution, others may become even more fearful of retaliatory actions by the offender. This is substantiated by the high numbers of offenders who reoffend and are undeterred by conviction. As a result, the authors emphasize the need for more aggressive prosecution of high-risk offenders and for greater efforts to ensure victim safety. In their view, low-risk offenders may be unlikely to reoffend, regardless of whether the case is prosecuted. For these offenders, following a victim's preference may best serve her immediate interests as well as those of society.

In a subsequent chapter, Andrew Klein explores the impact of the criminal justice system on offenders in greater detail. He reminds us that understanding variations in "chronicity" may be the key to identifying effective sanctions for offenders who reach the courts. In theory, the violent acts of a criminal offender are assessed and punished as discrete episodes, as the "system" makes few distinctions between offenders who are occasionally violent and those who are "generally violent." In fact, a large proportion of domestic violence offenders who reach the criminal justice system have no prior history of criminal offending. Most of these offenders simply do not reoffend, regardless of whether their cases are prosecuted and irrespective of the sentence if they are convicted. But there is a subset of batterers who have a diverse and lengthy history of criminal offending and who are likely to reoffend, also irrespective of their sentence.

In making this claim, it is important to be clear about which acts constitute abuse. For example, is reabuse limited to domestic violence, or is it defined as any new offense committed by the offender even if the victim is someone other than the original partner? Regardless of how it is measured, the extent of reoffending by a subset of chronic batterers who are generally violent is staggering. Klein believes this level of reoffending questions whether we should rely on current intervention strategies in these cases. Not only should the focus of intervention shift to this subset of chronic offenders, he argues, but also considerably more resources should be given to both the courts and corrections in order to enhance their capacity to rapidly prosecute and then incarcerate chronic abusers.

To help us better understand why police and prosecutorial interventions have had marginal utility at best in deterring future abuse by chronic offenders, it is important to understand how batterers process and understand their experiences with the criminal justice system. Keith Guzik draws on extensive interviews with batterers to analyze how arrest and prosecution affect how batterers understand what is happening to them. Supporting Goodmark's chapter as well as the chapter by Swan et al., Guzik highlights how typical domestic violence does not fit the typical stereotype often envisioned. Victims are often independent and self-sufficient. They are unwilling to tolerate abusive relationships and contact the police when confronted with an abusive partner. They also are willing to defend themselves from their abuser. To the extent that these women do not conform to the expectations of the traditional female, batterers feel threatened and often justified in their violent behavior.

He finds that some batterers do eventually realize their actions were wrong. For the most part, however, the lesson learned from punishment is different. He finds that batterers view their sanctions as inherently unfair and the result of a system biased against men in general and against them in particular. Rather than triggering inward reflections by abusers on the wrongness of their behavior, arrests and prosecutions trigger anger towards the criminal justice system, and perhaps against the victim as well. Overwhelmingly, respondents in some research believed that they had been mistreated by the police and courts.

Instead of accepting responsibility for their actions, they blame their victims and see themselves as the "real" victim in the relationship. Guzik's interviews help us understand why so many victims fear the outcome of arrest and/or prosecution. Many batterers, especially but not only those who are the most generally violent, are unrepentant, the prequel to further abuse, though this is not how they define their behavior. Clearly, the oft-heard victim concerns about retaliation are rooted in the offender's often acute sense of betrayal when he is arrested and his belief that the consequent stigma is unjustified by his acts.

Guzik also links the batterers' beliefs that they were wronged to the adversarial nature of the criminal justice system. The defense attorneys who represent batterers often help them justify their actions rather than accept responsibility for their behaviors. Instead of proceedings getting at the truth of what happened in a particular incident, they try to absolve their clients of wrongdoing in every possible way, helping them exit through legal loopholes or eliciting sympathy by portraying the offender as themselves the victim of stress or some dire circumstance.

When courts do convict batterers, the most common disposition is a mandate to attend a batterer intervention program. The vast majority of batterers attending these programs are there as part of a judicial sentence. California, Rhode Island, and other states mandate that all offenders convicted of a domestic violence offense must attend a batterer intervention program.

Rempel focuses on the administrative use of batterer programs by courts as a strategy to ensure batterer accountability. To the extent that these programs perform an important judicial service by providing batterer oversight through intensive monitoring, they may be able to prevent reoffending and provide greater protection for victims. But accountability depends on oversight, detecting violations or reoffenses, and a swift and consistent judicial response. This can be elusive. Rempel identifies the difficulties encountered with tracking compliance and maintaining reporting protocols.

In his chapter, social work professor Dan Saunders goes further, not only describing how batterer programs actually function but also assessing the dynamics that make accountability hard to achieve. To start, while there are some innovative and fully funded programs, most courts have inadequate investigatory staff and may even lack any personnel responsible for monitoring attendance, let alone the behavior, of adjudicated abusers. One reason for the low level of resource investment is that domestic violence cases are typically prosecuted as misdemeanors, the lowest level of offense. This means that many courts depend on batterer treatment programs or an emergency call from a victim to identify noncompliance. As Saunders notes, in approximately half of the cases, the services are being delivered by private for-profit programs whose funding can be affected if offenders fail to complete their entire program. Thus, the persons on whom the courts depend to monitor compliance have a vested interest in reporting success. Even some of the better programs lack the staff to closely monitor offenders and initiate contact with the courts.

For these and related reasons, most courts cannot be totally assured that offenders are attending these programs as required. But even when noncompliance is reported, as Rempel shows, a large proportion of courts do not impose any sanctions. As with the intervention programs themselves, judicial inaction may be the result of personnel shortages or slippages in communication. Rempel illustrates how these problems have been overcome to some extent by innovative practices. These include the use of specialized domestic violence courts and post-conviction status hearings that are closely monitored by a well-funded probation department and a judiciary that signals that it simply will not tolerate regressive behavior. In courts that have embraced these innovations, batterer treatment programs wield the most impact.

Even when offenders are closely monitored, there is only limited evidence that programs impact reoffending. Rempel wisely distinguishes between ending violent behavior—something few programs appear to do—and the more modest goal of ensuring offender accountability. This could potentially be achieved either by ongoing judicial compliance checks or intensive monitoring, or by a rapid and consistent court response to infractions immediately after a condition or rule of the program is violated. Moreover, these sanctions should be of sufficient significance to deter most batterers. He recommends that a short sentence to jail be used for more serious infractions such as termination from an intervention program. He also suggests considering a gradated system of sanctions for batterers who are noncompliant.

Dan Saunders is a bit more optimistic than Rempel about the prospects of batterer intervention. The approximately 2,500 intervention programs scattered throughout the United States vary widely in terms of their administration, format, and approach. Many of the negative conclusions about these programs are based on generalizations that fail to consider this variety. Using a single yardstick of success may not be appropriate. He describes the challenges posed to determining whether these programs are effective, including the general failure to agree on what constitutes a positive outcome and the best way to measure it. Should we only consider reoffending that results in arrest or focus primarily on victim reports of reabuse? While clearly not optimal, should a program count as a "success" if, after attendance in a program, a formerly chronic offender decreases the seriousness or frequency of his violent behavior? Should we look beyond the offender's behavior to assess the impact upon victim attitudes and behaviors? After all, many victims simply seek affirmation that the violence that they have experienced is not normal, healthy, or proper; that it will not be tolerated by society; and that the offender is expected to change his ways, not the victim. Many victims also hope that batterers mandated to attend intervention programs will get help with the issues that victims believe are behind batterers' abusive behavior, such as alcohol or drug abuse. Hopefully, if victims believe that a partner has reoffended despite this opportunity, they may become less tolerant of reabuse. Perhaps an increase in a victim's determination and gained confidence that she is not responsible for the abuse should be considered a measure of success, however indirect.

Saunders focuses on not only the divergent nature of batterer intervention programs and our lack of knowledge as to their effectiveness, but also the diverse range of offenders attending these programs. Like Andrew Klein, he observes that a small percentage of offenders will inevitably remain undeterred by intervention and continue their violent behavior after program completion. Saunders also stresses the interplay of substance abuse and personality disorders with abusive behavior, calling for more than one type of intervention as well as coordination with services for these problems.

No system has changed its response to partner abuse more profoundly since the domestic violence revolution began than the criminal justice system. Readers who complete this volume will gain an appreciation of not only how far the criminal justice system has come, but also where we can and should go from here. It is no small achievement that what was once a taken-for-granted facet of everyday life for millions of women and children is now considered criminal conduct. No one believes the steps taken thus far are sufficient to end a problem that has been with us for centuries. But even the small steps we have taken send a powerful message about the extent to which human progress demands we value and protect physical integrity, dignity, and autonomy in personal life.

NOTE

1. Patricia Tjaden and Nancy Thoennes (November, 2000). Full Report of the Prevalence, Incidence, and Consequences of Violence Against Women. Washington, D.C.: National Institute of Justice.

Chapter 1

The Real Crime of Domestic Violence

Deborah Tuerkheimer

At last, after a long history of legalized abuse by intimates, domestic violence is against the law in the United States. While the response of system actors—police, prosecutors, judges, and jurors—remains subject to legitimate critique, our statutes "on the books" prohibit the practice of battering. Formally, if imperfectly, domestic violence is a crime.

This, in short, is the narrative that has been generally accepted by academics, practitioners, and members of the public. Its central premise—that continued improvements in the criminal justice system's treatment of domestic violence will come from transforming the practices, procedures, and evidentiary rules that surround the enforcement of existing criminal statutes—has gone unchallenged.

This premise, however, is fundamentally flawed. Continuing efforts to enhance the enforcement of existing criminal laws, while important, are insufficient. This is because the laws themselves are in need of reform. Attending to our substantive criminal laws, as opposed to simply the procedures, rules, and customs that surround them, is the next stage of an ongoing criminal justice evolution.

Despite the conventional wisdom, domestic violence is not fully a crime. Or, more precisely, the domestic violence that is criminalized is only a subset of domestic violence as it exists outside the boundaries of law. While proscribing particular aspects of domestic violence, our criminal laws overlook its essential—indeed, its defining—characteristics. After elaborating on this disconnect between battering as it is practiced and battering as it is criminalized, the question of reform will be addressed.

BEYOND THE PHYSICAL

Outside the criminal law context, domestic violence is widely understood as an ongoing pattern of behavior defined by both physical and nonphysical manifestations of power. This is a remarkably uncontroversial proposition. For women whose lives it describes, the oft-described "power and control" dynamic is ubiquitous. Yet the boundaries of criminal law have remained largely impermeable to this accepted characterization of battering.

Social scientists, women's advocates, and feminist legal scholars have long recognized that the "struggle for power and control—the batterer's quest for control of the woman—[lies] at the heart of the battering process." As psychologist Mary Ann Dutton explains,

> Abusive behavior does not occur as a series of discrete events. Although a set of discrete abusive incidents can typically be identified within an abusive relationship, an understanding of the dynamic of power and control within an intimate relationship goes beyond these discrete incidents. To negate the impact of the time period between discrete episodes of serious violence—a time period during which the woman may never know when the next incident will occur, and may continue to live with on-going psychological abuse—is to fail to recognize what some battered woman experience as a continuing "state of siege."[1]

This continuing state of siege has become the focus of much scholarly commentary within both the social scientific community and the feminist legal academy. As a matter of both theory and practice, an accurate description of battering is "premised on an understanding of coercive behavior and of power and control—including a continuum of sexual and verbal abuse, threats, economic coercion, stalking, and social isolation—rather than 'number of hits.'"[2] Recognizing that power and control lie at the heart of battering necessarily broadens our understanding of what conduct constitutes domestic violence.

The most powerful evidence of the validity of these assertions is found in victims' accounts of the abusive relationship. Women's divulgences about the experience of abuse reveal that context is essential to understanding the nature and harm of battering; episodic physical violence, while often a devastating manifestation of the abuser's control, does not fully define its contours or map its reaches. This vast range of suffering—amidst and beyond the physical abuse—is a place where the criminal law "does not go."[3]

The suffering takes many forms:

> He used to fine me if I said anything considered out of order. All these sort of weird things, trying to get control, power.[4]

He almost burnt my work one time—three years of research and writing. He had lots of my papers out in the garden and the incinerator was burning. I had to beg and plead and agree to various conditions to get it off him.[5]

Within a couple of weeks, he started snarling at me about the way I laid the breakfast table. It was something stupid like the marmalade on the wrong side of the table.... I got to the stage of wondering about everything, if I was going to get it right or wrong.[6]

Things really started to go down hill when I went to university, there's no doubt about that.... I don't think there'd been any need for him to be violent to me [to that point in the relationship] because he had me so much in his control in other ways, financially, at home with the children.[7]

He would say things like "It took all my self-control last night not to get the bread knife and come upstairs and knife you." I never knew how far he could go. I just knew that I was in fear for my life.[8]

He always found something wrong with what I did, even if I did what he asked. No matter what it was. It was never the way he wanted it. I was either too fat, didn't cook the food right.... I think he wanted to hurt me. To hurt me in the sense ... to make me feel like I was a nothing.[9]

The physical stuff was bad though, but I think the silences were worse. They were psychological torture. You could never predict what would send him into one of these silences. Or how to get him out of them. These silences were the ultimate control.[10]

Evan Stark has recently drawn on his decades of experience as a researcher and forensic expert to document what he aptly calls the "chain of dominance"[11] that distinguishes domestic violence. For example, before killing his wife, one batterer

locked [her] out of their bedroom and forced her to sleep on the living room couch. She was limited to one meal a day, such as the slice of cold pizza found in the refrigerator. [The abuser] had taken the toilet paper from the downstairs bathroom and forbidden her to use the upstairs bathroom. He had taken her money and her car keys. He had forbidden her to go to work, speak to friends or family members on the phone, or watch TV. He had also kept her from touching her baby, except to breastfeed, and he had repeatedly threatened to kill her.[12]

Other illustrations of how domestic violence perpetrators operationalize power—using what Stark refers to as the "technology of coercive control"—include forcing the victim to eat off the floor; to answer her cell phone immediately; to walk in the snow without shoes; to sleep in her car; to quit her job because she talked to "the wrong person" at work; to record in a log book the details of how she spent her day, including whom she saw and what money she spent; and to cook dinner for the batterer and his girlfriend.[13]

Physical violence is an integral part of the abuse suffered by the women whose stories Stark tells. But violence is not an end in itself. Rather, by "appropriating their resources; undermining their social support; subverting their rights to privacy, self-respect, and autonomy; and depriving them of substantive equality," abusers are able to effectively control their victims in economic, political, and social spheres.[14] Using mechanisms of domination at once idiosyncratic and jarringly universal, batterers harm family pets; burn diplomas and photographs; harass victims' friends, coworkers, and family members; physically block access to transportation; and employ modern technology to accomplish effective 24-hour surveillance.[15]

As one final demonstration of the centrality of power and control to the dynamics of abuse, consider the lists of rules that one batterer created for his victim, who feared—based on past physical abuse and threats—that she would be beaten or even killed if she refused to follow her batterer's directives.[16] Included on these lists, which contained no less than 47 proscriptions, were the following edicts: vacuum daily "so you can always see the lines"; "CDs and cassettes in alphabetical order"; "refrigerator sorted by size and faced—as instructed"; "closets color-coordinated and sorted by length"; "no dishes left on counters or in sink ... wash and put away immediately"; "shower curtain always closed"; "everything kept clean, neat, and in its place"; and "fully stocked shelf just for [list maker] (lots of Hostess surprises!)." The category of "House Rules" prohibited men in the house, men on the telephone, and pictures of men, and concluded with the following, ultimate, decree: "BE A GOOD GIRL AT ALL TIMES."

Regardless of whether they are physical in nature, manifestations of power and control in a battering relationship harm victims. Indeed, the nonphysical abuse that is typically a critical component of the battering dynamic is often described by victims as the most painful and debilitating. Yet this injury is not redressed by law. As defined by existing statutes, battering bears little resemblance to the abuse suffered by more than half a million women each year.

Premised on a transactional model of crime that isolates and decontextualizes violence, the laws applied to domestic abuse conceal the reality of an ongoing pattern of conduct occurring within a relationship characterized by power and control. Law's failure to define accurately the nature and harm of domestic violence negates the experiences of victims and effectively places battering outside the reach of criminal sanctions.

AN INCOMPLETE EVOLUTION: CRIMINALIZATION IN HISTORICAL CONTEXT

The failure of criminal law to remedy domestic violence is best understood in historical context. So viewed, this failure is neither atypical nor coincidental, but rather one of many tangible proofs of the proposition that "criminal law is, from top to bottom, preoccupied with male concerns and male perspectives."[17]

Ambivalence surrounding criminalization efforts has enduring roots in the Anglo-American common law, which until the late nineteenth century provided for a husband's right to "command his wife's obedience, and subject her to corporal punishment or 'chastisement' if she defied his authority."[18] Integral to law's construction of the marital relationship was its defense of hierarchy, of which physical abuse was but one component.

The formal demise of the chastisement right in the late nineteenth century foretold the criminalization of domestic violence. By 1920, all states had made wife beating illegal.[19] Yet, as legal historian Reva Siegel writes,

> It would be misleading to look to the repudiation of [the] chastisement doctrine as an indicator of how the legal system responded to marital violence.... During the Reconstruction era, jurists and lawmakers vehemently condemned [the] chastisement doctrine, yet routinely condoned violence in marriage.[20]

Over time, the rhetoric of marital privacy grew and displaced a chastisement prerogative explicitly grounded in hierarchical norms. Until recently, privacy-based rationales for nonintervention in domestic crimes saturated the criminal justice system—from police to prosecutor to judiciary. Confronting a legal apparatus wholly unresponsive to battering, domestic violence advocates quite sensibly focused their reform efforts on forcing police and prosecutors to enforce the laws already on the books,[21] that is, to treat crimes "equally" whether the victim and perpetrator were strangers or intimates. Proponents of mandatory arrest and "no-drop" prosecution policies argued that constraining law enforcement discretion would tend to result in fuller enforcement of existing substantive criminal laws, thus improving the status quo.

In sociolegal context, this strategy seems eminently reasonable. And to a significant degree, it has proven successful—if success is defined as forcing criminal justice system actors to apply existing laws to domestic violence. Yet the evolution of criminal law's response to battering is incomplete. Because existing laws are themselves inadequate to remedy the harm of battering, even full enforcement of these laws cannot truly transform the legal response to domestic violence.

As we will see, legal paradigms in place when chastisement was a right are still intact, functioning to negate the quintessentially patterned practice of battering. Operation of these paradigms must be confronted if the criminal justice system is to move to the next stage of reform.

CRIMINAL LAW PARADIGMS

The laws currently used to prosecute domestic violence were created to redress criminal conduct of a fundamentally different nature. Statutes typically applied in domestic violence prosecutions—including assault, burglary, property destruction, violation of a restraining order, kidnapping, homicide, rape, and sexual assault—are generally characterized by a narrow temporal lens and a limited conception of harm. These paradigms of time and injury operate in tandem to obscure defining aspects of battering; ongoing patterns of power and control are not addressed, nor is the full measure of injury that these patterns inflict redressed.

The Problem of Time

Statutes criminalizing violence do not account for the perpetration of continuing acts. From the origins of our law, crime was conceived as occurring at a discrete moment, and this template endures. Put simply, the incident-focused criminal law contemplates an act transpiring at an ascertainable instant in time. As Judge Gerald Lynch has explained, the crime paradigm is "transaction-bound,"[22] meaning that, at least in theory, one could capture the commission of an archetypical crime with a conventional camera (i.e., one that takes still pictures).

This transactional model of crime fails utterly to describe domestic violence. A constricted temporal frame places the patterns of abuse that are a hallmark of battering outside of criminal law's reach. Conduct that cannot be reduced to a moment in time lies outside the bounds of existing statutes.

Expanding the law's temporal lens—replacing the hypothesized conventional camera with a video camera—is imperative if the continuum of violence that characterizes battering is to be criminalized. At the same time, law's conception of harm must also evolve.

The Problem of Injury

The transaction-bound nature of criminal law is compounded by its overly narrow conception of harm. Conventional crimes of violence, inflicted by a stranger, are generally contingent on physical injury or the imminent threat of it. As a result, these are the recognized indicia of harm. In contrast, nonphysical manifestations of power and control that characterize the abusive relationship (and, again, are often most devastating to its victims) are simply not recognized by the criminal law.

The problem goes beyond the disappearance of real injury. By using physicality alone to ascribe meaning, the law disregards the space between episodes of physical violence. The effect of isolating and atomizing violence in intimate relationships is to render context meaningless.

This decontextualization is of critical importance. Relationship provides the terrain on which a batterer's system of domination is enacted. Relationship is essential to grasping the full measure of harm inflicted by the abuser and suffered by the victim. Relationship connects and organizes what might otherwise seem to be random acts.[23] Structured to remedy paradigmatic violence between strangers, the criminal law negates context and the injury that is entrenched in it. The harm of battering is inflicted over time, yet systemic blindness to its defining conduct—conduct perpetrated on an ongoing basis and conduct that does not cause physical injury—negates the injury that results from unseen patterns.

It should by now be evident that basic features of existing criminal law structures are in deep tension with criminalizing the full spectrum of battering.

THE CASE OF MOLLY AND JIM

To fully appreciate the limitations of the current statutory regime, it is helpful to consider the movement of a domestic violence case through the criminal justice system. Because written judicial opinions (and even trials themselves) reflect legal structures that distort the realities of battering—thus inevitably reproducing those structures—we will consider how the lives of a real batterer and his victim might hypothetically encounter the criminal process.[24]

Jim and Molly were married less than a year after they met, and Jim began raping and beating Molly soon after. Throughout the course of the relationship, Molly was relentlessly subjected to Jim's domination, which functioned as the omnipresent backdrop to escalating physical abuse. Power and control were central to the battering dynamic. Molly was not permitted to go outside unless Jim was present. He forbade her to talk to the neighbors. He did not allow her to write to her family. He warned her that if she ever tried to end their relationship, he would "see to it that she never managed to leave with the baby." "He would take the rifle down from the wall when she was quiet for too long." Sexual abuse occurred "almost nightly."

One day, after years of abuse without any law enforcement intervention, Jim attacked Molly after finding her talking to a neighbor when he returned from work. He punched her repeatedly in the face, causing bruising, swelling, and pain.

After a neighbor called 911, the police responded and observed relatively minor injuries to Molly. (Here the account departs from reality. In actuality, law enforcement intervened only after Molly killed Jim and was charged with his murder. Jim had battered Molly for six years.) As is typical, we will assume that Jim was placed under arrest for the misdemeanor crime of assault.

What has Jim done to Molly over the course of their relationship that is defined as criminal by our justice system? Or, to ask the question in slightly different form, which aspects of Molly's suffering are deemed worthy of remediation? Because the law's constricted temporal lens does not see patterns of nonphysical abuse, Jim's ongoing scheme of domination is not illegal. Criminal statutes fail to reach battering behavior that defies capture in a moment in time; Jim is charged by the prosecutor with misdemeanor assault only.

When Jim appears before a judge or magistrate for arraignment, the judicial officer must determine whether bail is appropriate. This decision is based largely on the seriousness of the charges facing Jim. The degree of the offense alleged dictates the maximum sentence facing the defendant, which in turn impacts the judge's assessment of the need for bail to secure the defendant's return to court. Here, the arraigning judge knows only that Jim has been charged with assaulting Molly on one occasion and that Molly sustained misdemeanor-level injuries, subjecting Jim to misdemeanor-level penalties. In some jurisdictions, the judge may also consider Jim's potential for dangerousness in deciding whether bail should be set. But unless Jim has previously been convicted of a crime against Molly, the arraignment judge may have no information about Jim's long history of abuse, including his many threats to kill. The bail determination will be made accordingly.

When the prosecutor meets with Molly to discuss the case against Jim, the content of the interview is framed by the statutory definition of the crime of assault. The prosecutor assesses the strength of the case by focusing on how each element of the crime charged will be proven—and on defeating any possible defenses—should the case ultimately go to trial. What happened in the time period immediately preceding the incident is relevant to the prosecutor; what happened in the weeks, months, or years preceding it is not.

The prosecutor does not learn about the continuum of battering. The prosecutor does not learn about Jim's ways of isolating Molly, such as not allowing her to leave the house or write to her family. The prosecutor does not learn about the devastating physical abuse that occurred regularly; about the threats to kill Molly and her family; about the ongoing sexual abuse; about the time Jim sheared Molly's hair off, scraping her scalp with the blades, saying, "No one will look at you now, will they? No one will ever want you now."[25]

In response to questions from the prosecutor about the particular incident that is the basis for the pending criminal charge, Molly will not likely volunteer a fuller account of the abuse. Molly understands that the prosecutor is interested in *this one time.* And even were she inclined to attempt to move the prosecutor outside of the charging framework, how could

Molly possibly detail the inexorably linked dynamics of power, control, and violence that have dominated her life for the past six years? To whatever extent she does describe the various facets of Jim's scheme to subordinate her, Molly's confidence in the criminal justice system is unlikely to be inspired by the prosecutor's responses: that's not what he's charged with here (meaning that her experience has no legal significance), or that's not a crime (meaning that what he did to her is in fact legal).

Perhaps Molly discloses past physical violence that is criminal, and the prosecutor is willing to consider additional charges. But Jim cannot be prosecuted unless Molly knows the approximate date of the crime and is certain that she is accurately recalling the details of one particular incident, rather than distilling multiple incidents to a prototype. The patterned, ongoing nature of domestic violence makes this an often insurmountable obstacle. Given what has been endured, it is not surprising that domestic violence victims often blend, generalize, and summarize when narrating a history of abuse.

To ask the battering victim to isolate and recount with precision each incident of physical abuse—even assuming the theoretical possibility of cohering such a thoroughly decontextualized account—is to preordain failure. A legal system requiring this conceals that which is sufficiently ubiquitous to become indistinct.

In short, the criminal law's failure to account for an ongoing pattern of violence severely constrains the prosecutor's ability to do justice in these cases. It affects the charges that may be brought; the likelihood that an offer will be made on the case; the sentence that will be recommended to the judge on a plea; and, if the case goes to trial, the evidence and arguments that will be presented to judge and jury.

THE DOMESTIC VIOLENCE TRIAL

Acquittals in domestic violence cases occur more frequently than they should, largely as a result of the criminal law's failings. More specifically, juries (and judges acting as fact finders in nonjury trials) wrongly acquit—that is, they acquit in cases where the defendant is factually guilty of the crime charged—for reasons that derive from paradigmatic criminal law structures: jurors do not believe the victim; jurors do not see a motive for the defendant's actions; jurors are not moved by the victim's suffering. To account for these reactions, it is most helpful to juxtapose what we know about jury decision making with a description of evidence that generally is (and is not) presented in a domestic violence trial.

Victim Credibility

In many ways, trials are about storytelling and verdicts reflect which narrative was more persuasive to the jury. As legal scholar Mary

Coombs has observed, "Fact finders are more likely to believe stories that are coherent, internally consistent, [and] plausible"[26] and that accord with experience and cultural expectations. Empirical research into the psychology of credibility assessment has confirmed the validity of this model of cognition. Even the U.S. Supreme Court has emphasized the close nexus between narrative coherence and perceived credibility, proclaiming that "the prosecution with its burden of persuasion needs evidentiary depth to tell a continuous story."[27]

That the practice of battering finds no descriptive outlet in law may be fatal to the narrative coherence of the victim's account at trial. In domestic violence trials, the governing criminal statutes *themselves* dictate that the flow of evidence will be interrupted, that the natural sequence of narrative evidence will be broken, and that vital links will apparently be missing. Given that legal structures significantly distort what would otherwise be the battered woman's "true" (i.e., extralegal) narrative, we would anticipate that the stories victims are constrained to tell in court would hardly be persuasive to juries. The law forces the victim to testify in a manner that does not sound credible, for it is not her reality. Ripped from context, her account resembles something other than truth.

A domestic violence case I tried with a colleague, in which the jury acquitted the defendant of all charges, effectively illustrates this dynamic. The victim, Lourdes, had been battered by her husband throughout the many years of their marriage. He isolated her, used her undocumented immigration status as a mechanism of control, humiliated her, threatened to kill her, and physically and sexually abused her on an ongoing basis. For reasons discussed earlier, the defendant was prosecuted for the physical abuse that resulted in his arrest and the one other incident of physical violence that Lourdes could remember with sufficient precision. Apart from these two apparently (from the jury's perspective) isolated incidents, she was not allowed to testify about any of the ways in which the defendant exercised power and control over her. Lourdes's testimony was of course stilted, and her account virtually incomprehensible. Without context, the story simply did not cohere. One of the jurors whom I spoke with after the acquittal said, in words to this effect, that "something about her story just didn't seem right; she was strange." And, in the courtroom, she did seem strange. In this case, a battered woman whose story was mangled by legal structures became incredible.

By failing to criminalize what is quintessentially battering, the law guts the victim's story. As we have seen, an incoherent story is an unpersuasive story. And unpersuaded jurors must find a defendant not guilty.

Defendant Motive

Motive serves a unique function in a criminal trial. Evidence of motive is always relevant and, from a juror perspective, critical to making sense of the victim's story. As one leading teacher of trial advocacy suggests, "[P]eople do things for a reason. Jurors want to know not only what they did—the conduct—but also why they did it—the motivation."[28]

Jurors in domestic violence cases are typically not presented with the evidence they need to understand the defendant's motive. Law has decontextualized episodic physical violence from the battering relationship, depriving jurors of critical information.[29] Abstracted incidents are uprooted from their place of meaning. Jim beats Molly after he finds her outside the house talking to the woman next door—why? In the absence of a motive that can be causally linked to the alleged conduct, a fact finder might well entertain a doubt—and reasonably so—about whether the conduct in fact occurred. A jury cannot make sense of what motivates the defendant's actions without understanding that which the law masks.

This veiling of patterns of control obscures much that is relevant to the question of "motive"—the strand weaving together seemingly disparate mechanisms of power. Law shrouds an elaborate system of subordination, constructed and maintained to dominate.[30] Batterers make rules that their victims must follow.[31] They force their victims to internalize these rules and punish rule infractions.[32] Batterers reinforce their victims' connections to them through fear, emotional abuse, and social isolation.[33]

Yet a jury presented with evidence of isolated physical violence cannot begin to reconstruct this complex pattern of control. Left with the "why" question unanswered, a jury discredits the victim's account. What she's saying makes little sense, despite the fact—indeed, because of the fact—that her testimony is simply conforming to legal structures that deform her story.

Because the batterer's desire for power finds no expression in law, the jury in a domestic violence case is denied the evidence that would enable it to cobble together a motive for the conduct charged. An account of the full panoply of abuse—if allowed—would manifest a "systematic pattern of control and domination."[34] Only then would the jury be in a position to frame a meaningful account of the defendant's scheme.

Juror Apathy

A vote to convict a defendant of a crime is an expression of certainty beyond a reasonable doubt. As one veteran prosecutor in the New

York County District Attorney's office has often remarked, prosecutors "cannot win the jurors' minds unless they win their hearts."[35] Jurors presented with evidence of domestic violence out of context will naturally care less about the victim and what she has endured. This, in turn, makes jurors more likely to entertain doubts about whether the defendant's guilt has been proven to the requisite standard of certainty.

The law's decontextualization of battering thus has profound implications for jury functioning. As the U.S. Supreme Court has recognized,

> [W]hen a juror's duty does seem hard, the evidentiary account of what a defendant has thought and done can accomplish what no set of abstract statements ever could, not just to prove a fact but to establish its human significance, and so to implicate the law's moral underpinnings and a juror's obligation to sit in judgment.[36]

In domestic violence cases, jurors obligated to sit in judgment are presented with a narrative warped by law. The verdicts that they reach may reflect this failing.

EFFECTS OF INCOMPLETE CRIMINALIZATION

To the extent that the law functions in denial of the realities of domestic violence victims, it cannot truly remedy the harm of battering. This failure to adequately criminalize battering is an injustice that begets a multitude of wrongs. What are the implications of law's failure to define, and thus to condemn, battering?

For the sake of this discussion, let us assume that our current system could—with reform at the margins—function in domestic violence cases to convict defendants who are guilty of the crimes charged. Accepting this supposition focuses our inquiry on the inadequacies of existing statutes under which batterers may be prosecuted and convicted. This inquiry reveals that, in important ways, battering lives—as do batterers and their victims—outside the reaches of criminal law.

It is helpful to assume momentarily the perspective of the batterer charged under the existing criminal law framework. Presumably he assesses the wrongfulness of his conduct, at least in part, in relation to the formal charges that are brought against him. But the batterer will learn very little about the wrong of battering from the legal system's formal charge and the proof it allows. Unless we are willing to exempt the criminal defendant from law's prescriptive power, this seems unacceptable.

Even more importantly, battered women experience the law's failure—both as individuals and as members of a collective. When battering behavior goes unpunished, victims rightly perceive that whatever promise of justice the system offers has been broken. Batterers are not meaningfully condemned, the full spectrum of control is not deterred, and victims are uniquely situated to suffer for these failings.

A prosecutor who has handled domestic violence cases has in all likelihood heard, "But this (the crime formally charged) is not the worst that he did to me," usually followed by a painful story of what is. She calls for understanding at the very least and, beyond, for remediation, a fuller measure of justice. The prosecutor explains, "Only this is what the law says is criminal, only this can be spoken of in court, only for this may he be held accountable," and so on. A battered woman, upon confronting legal structures impervious to her stories, learns that the criminal law does not extend to the places of her suffering. This knowledge is constructive, shaping her understanding of what she has endured and of her place in society.

More broadly, failure to outlaw the pattern of violence and power that is experienced by battered women distorts communal understandings of the abuse that is inflicted in intimate relationships. We do not see battering for what it is. We do not see ourselves as victims or perpetrators of it. We cannot grapple honestly with its root causes or our own societal complicity in its perpetuation. Circumscribed by a collective narrowness of understanding, any social condemnation of domestic violence is, at best, misdirected to a practice that exists only in the landscape of law. Worse, what the law quietly calls legal remains socially legitimate.

PROGRESS?

In recent years, many state legislatures have enacted new laws in an effort to target domestic violence directly. Without exception, however, these statutes have simply replicated the structures already in place for criminalizing violence. Because, as I have described, these structures are inapplicable to battering, statutes that reproduce them are of limited utility.

Existing domestic violence laws are in essence assault laws that include a relationship component, often with enhanced penalty provisions.[37] Thirty-nine states have passed this type of assault-based crime,[38] which reflects an approach that is fundamentally flawed.

By remaining fully tethered to incidents and injuries, domestic violence statutes do not in any way expand the criminal law's definition of battering to reflect the realities of abuse. As a legislative solution to the problem of violence between intimates, this is woefully inadequate. Further, to the extent that existing laws against "domestic violence" are perceived as having criminalized battering, they may paradoxically function as barriers to meaningful reform.

There is, however, reason for hope. One important exception to the general rule of incident-based criminal statutes is the law of stalking.

Since 1990, every state has passed this type of legislation.[39] While statutory definitions vary, in most states "[t]he key components of the crime of stalking include multiple acts creating a pattern of intentional behavior that are credibly and reasonably believed by the victim to constitute a threat, implicit or explicit, against life or physical injury."[40] By criminalizing a continuing course of conduct, stalking laws codify the recognition that seemingly isolated events must be viewed in context in order for their meaning to be discerned. Identifying a pattern of behavior as criminal, the law accounts for the reality of stalking.

The nexus between domestic violence and stalking—tight and often lethal—makes stalking statutes an important component of law enforcement efforts to protect victims and hold batterers responsible for their behaviors. Stalking behavior is often triggered by some type of separation—or an expressed desire to separate—on the part of the victim. Feminist legal scholar Martha Mahoney calls this "separation assault" and notes that "it often takes place over time":

> Separation assault is the attack on the woman's body and volition in which her partner seeks to prevent her from leaving, retaliate for the separation, or force her to return. It aims at overbearing her will as to where and with whom she will live, and coercing her in order to enforce connection in a relationship. It is an attempt to gain, retain, or regain power in a relationship, or to punish the woman for ending the relationship.[41]

The concept of separation assault is closely, though not perfectly, aligned with social understandings of stalking. But when does a "batterer" become a "stalker"? The obvious pertinence of stalking laws to the paradigmatic fact pattern—an abuser unable to relinquish control pursues the victim attempting to extricate herself from the relationship—results in the reification of what comes to be known as stalking's onset. That is, defining separation as the necessary condition for stalking imbues separation with unwarranted meaning.

The practice of battering is not transformed by "separation." Rather, the desire to exert power and control continues to dominate the relationship. In a bizarre twist, what the law validates in the stalking context—that isolated incidents must be understood as pieces of a pattern of control—it denies in the pre-separation domestic violence context. The batterer's quest for power is considered only when the "relationship" is deemed to be "over." This rather simplistic doctrinal regime superimposes itself on realities far more complex.

But notice that the law does not formally distinguish between pre- and postseparation conduct in the context of abusive relationships. Interestingly, then, antistalking legislation may be used to prosecute a course of conduct that comprises the entirety of the battering relationship.[42] Embodying a legal recognition of crime that is neither coterminous with a discrete incident nor the sum of isolated constituent parts, the definition of stalking may thus allow for a fuller account of battering than does any other criminal statute currently on the books.

This application of stalking statutes was not contemplated by legislatures or courts. It does not comport with social understandings of stalking, nor does it truly capture the harm of battering. But it does show that the criminal law can redress patterned, context-dependent conduct, revealing the profound importance of framing crime as other than transactional in nature. A real crime of domestic violence must similarly depart from traditional paradigms.

CRIMINAL JUSTICE EVOLUTION

Domestic violence should be criminalized in a manner that corresponds to the realities of abuse. This requires a new statutory framework, one which rejects the notion that—apart from the identities of victim and perpetrator—battering is just like a barroom assault. Unless we are willing to concede that domestic violence *as it is truly experienced in the world* inevitably lies beyond the reach of the law, we must reconceptualize its criminalization.

To bring the law into alignment with reality, a statutory redefinition must reflect two fundamental characteristics of domestic violence: the patterned nature of abuse, and the centrality of power and control to the abusive dynamic.

Battering as a "Course of Conduct"

To capture the ongoing, patterned nature of domestic violence, it must be criminalized as a course of conduct. This necessarily expands the conventional temporal lens that views crime as occurring in an instant.

A course of conduct is a pattern of conduct composed of a series of acts over a period of time, however short, evidencing a continuity of purpose. This definition finds precedent in the substantive criminal law, which has at times incorporated the proposition that the legality of acts must be assessed in context. For instance, state statutes defining harassment, menacing, a course of sexual conduct against a child, and, as I have discussed, stalking all depart from the transaction-based norm and criminalize a course of conduct. Federal criminal law has similarly codified a model of crime premised on an ongoing pattern of conduct.[43] From a doctrinal perspective, there is nothing revolutionary about criminalizing domestic violence as a course of conduct.

But note how reframing the definition in this manner dramatically refocuses the lens through which evidence is filtered. Context is now relevant, as is relationship. Physical manifestations of power are no longer understood as the sole incidents of battering. What were seemingly disconnected events become woven together by the thread of control. In short, the ongoing, patterned nature of battering is reflected in the legislative language which purports to criminalize it.

The Heart of Battering: Power and Control

A statute criminalizing battering must import to criminal law the constructs of power and control. Domestic violence cannot be described accurately without reference to these concepts that, as we have seen, lie at the heart of battering.

How should this premise be legally operationalized? I have proposed that battering be defined in part as an intentional course of conduct likely to result in substantial power or control over the victim. By emphasizing the natural consequences of the abuser's pattern of activity, as opposed to the ultimate outcome of his efforts, this formulation avoids a singular inquiry into the victim's powerlessness.[44] The practice of battering would be truly rendered by the prosecution's satisfaction of its burden of proof.

Admittedly, in contrast to the "problem of time," which can be rather easily addressed by adopting a course of conduct template, what I have referred to as "the problem of injury" is somewhat more complicated. As we have seen, the harm suffered by a battered woman is inextricably bound up in the abuser's exercise of power and control. Yet because injury of this nature differs so dramatically from archetypical physical injury, the criminal law offers little in the way of precedent to rely upon in framing a workable definition of these constructs.[45]

That said, I offer the following as a starting point for discussion. Evidence of power and control may include, but is not limited to: physical or mental torture; physical force or actual or implied threats of physical force; isolation from others; interference or threats to interfere with parental rights or responsibilities; interference or threats to interfere with opportunities for education or skills training; destruction of property; restraint on movement; exploitation of needs for food and shelter; interference with the use of mail, telephone, or money; sexual abuse or exploitation; and threats to undermine immigration status.

By delineating a nonexhaustive list of mechanisms of domination commonly employed by batterers, a battering statute bridges the gap between the law and the lives of battered women. Ironically, where this chasm is at its deepest, the challenge of reforming criminal law structures is most daunting. Yet here is precisely where reform is urgently needed. Until the constructs of power and control are somehow incorporated into our law, the harm of domestic violence cannot be adequately described. Without description, there can be no remediation.

Other Considerations

Three additional implementation-related questions are worthy of brief mention, though I do not purport to answer them here.[46]

First, how should the statute be named? "Battering" and "domestic violence" are the obvious contenders, but "aggravated battering" (or "aggravated domestic violence"), "domestic abuse," and "intimate partner abuse" are other possibilities. Each name has its merits and its drawbacks, some practical and others conceptual, none of which can be assessed in the abstract without reference to the statutes already on the books of the enacting jurisdiction. My point here is simply to note that naming matters.

Second, how should the requisite relationship between perpetrator and victim be statutorily defined? This, too, may be impacted by already existing language in the criminal and family codes of the enacting jurisdiction. But the question of relationship raises a number of important concerns. Most fundamentally, should the statute be drafted in a manner that makes it applicable to child abuse, or should its applicability be limited to the abuse of adult partners? (I strongly advocate the latter.) Should the statute cover elder abuse, regardless of whether there is a familial relationship between abuser and victim? Should the statute criminalize violence in teen dating relationships, even in the absence of sexual activity between the partners? How these questions are answered has implications that are not only tactical (insofar as they relate to the likelihood of legislative success) but also deeply substantive.

Finally, any discussion of implementation must include an acknowledgment that significant resistance to change will invariably attend any legislative effort to fundamentally shift how the crime of domestic violence is defined. How can this resistance be surmounted?

The answer to this question lies in the stories of domestic violence victims and their willingness to share them with those in a position to enact statutory reform. Change will come only when the disconnect between law and the lives of battered women is made salient.

Though the application of existing legal structures to domestic violence represents tremendous progress, new laws are needed to account for truths antithetical to existing criminal law paradigms. A course of conduct crime represents the next stage in the evolution of law's growing responsiveness to the harm of battering. Outside law, the meaning of domestic violence is transformed by a redefined crime of battering. What once was socially invisible can be called by its name, and conduct that was condoned may now be condemned. This next move, then, is critical.

CONCLUSION

Given that domestic violence was once legally authorized, the development of a criminal justice system response to battering may be viewed as a story of progress. Without minimizing that progress, a fuller account of the status quo reveals that criminal law's evolution in this area is not complete. The laws that exist to remedy paradigmatic stranger violence, no matter how rigorously they are enforced, cannot remedy domestic violence.

Law's failure to redress ongoing, patterned, and nonphysical manifestations of the abuser's effort to dominate his victim means that domestic violence has been criminalized in a manner that negates the essence of battering. As a consequence, battering as it is experienced in the world lies outside the criminal law. Under current statutory definitions of domestic violence, deep and pervasive suffering by battered women is not redressed, and the infliction of such suffering is not condemned.

The failure of criminal law to recognize and remedy harms to women is not new, nor is it inevitable. Reforming legal structures to recognize the violent exercise of power and control in intimate relationships represents the next phase of law's evolving response to the practice of battering. The time has come to truly criminalize domestic violence.

AUTHOR NOTE

Many of the ideas expressed in these pages first appeared in D. Tuerkheimer, "Recognizing and Remedying the Harm of Battering: A Call to Criminalize Domestic Violence," *Journal of Criminal Law and Criminology* 94 (2004): 959. Reprinted by special permission of Northwestern University School of Law, The Journal of Criminal Law and Criminology.

NOTES

1. M. A. Dutton, "Understanding Women's Responses to Domestic Violence: A Redefinition of Battered Woman Syndrome," *Hofstra Law Review* 21 (2003): 1191, 1208 (quoting Sue Osthoff, director, National Clearinghouse for the Defense of Battered Women).

2. E. Schneider, *Battered Women and Feminist Lawmaking* (New Haven, CT: Yale University Press, 2000): 65.

3. As Professor Mari Matsuda has insightfully observed, "The places where the law does not go to redress harm have tended to be the places where women, children, people of color, and poor people live." See M. J. Matsuda, "Public Response to Racist Speech: Considering the Victim's Story," *Michigan Law Review* 87 (1989): 2320–2.

4. L. Kelly, "Surviving Sexual Violence," University of Minnesota Press (1988): 129. Liz Kelly's study of a range of sexual violence, based on interviews with 60 women, is a rich source of firsthand accounts of battering.

5. Kelly, "Surviving Sexual Violence," 129–30.

6. Ibid., 131.

7. Ibid., 129.

8. Ibid., 133.

9. K. Fischer et al., "The Culture of Battering and the Role of Mediation in Domestic Violence Cases," *SMU Law Review* 46 (1993): 2117, quoting K. Fischer, "The Psychological Impact and Meaning of Court Order of Protection for Battered Women" (unpublished Ph.D. thesis, University of Illinois, Urbana-Champaign, 1992), on file with Karla Fischer.

10. C. Fedders and L. Elliot, *Shattered Dreams: The Story of Charlotte Fedders* (New York: HarperCollins, 1987): 92–93. Fedders's account of her 17-year marriage contains vivid descriptions of nonphysical as well as brutal physical abuse.

11. E. Stark, *Coercive Control* (Oxford, England: Oxford University Press, 2007): 229.

12. Stark, *Coercive Control*, 2.

13. Stark, *Coercive Control*.

14. Stark, *Coercive Control*, 13.

15. The domestic violence cases discussed by Evan Stark reflect these varied means of control. See Stark, *Coercive Control*.

16. Ibid., 314–19.

17. S. J. Schulhofer, "The Feminist Challenge in Criminal Law," *University of Pennsylvania Law Review* 143 (1995): 2151.

18. R. B. Siegel, "'The Rule of Love': Wife Beating as Prerogative and Privacy," *Yale Law Journal* 105 (1996): 2117, 2123.

19. C. Hanna, "No Right to Choose," *Harvard Law Review* 109 (1996): 1849, 1857.

20. Siegel, "'The Rule of Love,'" 2117, 2130.

21. Marital rape is the exception to this generalization. Not until 1990 was marital rape considered a crime in every state. L. R. Eskow, "Note: The Ultimate Weapon? Demythologizing Spousal Rape and Reconceptualizing Its Prosecution," *Stanford Law Review* 48 (1996): 677, 681–82. Even now, in a majority of states the criminal justice system treats marital rape differently from nonmarital rape. J. E. Hasday, "Contest and Consent: A Legal History of Marital Rape," *California Law Review* 88 (2000): 1373, 1375.

22. G. E. Lynch, "Rico: The Crime of Being a Criminal, Parts III & IV," *Columbia Law Review* 87 (1987): 927, 932.

23. This legal discounting of nontransactional realities has important evidentiary implications. In law, what gives life to a substantive criminal statute is the evidence that bears on its proof. Evidence is considered relevant only if it supports a factual proposition "of consequence" to the determination of the legal action. Put differently, the elements of a crime—defined statutorily—dictate what is, and what is not, meaningful from a criminal justice perspective. Imposing this framework on the substantive criminal law, which focuses myopically on physical injury occurring at a moment in time, renders legally irrelevant a great deal of battering conduct.

24. The relationship between Molly and Jim is documented by Angela Browne in her description of interviews with women charged with killing or attempting to kill their batterers. Browne's powerful account provides a wealth

of information about the patterns of violence in intimate relationships. See generally A. Browne, *When Battered Women Kill* (Free Press, 1987).

25. See Browne, *When Battered Women Kill*.

26. M. I. Coombs, "Telling the Victim's Story," *Texas Journal of Women and the Law* 2 (1993): 277, 288–89.

27. *Old Chief v. United States*, 519 U.S. 172 (1997).

28. T. A. Mauet, *Trial Techniques*, 5th ed. (New York: Aspen Publishers, 2000): 26.

29. While largely beyond the scope of this discussion, it bears mentioning that the evidentiary rules exacerbate the criminal law's hostility to motive-related evidence in domestic violence cases. Because conduct not specifically charged in a prosecution is conceived as "other acts," it is generally excluded in service of the prohibition on evidence of a defendant's "character" or disposition. For a more thorough analysis of this problem, see D. Tuerkheimer, "Recognizing and Remedying the Harm of Battering: A Call to Criminalize Domestic Violence," *Journal of Criminal Law and Criminology* 94 (2004): 959, 989–99.

30. See K. Fischer et al., "The Culture of Battering and the Role of Mediation in Domestic Violence Cases," *SMU Law Review* 46 (1993): 2117, 2126–32.

31. Fischer et al., "The Culture of Battering."

32. Ibid.

33. Ibid.

34. Ibid.

35. P. Casalaro, assistant district attorney, New York County District Attorney's Office, personal communication.

36. *Old Chief v. United States*, 187–88.

37. N. Miller, *What Does Research and Evaluation Say about Domestic Violence Laws? A Compendium of Justice System Law and Related Research Assessments* (Alexandria, VA: Institute for Law and Justice, 2005): 54.

38. Miller, *What Does Research and Evaluation Say.*

39. Ibid., 62.

40. Ibid., 62–63.

41. M. Mahoney, "Victimization or Oppression? Women's Lives, Violence and Agency," in *The Public Nature of Private Violence: The Discovery of Domestic Violence*, ed. M. Albertson Fineman and R. Mykitiuk (1994), 65–66.

42. I have found no indication that this prosecutorial practice is widespread. New York County is one jurisdiction that has applied stalking laws in this manner. L. E. Busching, bureau chief, Family Violence and Child Abuse Bureau, New York County District Attorney's Office, personal communication, December 17, 2003.

43. For instance, in the federal system, the Racketeer Influenced and Corrupt Organizations Act (RICO) makes it illegal to "conduct or participate . . . in the conduct of [an] enterprise's affairs through a pattern of racketeering activity," 18 U.S.C. 1962(c)(2002).

44. A statute could require proof that the victim was *in fact* dominated and controlled as a result of the defendant's conduct. But this is problematic from an evidentiary perspective, as it suggests (or at least does not preclude) that the victim must be completely subordinated for the defendant to be convicted.

It is also troubling phenomenologically, since a focus on the victim's domination will tend to obscure evidence of agency.

45. While many financial and property-related crimes include reference to control, the meaning of the concept is sufficiently distinct in these contexts that analogy is not particularly helpful.

46. I have acted as a consultant to a number of advocacy groups working to enact a statute that criminalizes domestic violence as a course of conduct. In my experience, the issues discussed here inevitably arise and are best addressed at an early stage of the legislative process.

The model statute that I have previously drafted reads as follows:

> A person is guilty of battering when:
>
> He or she intentionally engages in a course of conduct directed at a family or household member; and
>
> He or she knows or reasonably should know that such conduct is likely to result in substantial power or control over the family or household member; and
>
> At least two acts comprising the course of conduct constitute a crime in this jurisdiction.

"Family or household member," means spouses, former spouses, adults related by consanguinity or affinity, an adult with whom the actor is or has been in a continuing relationship of a sexual or otherwise intimate nature, and adults who have a child in common regardless of whether they have been married or have resided together at any time.

Chapter 2

Battered Women Who Fight Back against Their Abusers[1]

Leigh Goodmark

The provision of formal services to survivors of domestic violence often hinges on an image of a stereotypical victim—white, straight, and above all, passive in the face of her partner's power and control. The battered women who seek the assistance of these formal systems frequently fail to conform to this stereotype, however; women who fight back against their abusers are one example. Though some have recognized that this stereotype is not representative, the systems that serve battered women, particularly the legal system, have been slower to change their perceptions of who battered women are. This chapter explores the dissonance between the stereotypical victim and the stories of women who fight back and asks how systems can become inclusive enough to hear and respond to the stories of "nonconforming" victims.

Over the past 30 years, the public, media, and the legal system have coalesced around a stereotypical image of the victim of domestic violence. Before the birth of the battered women's movement, the popular assumption was that domestic violence only happened to "them"— poor African American women who lived in slums. To counter this image, battered women's advocates insisted that domestic violence was prevalent among all races, ethnicities, religions, and socioeconomic brackets. This argument, coupled with the belief that victims of "battered woman syndrome" remain in abusive relationships because of "learned helplessness," changed the portrait of intimate partner violence, replacing one stereotype with another. The victim morphed from a low-income woman of color to a passive, middle-class, white woman cowering in the corner as her enraged husband prepares to beat her again. This woman would *never* fight back.

But many women do. Who fights back? The potential responses to this question are endless. African American women. Lesbians. Poor women. Women with limited options to address the violence done to them. Women who lack access to resources. Women whose immigration status prevents them from asserting their rights. Women who may be afraid or unwilling to turn to the police or other professionals for assistance. Women who are conflicted about turning to the civil legal system and who find that when they do, and when they are honest about how they have defended themselves, they are penalized for exercising one of the few options open to them to prevent or escape from an assault.

A battered woman who fights back defies the societal expectation of a "victim" and, as a result, complicates her attempts to secure assistance through the legal system. Attorneys who represent these women, in turn, silence these stories of resistance or self-defense in order to meet the legal system's expectations of battered women as "victims." This type of editing has very real implications for both battered women and their advocates.

THE CHARACTERISTICS OF WOMEN WHO FIGHT BACK

Studies of women who use force against their partners indicate that overwhelmingly large numbers of those women have been battered. Moreover, researchers agree that the vast majority of women who use violence do so to defend themselves or their children or to prevent an impending attack. In a recent study, 95 percent of women arrested for domestic assaults had used violence in reaction to a partner's violence. The study's author explains, "Typically, women's use of force is in response to their current or former partner's violence or can be characterized as a reaction that results from past abuses and their relative powerlessness in the relationship."[2] While few would argue that humans have the right to defend themselves from impending attacks, it is hard to imagine men being asked, as women are, why they fought back when being assaulted.

Self-defense is not their only motive. Women also use violence to stand up for themselves in an attempt to salvage their self-worth, to get their partners' attention, to earn their partners' respect, to retaliate for threats against their families, and to retaliate for their partners' abusive behavior. Evan Stark argues that women often use violence to express their identities as beings independent of their controlling partners. Describing Nathaline Parkman, a 35-year-old African American woman who stabbed her abusive partner the day after he threatened to cut her, Stark writes,

> The main damage Nate suffered had less to do with physical or psychological trauma—though both were present—than with her feeling that Larry had so circumscribed her capacity to freely act that she was dying as a distinct person.... What drove her into the street that night was the existential threat to her standing as a free woman, the fact that Larry intended to subordinate her purposes to his as well as hurt her physically, to make her his thing. This, she could not allow.[3]

Women may also use violence because they lack (or believe that they lack) other options to address the violence against them. Susan Miller has organized women's use of violence into two categories: defensive behavior (the attempt to escape or avoid a violent incident against the woman or her children, typically after the man has already used violence against her) and frustration responses (expressive acts conveying the woman's frustration over her inability to escape the violence or control the violent situation).[4]

Research amply documents that men use violence to exert coercive control over their partners. Sociologist Michael Johnson describes situations in which women respond physically to coercive control (as opposed to their partner's assaults) as "violent resistance."[5] Few women who fight back are seeking to exercise control or induce fear in their partners, and even fewer are successful in doing so. Typically, neither the women nor their partners believe that the women's violence makes their partners fearful for their safety. In fact, one study reported that men were frequently amused and laughed when their partners initiated violence, suggesting that the men did not take their partners' violence seriously.[6] Ironically, women's use of force may lead to escalation of the violence and make women who fight back more vulnerable to serious injury. Women are generally unsuccessful in achieving their goals through violence. They are unable stop the violence against them, and they cannot alter the behaviors of their abusive partners to conform to their will.

How do women feel about using violence against their partners? Although many women who fight back perceive that they have no choice but to use violence to defend themselves or their children, they are nonetheless conflicted about what they have done. While they recognize that their actions may be illegal, they also believe them to be morally justified. But their belief in the morality of their actions does not prevent women who fight back from reacting negatively to having done so. Women who use violence experience higher levels of depression and fear or anxiety than violent men and often feel guilty about their actions.

Women who fight back are more likely to admit to using violence than men and to take responsibility for their violent behavior. These women tend to include a great deal of detail in their stories, including exactly where they struck their abusers and how hard they hit. Their willingness to admit and minutely recount their violence may relate to how violence by women is perceived in society.

Women who fight back undermine societal assumptions about appropriate gender roles and how battered women should respond to violence. As Shamita Das Dasgupta argues, "[S]ocieties that believe in the stereotype of feminine passivity and tolerance ... may perceive a woman who uses violence against her intimate partner as 'unnatural,' 'freakish,' and 'criminal by nature,' and deal with her accordingly."[7] Once a battered woman uses violence, her status as "victim" is imperiled. Sue Osthoff explains, "[A] practitioner may not go so far as to conclude that the woman who used force is the batterer; he or she may simply conclude that, if the woman used violence, she could not be battered."[8] This problem is more acute for women who have been charged with assaulting their partners. While Ostoff notes that "battered women who become defendants frequently find that their entire history of victimization gets erased when they are labeled perpetrators,"[9] in her study of women who fight back, Susan Miller found that some police officers were beginning to express "a sense of understanding, if not even tacit approval" of the actions of women who fight back. Some of the officers Miller interviewed "applaud women's initiative because they are not putting up with guys' shit anymore. Instead of taking it, like the past hundred years, women are giving it back."[10] The views expressed by these officers, however, are not the norm. Because they are socialized to refrain from using violence, women may understand their violence as "a violation of their socially prescribed gender role," making these "transgressions" more memorable.

The narratives of women who fight back, then, must strike a delicate balance. Battered women who fight back may be fearful but are not passive—they actively resist their abusers. While these women tell compelling stories of being abused and of taking action to stop that abuse, they must also combat the stereotype that they defy: the weak, passive, and helpless battered woman. Consider, for example, the following exchange between a prosecutor trying the case of a battered woman who killed her abuser and a witness who had known both parties. Responding to the prosecutor's question about how Dianne reacted when abused by her husband, the witness stated, "You know, Dianne was really calm. You know, Dianne would be really calm until he smacked her and then she'd smack him back. I never seen her do anything to him, you know, it was always him doing it to her, and then she would fight back." The prosecutor then remarked, "She could probably hold her own, though," to which the witness replied, "Well, she tried. No, not, well, I don't think she could hold her own, but she was pretty tough, she's a pretty tough girl, you know."[11] The prosecutor used this exchange to bolster his contention that because Dianne could defend herself, she could not possibly be battered. Explaining their active resistance to judges schooled in battered women syndrome and the paradigmatic victim poses real challenges for women who fight back.

The literature on women who fight back is incredibly dynamic. There is some evidence, for example, that despite stereotypes of Asian women as passive and submissive, South Asian women actively resist the violence against them, some (though relatively few) through the use of physical force.[12] Social science research has focused most closely on two groups of women who defy the victim stereotype: African American women and lesbians. Research also offers a variety of suggestions as to why these women might be likely to fight back. A survey of the reasons that these women might fight back is offered here, to give a sense of the diversity of the stories that these women would tell, if given the chance. Not every theory applies to every woman. But the multitude of theories suggests a vast range of narratives that women could bring to courts when seeking protection. These narratives may be particularly hard for courts to assimilate, however, given what they have come to believe about battered women.

COMMUNITY AND SOCIETAL CONSTRAINTS

While many victims of domestic violence bear the burden of remaining silent about their abuse, African American women may feel particularly pressured to keep their affairs private. African American women may feel that to break the silence is to bring further shame and disapprobation on African American men from the wider society. In communities that stress and prioritize race over gender, African American women are warned that to disclose the violence to authorities would mean "putting another 'brother' in prison." Women who have reported violence by African American men to state actors have been criticized for racial disloyalty and accused of perpetuating and reinforcing negative stereotypes of African American men as violent. Low-income African American women who turn men in to the police are sometimes labeled "snitches," which can make them more vulnerable in the projects.[13] African American women suffer as a result of these attitudes. As Tricia Bent-Goodley explains,

> When the perception that racism is a more serious issue than sexism develops, African American Women deny an equally important part of their identity. As these women deny their unique experiences as women to protect their partners, they put themselves at a greater risk of physical harm and do not allow their partners to be held accountable for their behavior. This internal barrier undermines the woman's mental health,

because it denies the differences that she experiences based on gender and creates feelings of confusion, guilt, and shame for differentiating between her needs and that of her partner.

Despite the urging of black feminists to reject the privileging of racial loyalty over women's safety, the "political gag order"[14] contributes to African American women's reluctance to reach out to state systems for help.

Because domestic violence has been widely perceived as male violence against women, some lesbians believed that their community was immune from such violence. "Most lesbians," Joan McClennen writes, "want to maintain the image of their community as one of utopian peace and love,"[15] a haven from a violent, heterosexist world. In the ideal, lesbian relationships were thought to be based on nonviolence and egalitarianism. Acknowledging lesbian battering, therefore, "would mean shattering a utopic vision of a peaceful, women-centered world."[16] Lesbians who report intimate partner violence have been considered traitors, airing the community's dirty laundry before a homophobic society. The myth of the lesbian utopia has discouraged lesbians from addressing woman-on-woman violence within the community and may silence women who might otherwise seek assistance. The lesbian utopia operates in the same way that the "gag rule" does in African American communities; by refusing to acknowledge the existence of violence, the community seeks to insulate itself from criticism by the majority. For individual battered lesbians, however, the lesbian utopia feels more like a prison.

Homophobia also prevents battered lesbians from seeking outside assistance. In 1986, Kerry Lobel noted that by acknowledging that domestic violence occurred within lesbian relationships, "we risk further repression";[17] that fear still exists among some lesbians over two decades later. The silence of battered lesbians is a function not just of the unwillingness of lesbians to admit that violence happens in relationships between women, but also of the fear that such violence will be used to justify further discrimination against and hatred of lesbians.

Abusers use homophobia to prevent their victims from reporting. The abuser may threaten to reveal a closeted lesbian's sexual orientation to her family, friends, and coworkers if she discloses the abuse or seeks assistance. The abuser may also attempt to convince the victim not to "out" her by asking for help. Additionally, if the victim has "internalized society's negative perceptions of homosexuality," the "shame and doubt" that she feels—and the abuser's reinforcement of those feelings through the message that because she is a lesbian, she deserves to be battered—may keep her from reporting abuse as well.

Homophobia contributes to the isolation of battered lesbians. Battered lesbians are less likely to seek the assistance of friends or family, particularly when those potential sources of support are homophobic. The battered lesbian may not even be able to turn to her own community for support; she may worry about confidentiality or be unable to access resources in her immediate surroundings. Geography, fear, and lack of connection to other lesbians all serve to isolate lesbian victims. Isolation may be a deliberate tactic of the abuser as well; the abusive partner may use isolation to make the battered lesbian bond to her more closely. Given the disapproval of homosexuality among many in the African American community, isolation is a particular problem for African American lesbians.

SELF-IMAGE

> Part of my problem is that I am a strong Black woman. I am angry, and some people think I am too loud. So even though he beat me almost to death, I beat him too. If I had been as strong as he was, we'd both be in trouble. But since I wasn't as strong, he got away with almost murdering me. It's as simple as that. The broken bones, the scar where he cut my face ... all of those are because he was stronger outside, and I was stronger inside. By that I mean I'm not [a] regular battered woman, because he got his share of licks. It wasn't until he started playing the mind games on me that I was really vulnerable to him.[18]

Johnetta, like many African American battered women, had difficulty reconciling her experience with that of a "regular battered woman." Her sense of herself as a strong, independent woman clashed with the stereotypes of battered women as passive and weak. Fighting back enables Johnetta and other women like her to express their sense of themselves as powerful, resourceful, and self-sufficient. One African American woman who did not fight back felt that she had betrayed her "birthright" because she did not have a story of retaliating against her partner; her "image of African American women was that they stood up for themselves."[19]

Some African American women are taught from an early age that they need to be able to protect themselves. Selma stated, "I would *never* have done anything like that if I wasn't well trained by my family to take care of myself and if I hadn't learned from my husband that men will do anything to get me, and I'd better try to protect myself when a man was coming to hurt me."[20] African American women whose sense of self is firmly tied to their strength may be reluctant to back down from their abusers and more likely to minimize their victimization, particularly in the face of the pressing problems confronted by other family members and friends in the community. According to Juanita, a 26-year-old African American woman,

> [S]ince my family and friends always thought I could take care of myself, they never even thought that my problems would be so bad as they were. No, there was so much suffering around, everyone thought mine was lightweight.[21]

The notion of "strength" transcends the physical. African American women are also more economically independent of their partners than white women. Without the financial impetus to remain in the relationship, African American women may be less willing to tolerate physical violence and more likely to fight back.

Battered lesbians may also feel constrained from reporting their abuse by pressure from within the lesbian community to appear strong and unafraid. The lesbian community may hold victims responsible for their abuse because they have failed to assume power, a tenet of lesbian feminist culture. As Barbara Hart explains, "As a lesbian community, we identify with the power, control and anger of lesbians who batter.... We view lesbians who are battered as weak sisters."[22] Some battered lesbians report that their friends view violence as a normal part of problem solving; a friend told one battered lesbian that "a good fist fight would clear the air."[23] Battered lesbians who do seek assistance are dismissed or ridiculed by the community. "Victim" is used as a pejorative: "Don't be such a victim. You're acting like a victim."[24] When those strong women do fight back, however, the guilt they feel as a result of doing so may keep them from seeking help.

STEREOTYPING AND CREDIBILITY

Violence against women has been framed in terms of patriarchy, misogyny, sexism, and male dominance, leaving no theoretical room for female perpetrators of intimate partner violence. Violence is a male trait; women are viewed as calmer, gentler, and better able to resolve conflict without resorting to violence. As a result, battered lesbians often face hostility and disbelief when they report being abused by their partners. This negative response has come not just from the larger society, but from some within the lesbian community as well.

Despite research to the contrary, battering in lesbian relationships is frequently described as mutual violence, with both partners being equally powerful and equally culpable. One reason for this characterization is the lack of a male abuser to whom primary aggressor status can be attributed. Amorie Robinson writes, "In same-sex relationships, gender cannot be used to distinguish between the aggressor and victim. Consequently, mental health professionals, researchers, and police have often perceived lesbian battering as an 'equal fight' or mutual battering."[25] The lesbian community's acceptance and encouragement of self-defense may contribute to this perception. The battered lesbian is told that she ought to fight back, but when she does, the community labels her mutually abusive. Batterers encourage this characterization, arguing that any use of violence, defensive or otherwise, constitutes abuse, and use the label "mutual batterer" to minimize their own actions. Battered lesbians, too, have contributed to this stereotype through their willingness to accept guilt for taking defensive action. Barbara Hart explains:

> It is as if they have concluded that absent any violence they can with clarity identify themselves as victims of the abuser, but once they have been violent, especially if it has worked in the immediate situation to stop the batterer, they are compelled to see themselves as equally culpable—as batterers—and as obligated to fight back every time or otherwise to accept the ultimate responsibility for the battering.[26]

Framing the violence as mutual and belittling it as a "catfight" allows system actors to dismiss the stories told by battered lesbians as overblown and unrealistic, and therefore unworthy of belief, or as involving violence too trivial to waste the court's time with. The battered lesbian's inability to see herself as a victim because she has used violence may prevent her from conveying a coherent narrative of victimization—the kind of narrative that a court wants to hear.

Battered lesbians may fight back more often because of their parity in size and strength with their partners. But misperceptions about women's "roles" within their relationships based on differences in size and appearance cast doubt on victims' stories of abuse. Bluntly put, batterers are not always butch. "Many battered lesbians are women of substantial physical prowess and power; women who are objectively very much more powerful than their assailants. They are women who choose not to use this power to control the perpetrator or would do so only to protect themselves or stop the batterer."[27] Nonetheless, the perception that batterers are butch and victims femme makes it more difficult for larger, more physically imposing women to persuade others that they have been abused. One important criterion that friends of battered lesbians use to assess the validity of their claims of abuse is their physical size and demeanor relative to that of their partners. Butch women abused by their femme partners have described the shame they felt when others assumed, based on their size or appearance, that they must be the perpetrators, as well as the difficulties they faced in securing assistance.

ACCESS TO SHELTER AND DOMESTIC VIOLENCE SERVICE PROVIDERS

Untangling the social science research on the impact of access to resources on women's decisions to fight back is more complicated. Some writers suggest that access to resources has a strong influence on African American women's decisions to use violence. Some African American women, for example, report that they will not turn to formal social services because they have had past negative encounters with the social service provision system. Having encountered social service systems that are not culturally competent, and that may even feel hostile, they are unlikely to avail themselves of those services. Other African American women perceive that the supports and services created to assist battered women are intended to be used only by white women. When African American women are willing to turn to service systems for assistance, their efforts may be thwarted. African American women, especially those living in the South and urban areas, have greater difficulty accessing shelters than white women. Particularly for poor African American women living in depressed urban areas, simply reaching the available social services may be impossible. As Bent-Goodley explains, "Transportation constraints, lack of money to get to appointments, and fear of entering a perceived hostile environment often result in a decreased likelihood of African Americans keeping appointments and fully participating in services."[28] When they do seek shelter, African American women may confront racism among staff and residents and may clash with shelter staff interested in assisting only worthy—stereotypically meek and unassertive—victims. Other studies, however, contend that African American women use services at the same rates as or greater rates than do white women, and that the greater use of services by African American women has contributed to the decline in the number of homicide deaths among African American men. These studies call the argument that limited access to services may make African American women more likely to fight back into question.

Battered lesbians may also have difficulty accessing resources to address interpersonal violence. Despite increases in federally funded services for battered women, resources like shelters are still scarce in many communities. Lesbians perceive mainstream shelters as the province of heterosexual women—which is ironic, because lesbians have played key roles at every point in the development and maintenance of shelters. Although lesbians were integral to the growth and success of the battered women's movement, the view that shelters are the province of straight women is sometimes shared by shelter residents and staff, who express discomfort at the idea of living and working with lesbians. Even professionals who are open to assisting battered lesbians may feel precluded from doing so by the homophobia of the residents or the organization.[29]

Battered lesbians may also find that service providers buy into the gendered nature of violence, the idea that violence done by women cannot be as serious as that perpetrated by men, and the myth of mutuality. Service providers may be less willing to expend scarce resources on women whose victimization seems trivial. The battered woman's appearance may also prevent the battered lesbian from receiving services. As Janice Ristock explains, "[S]ervice providers are more likely to respond positively to battered women if they conform to stereotypes of 'respectable femininity'";[30] butch lesbians need not apply for assistance. Black lesbians may find that professionals use race as a proxy for masculinity when assessing violence between women, disadvantaging African American lesbians being battered by white partners. Fighting back may further jeopardize the battered lesbian's ability to access services. Admitting to the use of violence may lead to the recharacterization of the victim as a batterer, rendering her ineligible for shelter, counseling, and other assistance.

Shared gender gives the perpetrator of violence the opportunity to foreclose access to services. The batterer, using her gender to assert her status as the victim, may have already applied for or be receiving services from the sole provider in the area. The batterer who, after separation, learns that her victim is living in shelter or participating in a program may use her gender to gain entry to the victim's safe space. Worse yet, the batterer may be employed by that service provider or be friendly with the staff of the organization. If the abusive partner discredits the battered lesbian in the advocacy community, the latter may find her access to services sorely limited.

CONFRONTING THE LEGAL SYSTEM

Given the culture of secrecy that surrounds domestic violence in many African American communities, African American women may be deeply conflicted about turning to the legal system, and their relationship with the system is an ambivalent one. Some women simply refuse to involve the police. Kim, a battered African American woman, recounted her decision not to call the police:

> Call the police? Never!... [I] just never could really trust that they would help me and not just use my 911 call as one more excuse to beat up a Black man.... I learned early in my life the cops were dangerous to my people. They were to be avoided at all costs.[31]

In sociologist Neil Websdale's survey of poor African American women in Nashville, Tennessee, Alicia explained that some African American women will not call the police to the projects because doing so means giving up the very little privacy that these women have or because the women are involved in other illegal activities.[32]

Although African American women are more likely than white women to call the police for assistance, they are often dubious about what the police will actually do for them. Similarly, African American women who turn to the courts know that there is no guarantee that they will find assistance there. Social scientists have suggested that stereotypes that depict African Americans as more prone to violence than whites have depressed law enforcement and judicial responses to violence in the African American community. Stories about negative interactions between African American women and the legal system are common. Janet, a battered African American woman who went to court for assistance, described her experience:

> When I finally went for help they asked why I waited so long.... I could tell that the judge didn't believe me, especially because he went on and on about how I "seemed so smart and all." Now what's that supposed to mean? That he's dumb? I don't want any white judge talking about my man that way. Or did he mean that the sisters ... are dumb? Either way, it was a put-down that I didn't appreciate at all. So to answer him, *that's* why I didn't go for help sooner.[33]

Such experiences can have long-lasting ramifications; after battered women learn that the systems put in place to address the violence against them are not responsive to their needs, they are less likely to turn to those systems a second time. Given that the legal system is the primary means for responding to domestic violence in American society, the removal of that system as a real option for African American women may leave them grasping for other alternatives to address the violence they face.

Battered lesbians do not perceive the police as helpful.

> [O]ne woman wrote on her questionnaire that the officers who responded to her call for help insulted her by calling her a "queer devil." She wrote that they told her that she deserved trouble because she is a lesbian.... During the interviews, another woman said, "I called the police, but nothing was done about it. I kept thinking, 'No one cares because I am a lesbian.' The police basically took the attitude, 'So two dykes are trying to kill each other; big deal.'"[34]

Given the history of homophobia within the police community, battered lesbians are understandably wary of requesting police assistance. In her groundbreaking study of lesbian domestic violence, sociologist Claire Renzetti found that only 19 of the 100 battered lesbian women she surveyed called the police; of those 19 women, 15 characterized the assistance they received as a little helpful or not helpful at all.[35] Studies suggest that police are less likely to intervene in same-sex domestic violence cases. Like other professionals, police may be unwilling to intervene because they perceive the violence as mutual or because they minimize the violence that women do. The rise in the numbers of arrests of women and dual arrests suggests that police may be unwilling or unable to determine who the primary aggressor is in these cases. Recognizing this problem, some communities have worked diligently to improve police response to same-sex violence cases. The District of Columbia, for example, created a special unit to respond to same-sex violence calls, headed by an openly gay police officer.

Lesbians may be even less likely to seek assistance through the courts than they are to call the police; in Renzetti's study, only 2 percent of the women surveyed said they would find the legal system or courts helpful in resolving their problems. This reluctance to turn to the courts reflects both a general sense that the courts are not helpful to battered women (even straight women) and specific concerns about the treatment of lesbians.

Renzetti's inquiry presupposes that lesbians can access civil remedies. Some state laws, however, explicitly exclude lesbians from protection order laws; others do so implicitly, by virtue of the relationships covered by the statute. Even where court remedies are available, however, the prospect of appearing in a civil court can be daunting. Sandra Lundy recounts,

> As a lawyer, I know from experience that litigating openly queer cases in civil court is never easy. You can be sure that somehow, somewhere, when you least expect it, homophobia will rear its ugly head in the courtroom, derailing your arguments, upsetting your client, making it impossible to be heard.[36]

Given the courts' unfamiliarity and discomfort with same-sex violence, judges may demand more evidence of the violence, proof that may be impossible to provide given the private nature of battering and the reluctance of battered lesbians to seek outside assistance. Although judges and courtroom staff may be respectful of victims, battered lesbians may nonetheless be ridiculed by those watching the proceedings. The myth of mutual abuse frequently leads to the issuance of inappropriate mutual restraining orders, sending the victim the message that she has not been believed and that she is not entitled to any greater protection than her abuser. Even when orders are granted, those orders may not be strictly enforced, making their worth questionable. Faced with those challenges, it is unsurprising that few battered lesbians see the court system as a viable source of assistance.

THE IMPORTANCE OF OWNING NARRATIVES

Notwithstanding the dominant image of the passive victim, battered women do fight back. Because theirs is not a story that courts are conditioned to hear, however, it is a story that advocates frequently discourage their clients from telling. Revealing that a battered woman has used physical violence against her abuser may blind the judge to her need for protection. So advocates ask their questions narrowly and prepare their clients carefully, omitting any mention of the force that victims use. Victims' stories go untold in the name of securing assistance.

The stories of battered women who fight back are remarkably diverse. They are stories of fear, frustration, anger, protectiveness, lack of options, lack of resources, self-image, racism, and homophobia. But in the hands of advocates, those stories frequently get distilled down to the story of the paradigmatic victim, the stock narrative, minus any violence the woman might have done, no matter what her reason. The choice to exclude violence from the narratives of battered women who fight back is logical from an instrumental perspective. But the failure to tell judges the unedited stories of battered women who fight back has ramifications for both battered women and advocates. The inability to tell their stories may prevent battered women from healing and exacerbate doubts about battered women's credibility. The silencing of battered women's voices undermines their autonomy and highlights a troubling trend in the battered women's movement—replacing women's stories and experiences with professional judgments about what is best for battered women. Battered women who fight back tell stories that judges don't expect to hear. Coupled with concerns about judges' perception of the credibility of battered women, it is hardly surprising that advocates edit women's violence out of their stories.

Over time, stories coalesce around familiar themes and characters, and those stock narratives, or skeletons, frame how we come to view unfamiliar people and situations. Deviating from the stock narrative may create cognitive dissonance for the hearer; stories that depart from the expected may not be easily heard. The legal universe is constructed on these stock stories; skeletons "are part of a line of precedent that reflects a universalized narrative."[37] We create similar skeletons of people. "Our culture," Mark A. Fajer explains, "contains a wide variety of assumptions, both good and bad, about categories of people. Although not everybody believes in the strongest versions of these assumptions— that every member of the group strongly displays the characteristic— most people understand that our society connects certain traits with certain categories."[38] One obvious connection of a category and a trait in the context of domestic violence is battered women and passivity.

It is hardly surprising that lawyers organize their cases around these stock characters and stories, seeking to situate their clients' narratives within the skeletons of past successes. The failure to conform can be disastrous for the litigant. "Pre-understandings" of group characteristics impede true understanding when a group member exhibits characteristics that are markedly different—like fighting back. In the court context, the inability to overcome a pre-understanding of a "battered woman" as "passive" could easily preclude the woman who fights back from being able to persuade a judge that she needs protection; the judge would instead create a story that reflects his own beliefs about how battered women are expected to behave, and rule accordingly. The lawyer's role is to prevent the judge from reconstructing the client's story in a way that undermines the client's goals for the representation. For a victim of violence, if the goal is to secure a protective order, the lawyer must attempt to persuade the judge of a narrative that fits the narrow bounds of what is actionable under the law. If the woman's goal is to publicly tell a story that may be difficult for the judge to hear, though, the lawyer's role might be to create space for that story, notwithstanding the impact on the outcome for the case. One woman's decision to tell a different story can pose a danger for other litigants. As Mary Coombs explains in the context of rape victims, "[U]nsuccessful narrative structures help reconfirm the very … myths that make future cases hard to win."[39] When unconventional narratives are not persuasive, later litigants who tell similar stories may find it difficult to prevail.

Battered women enter the courtroom at a disadvantage. Social science research establishes that women are generally perceived as less credible than men (and, occasionally, as no more credible than children). The claims of battered women are viewed with a great deal of suspicion; the credibility of battered women is challenged at every turn. Judges share their cynicism about battered women's claims with their colleagues; the judicial grapevine buzzes with the received wisdom that women seek protective orders only to gain advantage in divorce and custody proceedings. The materials produced to aid judges with their determinations reflect this incredulity; in one bench book dedicated to family law matters, judges are told to view the claims of battered women with a healthy dose of skepticism. While it is rare to see such advice in print, advocates and judges have both described the disbelief with which battered women's claims are received.

Judicial doubt intensifies when women describe how they fight back against their abusers. While the stories that clients tell their lawyers reveal a range of human behaviors, stories that challenge judicial pre-understandings of victim characteristics are likely to raise doubts about the victim's credibility. Women who fight back enter the courtroom with their credibility in question by virtue of their failure to comply with the prevailing victim stereotype. As evidenced by the stories told above, women who fight back are not seen as needing protection, and their claims are routinely downplayed (particularly in the cases of lesbian victims) or dismissed.

In heterosexual couples, arguments about similarities in the rates of violence among men and women may be at play as well. An entire literature disputing the prevalence of men as perpetrators of interpersonal violence has emerged; some see this literature as a backlash against the gains that the battered women's movement has made over the past 30 years. Backlash or not, doubters have certainly succeeded in pressing the public case for proportionality—the proposition that, within relationships, men and women are equally violent. Despite the reasoned responses to these claims (that men's violence is more serious, more damaging, and more likely to be a means of controlling their victims), those preaching proportionality have made some inroads into society's understanding of what interpersonal violence is. Judges are not immune; when women describe how they fight back, those judges with whom the proportionality argument resonates may be likely to simply categorize those women as violent rather than explore the context for women's violence and the justification for its use.

Race compounds the credibility deficit for African American women who fight back. Studies show that African American women, as witnesses and litigants, are far less likely to be believed by judges and jurors. By virtue of the color of their skin, argues Linda Ammons, black women are "suspect, unless they prove otherwise."[40] African American women who fight back are the most suspect of all; African American women who fight back are less likely to be seen as testifying truthfully about the assault than passive African American women.

To convince judges of the credibility of women who fight back, an essential element of most protective order cases given the private nature of domestic violence and the frequent lack of evidence other than the victim's testimony, advocates might be sorely tempted to edit unhelpful details out, to "spin the victim's demeanor as consistent with the myth of the helpless battered woman."[41] The failure to reinterpret the narrative in a manner that meshes with a judge's preconceptions could prevent the client from securing the relief she seeks—the relief that she asked the advocate to help her obtain.

The process of coming to court to seek protection is not one undertaken lightly by most victims. Having been assaulted by someone she likely loved and trusted, the battered woman then must decide whether to make that violence public by sharing it with court staff, judges, and advocates. She may come to court knowing that taking that step is likely to anger her abuser further or irrevocably change her relationship. Calculating all of the variables—her needs, her fear, her love for her partner, and so many more—she decides to tell her story. It is essential that she find a listener willing to hear and accept that story.

> Those whose stories are believed have the power to create fact; those whose stories are not believed live in a legally sanctioned "reality" that does not match their perceptions.... [T]here are few things more disempowering in law than having one's own self-believed story rejected, when rules of law (however fair in the abstract) are applied to facts that are not one's own, when legal judgments proceed from a description of one's own world that one does not recognize.[42]

A judicial determination that her story is not credible can be crushing for a battered woman who summons the courage to come before the court and describe her abuse. Such a ruling rejects her reality, recreates her life in a way that clashes with her own experiences, and, ultimately, denies her the court's protection. Once dismissed, these women may then be less likely to seek the assistance of the courts again.

Given how high the stakes are for women seeking the court's assistance, the compunction that battered women and their advocates feel to tell stories that jibe with the court's preconceptions about victims of violence makes perfect sense. But the failure to allow, to encourage, battered women to tell their stories as they see fit has a price as well.

The stories we tell give us the opportunity to define ourselves. Self-definition can be particularly important for marginalized groups whose identities have been constructed by a dominant culture as a means of silencing and oppression. When lawyers edit the stories of battered women, they lie about who they are and how they perceive the world around them. When those stories are accepted by others as truth, women are forced to live that lie. For the battered woman who fights back, that lie—that she is the passive, weak, dependent, stereotypical victim—contradicts the actions that she has taken to protect herself and can undermine her self-image and self-worth as well as her standing in her community.

The failure to tell the stories of women who fight back not only denies the experiences of the individual women, but also undermines the credibility of the women who will come after them seeking assistance from the courts. Until judges grow accustomed to hearing the diversity of battered women's stories, they will continue to look askance at nonconforming narratives. Skilled advocates can help judges to understand these stories, working with clients to shape and present the true narratives in ways that judges might accept. But given the dearth of representation for victims of domestic violence, few women have such advocates. Women without counsel "cannot benefit from the techniques of 'demeanor repackaging'" used to make the stories of women who fight back more palatable to judges.[43] When advocates counsel women who fight back to edit their stories rather than helping judges to reformulate their notions of who a battered woman is, they deny unrepresented women the opportunity to gain from the telling of their clients' stories as well. The failure to tell these narratives may even increase the danger to women who fight back. Martha McMahon and Ellen Pence argue that,

> Women who fight back become increasingly vulnerable to their abusers if the advocacy community does not recognize their actions as legitimate responses to being beaten. The idealized image of the perfect victim and the naïve notion that there is a healthy or proper way of being abused makes women who fight back ... more vulnerable to both the abuser and the institutions to which they turn for help.[44]

When advocates are unwilling to accept that women fight back and to present fighting back as a coping strategy, they are complicit in the silencing of their clients and in the creation of additional hurdles for other women.

The silencing of women who fight back is particularly ironic given the theoretical foundations of advocacy for battered women. Recognizing that battered women had been denied agency and authority in their relationships, a belief in a woman's right to self-determination was one of the cornerstones of the nascent battered women's movement. The movement's focus on the empowerment of battered women attracted many advocates to the work. As the movement has become more professionalized, however, "sisters" have become clients, and the voices of battered women have been muted in favor of deference to the judgment of the social workers, counselors, lay advocates, and lawyers working with them. One unintended consequence of the credentialing of the battered women's movement may be the failure of these professionals to acknowledge the diversity of battered women's stories.

The pressure that advocates exert to edit the stories of women who fight back constitutes a sort of substituted judgment. It underscores advocates' assumptions, based on their experiences, that women who fight back will not be eligible for relief unless their stories echo the prevailing narrative. It devalues the rational and legitimate choice that a woman makes to fight back. Editing a woman's decision to fight back out of her story suggests to the woman that her decisions are unjustifiable, her actions aberrant. Battered women choose to fight back to preserve their autonomy and sense of self; those choices are denigrated when that portion of their narratives is stifled. Each time an advocate counsels a woman to tailor her story without appreciating that decision or giving her the opportunity to tell her story as she chooses, that advocate turns her back on the principles that undergirded the battered woman's movement and does violence to her client.

Attorneys have tremendous power in shaping the stories of their clients; even if the lawyer hews closely to the story told by the client (and not all do), it is the lawyer's voice, the lawyer's choice of words, and the lawyer's tone and inflection and pacing that structure the narrative heard by the court. Lawyers can misuse that power in a number of ways: by silencing client voices, by omitting particular kinds of narratives, by presenting only narratives that are acceptable to the legal system, and by requiring client obedience to the lawyer's translation of the story. When lawyers rewrite client stories without client input or approval, they take from clients the power to decide how they want to be presented and exclude the client from the strategic choices that will shape her case.

Reconstructing client narratives in ways that are not consistent with their choices, feelings, and perspectives on the violence is disempowering for battered women. M. Joan McDermott and James Garofalo suggest that battered women are disempowered when they are told to reconstruct their stories in order to make them more palatable to the legal system. This reshaping is disempowering, they argue, because it suggests that women's

> own stories lack the legitimacy of real, prosecutable criminal victimization. Ironically, the practice of conveying to victims the idea that "you're only a victim if ..." is the very practice that the women's movement has fought long and hard against for victims of domestic battery and sexual assault.[45]

The disregard for women's lived experiences may make them feel "absent, impotent, even desperate,"[46] a far cry from what most advocates hoped to achieve when they began working with battered women.

In one final irony, sometimes the reframing simply cannot contain the client's lived experience. Stark describes how Emily D. initially resisted her attorney's pressure to present herself as a passive victim. Although Emily later relented, the stock victim story simply could not be squared with Emily herself—"aggressive, demanding, even 'rude.'" As Stark recounts, "The more Emily D. was advised by her attorneys to behave like the stereotypic victim the court expected, the more inappropriate her behavior became."[47] The lawyers' determination to substitute their judgment for Emily D.'s ultimately undermined the client's case. Even when clients assent to the editing of their stories, then, when those stories are not consistent with the client's experiences as she understands and expresses them, that conflict can manifest itself in ways that undermine her credibility. Lawyers who counsel clients to change their stories in order to help them "win" might, in fact, be achieving just the opposite result.

REWRITING THE VICTIM NARRATIVE

The creation of the stereotypical battered woman is not solely a function of what the courts and media have been taught to expect, but also of what the advocacy community has chosen to present to those systems despite its increasing awareness of the diversity of battered women. This narrowing of the range of acceptable victims began during the early years of the movement, and continues each time that an advocate edits a client story because she believes that otherwise the client cannot prevail. The failure to allow clients to tell unedited narratives increases the barriers that nonstereotypical victims face when they seek assistance. Particularly for unrepresented women, who have no advocates to craft acceptable stories, the results have been devastating.

To the extent that lawyers doubt that clients' stories will be credible or persuasive, they perpetuate untruths about clients who fight back— that they are not believable, that they are wantonly violent, and that they are not victims of abuse. Why should judges change their minds about these women and reassess the stories they tell if their lawyers have no faith in those stories either?

Lawyers must be willing to tell counterstories—alternate narratives that subvert the received wisdom and describe clients' authentic experiences with their violent partners. Counterstories bring into stark relief the gulf between judicial assumptions about battered women and real women seeking the court's protection. Faced with this juxtaposition of the paradigmatic victim and the living, breathing plaintiff telling a very different story, judges may have to rethink the stereotypes on which they rely. One counterstory might be easy for a judge to reject; regular exposure to these stories, however, should make a judge question the basis for his or her beliefs about battered women.

Collaboration between lawyer and client is essential in the construction of counterstories. Power imbalances are inherent in the attorney-client relationship; to redress that imbalance, "room for client voice ... must be carved out of lawyer-dominated space."[48] The need for collaboration also addresses the concern about the instrumentality of client stories. The decision to tell a counternarrative must be the result of discussion about the goals of the representation and the advocate's approach to his or her work with battered women, as well as thoughtful counseling about how the legal system is likely to view the client's claims. Through that conversation, the advocate and client must decide what empowerment means for that woman, particularly if they believe that testifying to how she fought back and winning her case are mutually exclusive goals. The lawyer has no right to assume that the client would always choose to "win" over telling a particular story. Advocates should share their experiences with the legal system, not only to give the client a sense of what she might face should she decide to tell her own story, but also to provide the client with a sense of the importance of her story within the larger context of the legal system and of the battles that women without counsel face when they tell unmediated narratives. Battered women might be more willing to share their stories regardless of the consequences if they understood how doing so could benefit the women who come after them. The advocate and the client must discuss short- and long-term goals, not only around what the legal system can offer by way of immediate protection, but also in terms of additional legal options, how her choices will affect her family and other relationships, how telling her story relates to her sense of herself, and any other concern that the client puts on the table. Only after these discussions have taken place can the client make an informed choice about how to formulate her legal narrative. Creating space for that choice, and providing context for making the choice, recognizes the client's autonomy and underscores the advocate's commitment to empowerment, both for her own client and for the battered women she cannot represent.

The lawyer must also recognize that the client may not yet have found her voice or may be unsure of the story she wants to tell. Traumatized, defiant, angry, grieving the loss of the relationship, and ashamed of her action or inaction, the client's story may change depending on the emotions she feels and the acceptance or resistance she meets as she begins to articulate her narrative. Her story may be in transition and may remain in flux over the life of the case. Leslie Espinoza cautions, "Lawyer interaction with a client who has been abused should allow the client the space to construct a story in her own time."[49] The lawyer must avoid the temptation to see the initial client story as the "truth" and adhere to that narrative regardless of how the client's understanding of her story evolves over time.

Moving away from the paradigmatic victim through counterstories is neither a quick nor easy task. Some have asked whether, given the many pitfalls it poses for battered women, it is worthwhile to attempt to tell these stories in the legal system at all. The dearth of other avenues to address violence, however, and the benefits that can accrue to those who are successful in bringing legal claims, both by way of protection and by way of the validation that can come from telling a story and having the system respond positively as a result, make it imperative that advocates attempt to create a forum for the stories of women who fight back in the legal system. To make such space, judges "must first be convinced of some inadequacy in the old" story before being open to a new one; as a result, "story change is ... both difficult and incremental."[50] But the difficulty of the endeavor is hardly a reason to continue to perpetuate a stereotype that does not reflect, and indeed undermines, the lived experiences of battered women who fight back and ask the legal system for protection.

Janice Ristock writes, "My work on lesbian abuse seeks to tell troubling tales."[51] Too often, however, advocates for battered women substitute safe stories for troubling tales, editing the violence that their clients do out of the stories that they tell judges. While those omissions may be instrumental in the sense that they may help women to attain the short-term goal of securing the protection of the court, in the long run—by enabling the paradigmatic victim to remain the gold standard for the court system—such omissions undermine the opportunities available to women who fight back. By telling counterstories, advocates can show judges the variety and complexity of the stories of battered women and provide spaces in which those stories can be heard.

NOTES

1. This chapter is adapted from "When Is a Battered Woman Not a Battered Woman? When She Fights Back," *Yale Journal of Law and Feminism* 20 (2008).

2. S. L. Miller, *Victims as Offenders: The Paradox of Women's Violence* (New Brunswick, NJ: Rutgers University Press, 2005), 131.

3. E. Stark, *Coercive Control: The Entrapment of Women in Personal Life* (New York: Oxford University Press, 2007), 165–66.

4. Miller, *Victims as Offenders*, 116–20.

5. M. P. Johnson, *A Typology of Domestic Violence: Intimate Terrorism, Violent Resistance, and Situational Couple Violence* (Boston: Northeastern University Press, 2008).

6. L. K. Hamburger and C. E. Guse, "Men's and Women's Use of Intimate Partner Violence in Clinical Samples," *Violence against Women* 8 (2002): 1314.

7. S. Das Dasgupta, "Just Like Men? A Critical View of Violence by Women," in *Coordinating Community Response to Domestic Violence: Lessons from Duluth and Beyond*, ed. M. F. Shepard and E. L. Pence (Thousand Oaks, CA: Sage, 1999), 214.

8. S. Osthoff, "But Gertrude, I Beg to Differ, a Hit Is Not a Hit Is Not a Hit: When Battered Women Are Arrested for Assaulting Their Partners," *Violence Against Women* 8 (2002): 1527.

9. Osthoff, "But Gertrude," 1529.

10. Miller, *Victims as Offenders*, 66.

11. K. J. Ferraro, "The Words Change, but the Melody Lingers: The Persistence of the Battered Woman Syndrome in Criminal Cases Involving Battered Women," *Violence Against Women* 9 (2003): 116.

12. M. Abraham, "Fighting Back: Abused South Asian Women's Strategies of Resistance," in *Domestic Violence at the Margins: Readings on Race, Class, Gender, and Culture*, ed. N. J. Sokoloff with C. Pratt (New Brunswick, NJ: Rutgers University Press, 2005), 259.

13. N. Websdale, "Nashville: Domestic Violence and Incarcerated Women in Poor Black Neighborhoods," in *Domestic Violence at the Margins*, 142–56.

14. J. Y. Taylor, "Talking Back: Research as an Act of Resistance and Healing for African American Women Survivors of Intimate Male Partner Violence," in *Violence in the Lives of Black Women: Battered, Black and Blue*, ed. C. M. West (New York: Routledge, 2002), 149.

15. J. C. McClennen, "Partner Abuse between Lesbian Couples: Toward a Better Understanding," in *A Professional's Guide to Understanding Gay and Lesbian Domestic Violence: Understanding Practice Interventions*, ed. J. C. McClennen and J. Gunther (Lewiston, NY: Edwin Mellon Press, 1999), 78.

16. S. E. Lundy, "Abuse That Dare Not Speak Its Name: Assisting Victims of Lesbians and Gay Domestic Violence in Massachusetts," *New England Law Review* 28 (1993): 286.

17. K. Lobel, "Introduction," in *Naming the Violence: Speaking Out about Lesbian Battering*, ed. K. Lobel (Berkeley, CA: Seal Press, 1986), 7.

18. B. E. Richie, *Compelled to Crime: The Gender Entrapment of Battered Black Women* (New York: Routledge, 1996), 95.

19. V.A. Moss et al., "The Experience of Terminating an Abusive Relationship from an Anglo and African American Perspective: A Qualitative Descriptive Study," *Issues in Mental Health Nursing* 18 (1997): 443.

20. Richie, *Compelled to Crime*, 114.

21. Ibid., 94.

22. B. Hart, "Preface," in Lobel, *Naming the Violence*, 14.

23. C. Renzetti, *Violent Betrayal: Partner Abuse in Lesbian Relationships* (Thousand Oaks, CA: Sage, 1992), 102–3.

24. M. L. Dietrich, "Nothing Is the Same Anymore," in Lobel, *Naming the Violence*, 158.

25. A. Robinson, "'There's a Stranger in This House': African American Lesbians and Domestic Violence," in West, *Violence in the Lives of Black Women*, 128.

26. B. Hart, "Lesbian Battering: An Examination," in Lobel, *Naming the Violence*, 184.

27. Hart, "Lesbian Battering," 185.

28. T. B. Bent-Goodley, "Perceptions of Domestic Violence: A Dialogue with African American Women," *Health and Social Work* 29 (2004): 308.

29. N. Hammond, "Lesbian Victims and the Reluctance to Identify Abuse," in Lobel, *Naming the Violence*, 196.

30. J. L. Ristock, *No More Secrets: Violence in Lesbian Relationships* (New York: Routledge, 2002), 101.

31. Richie, *Compelled to Crime*, 95.

32. Websdale, "Nashville," 145.

33. Richie, *Compelled to Crime*, 96.

34. Renzetti, *Violent Betrayal*, 91.

35. Ibid., 90–91.

36. S. E. Lundy, "Equal Protection/Equal Safety: Representing Victims of Same-Sex Partner Abuse in Court," in *Same Sex Domestic Violence: Strategies for Change*, ed. B. Levanthal and S. E. Lundy (Thousand Oaks, CA: Sage, 1999), 43.

37. C. P. Gilkerson, "Poverty Law Narratives: The Critical Practice and Theory of Receiving and Translating Client Stories," *Hastings Law Journal* 43 (1992): 911.

38. M. A. Fajer, "Authority, Credibility, and Pre-Understanding: A Defense of Outsider Narratives in Legal Scholarship," *Georgetown Law Journal* 82 (1994): 1847.

39. M. I. Coombs, "Telling the Victim's Story," *Texas Journal of Women and the Law* 2 (1993): 291.

40. L. L. Ammons, "Mules, Madonnas, Babies, Bathwater, Racial Imagery and Stereotypes: The African American Woman and the Battered Woman Syndrome," *Wisconsin Law Review* 1995 (1995): 1042.

41. L. S. Kohn, "Barriers to Reliable Credibility Assessments: Domestic Violence Victim-Witnesses," *American University Journal of Gender, Social Policy and the Law* 11 (2003): 735.

42. K. Lane Scheppele, "Forward: Telling Stories," *Michigan Law Review* 87 (1989): 2079.

43. Kohn, "Barriers," 735.

44. M. McMahon and E. Pence, "Making Social Change: Reflections on Individual and Institutional Advocacy with Women Arrested for Domestic Violence," *Violence Against Women* 9 (2003): 71.

45. M. J. McDermott and J. Garofalo, "When Advocacy for Domestic Violence Victims Backfires: Types and Sources of Victim Disempowerment," *Violence Against Women* 10 (2004): 1259.

46. E. Stark, "Re-presenting Woman Battering: From Battered Woman Syndrome to Coercive Control," *Albany Law Review* 58 (1995): 1011.

47. Stark, "Re-presenting Woman Battering," 1013–14.

48. A. V. Alfieri, "Reconstructive Poverty Law Practice: Learning Lessons of Client Narrative," *Yale Law Journal* 100 (1991): 2140.

49. L. G. Espinoza, "Legal Narratives, Therapeutic Narratives: The Invisibility and Omnipresence of Race and Gender," *Michigan Law Review* 95 (1997): 908.

50. A. A. Taslitz, "Patriarchal Stories I: Cultural Rape Narratives in the Courtroom," *Southern California Review of Law and Women's Studies* 5 (1996): 435.

51. Ristock, *No More Secrets*, 28.

Chapter 3

Women's Use of Violence with Male Intimate Partners

Suzanne C. Swan
Jennifer E. Caldwell
Tami P. Sullivan
David L. Snow

Are women just as violent as men in their intimate relationships? Or, is women's violence fundamentally different from men's violence? This chapter examines these two competing perspectives about women's violence in their intimate relationships. Our major conclusions are that women's violence usually occurs in the context of violence against them by their male partners. In general, women and men perpetrate equivalent levels of physical and psychological aggression, but men perpetrate sexual abuse, coercive control, and stalking more frequently than women; women also are much more frequently injured during domestic violence incidents. Women and men are equally likely to initiate physical violence in relationships involving less serious "situational couple violence"; in relationships in which serious and very violent "intimate terrorism" occurs, men are much more likely to be perpetrators and women victims.

Women's physical violence is more likely than men's violence to be motivated by self-defense and fear; men's physical violence is more likely than women's to be driven by control motives. Even in mutually violent relationships, women suffer more negative effects than men. Because of the many differences in behaviors and motivations between women's and men's violence, interventions designed to stop or prevent violence in intimate relationships that are based on male models of partner violence are not effective for many women.

BACKGROUND

> He was drunk and I was drunk.... He says you ain't going anywhere, and I said I am. I pushed him and he pushed me to the floor. I got up and I just tore into him. I scratched him right on the neck and he punched me in the mouth and cut inside of my lip. Next thing I know, I'm standing in the hallway, there's cops handcuffing me. (Christina, describing the incident that got her arrested)[1]

One of the major accomplishments of the domestic violence revolution that began in the 1970s was to force criminal justice systems to hold domestic violence offenders accountable and to provide protection to victims. A testament to this success is that all states now have increased police authority to make arrests without a warrant in domestic violence cases, and the majority of states have mandatory arrest provisions (i.e., arrest is mandated when there is probable cause to believe domestic violence has occurred) or preferred arrest provisions (i.e., arrest is the preferred response in cases of domestic violence). These reforms in domestic violence laws were prompted by cases such as *Thurman v. City of Torrington* (1984).[2] Although Tracy Thurman left her violent husband, he continued to stalk and abuse her. She repeatedly sought police protection from him, to no avail. Finally, her husband was placed on probation after smashing the windshield of her car while she was in it. Mr. Thurman violated his probation by threatening to shoot Mrs. Thurman and her son, but the police still would not arrest him. When he came to her home and demanded to speak to her, Mrs. Thurman called the police and told them she feared for her life. Ten minutes later, Charles Thurman stabbed her in the chest, neck, and throat. A police officer arrived 15 minutes after the stabbing and watched as Mr. Thurman kicked his injured wife in the head. Mrs. Thurman won $2.3 million in a lawsuit against the Torrington (Connecticut) Police Department, and changed how police across the nation responded to domestic violence.

Two outcomes relevant to the present discussion of women's violence against partners resulted from the creation of stronger domestic violence arrest protocols. The first is an intended consequence of the reforms: there has been a dramatic increase in the numbers of individuals arrested for domestic violence offenses. Rates of arrest for domestic violence calls have increased from 7 to 15 percent in the pre-reform era to a national average of 49 percent in the year 2000 for domestic violence between intimate partners.[3] The second change is an unintended consequence of the stronger arrest protocol, and that is that the proportion of women being arrested for domestic violence offenses also has grown dramatically. Following the implementation of mandatory or preferred arrest policies, the arrests of women for domestic violence rose from 5 to 17 percent in California; 23 to 35 percent in Concord, New Hampshire; and 13 to 25 percent in a Minnesota county.[4] On a national level, Hirschel et al.'s analysis of all assault and intimidation cases in the U.S. National Incident Based Reporting System for the year 2000 found that 23.4 percent of those individuals arrested were female.

These findings raise many questions about women's violence against male intimate partners. Are these women who are arrested for domestic violence *batterers*? Do their partners live in fear of them the way many battered women fear their violent partners? Do they control every aspect of their partners' lives through threats of violence, isolation, and emotional abuse, as male batterers do? Do they use other forms of abuse, such as sexual abuse and stalking? Or, are some of the women practicing what sociologist Michael Johnson calls violent resistance— that is, are they victims fighting back against their abusers?[5]

Further questions are raised about judicial responses and treatment for these women. Mandatory and preferred arrest policies were originally enacted with batterers like Charles Thurman in mind. What if, after enduring years of abuse, Tracy Thurman beat her husband? Should she be arrested? If she is arrested, what sort of treatment should she receive? Most states provide court-mandated domestic violence perpetrator treatment to individuals who have committed a domestic violence offense (see chapter 8 in this volume by Saunders). These treatment programs, like current arrest policies, were designed for male batterers like Charles Thurman. For example, almost all states that have standards for court-mandated treatment programs provided to domestic violence offenders stipulate that the program must conceptualize domestic abuse as a form of power and control, in which an abuser uses violence to enact power and control over a victim. This framework stems from an early, very influential domestic violence perpetrator treatment program, the Duluth model, based on the feminist theory that patriarchal ideology, which encourages men to control their partners, causes domestic violence.

If Tracy Thurman were to be arrested for beating her husband, would the typical domestic violence perpetrator treatment program that is available in most states be appropriate or helpful for her? Does her behavior fit the conceptualization of a patriarchal abuser using violence to enact power and control over a victim—in this case, her husband? In fact, many women who are arrested for domestic violence are court-mandated to attend these kinds of programs. In all likelihood, the typical domestic violence perpetrator treatment program would not be helpful for Tracy Thurman or for Christina (quoted at the beginning of this section) because their motives for using violence, the context for their use of violence, and the types and patterns of violence used are very different from those of men like Charles Thurman.

While the criminal justice system struggles to respond appropriately to female domestic violence offenders, a debate about gender and intimate partner violence has been occurring among researchers for decades, and to this day remains unresolved. The debate concerns whether women are really "just as violent as men" toward their intimate male partners, or whether there are qualitative, essential differences between men's and women's violence against partners. Writings reflecting the theme that women's violence is equivalent to that of men's (often called the "gender symmetry" argument) typically cite the numerous survey studies of physically violent behavior using the Conflict Tactics Scale, a very widely used instrument that assesses aggression toward an intimate partner. The instrument is a checklist of behavioral acts of physical aggression, ranging from pushing and slapping to beating up, choking, and weapon use. Respondents indicate how many times in the past year they enacted the behavior toward an intimate partner, and how many times their partner enacted that behavior toward them. Over 100 studies and a large meta-analysis,[6] all using the Conflict Tactics Scale or measures like it, have found that women and men self-report very similar rates of physical aggression toward their partners. Some studies, particularly those with younger samples, find that women are more likely than men to self-report physical aggression toward partners.

Proponents of the theme that women's violence is fundamentally different than men's violence point out that the Conflict Tactics Scale does not assess the context, motivation, or impact of the aggressive behaviors. For example, two respondents may both state that they hit their partners. It is not possible to determine if the hit was the first blow, enacted to force the partner to obey a command; or if the hit was an effort to defend oneself from being attacked. Similarly, one cannot know if the hit resulted in crushing an organ, breaking a bone, or only mild discomfort. Thus, what appears to be equivalence in men's and women's aggression may, in fact, reflect behaviors with very different motives and consequences. Another problem with using Conflict Tactics Scale–based studies to conclude that women's violence is just like men's is that the majority of these studies assess only physical aggression. Studies that examine other types of interpersonal violence, such as sexual assault and stalking, find higher rates of males than females committing these behaviors.[7,8]

Meanwhile, as scholars debate the question of gender symmetry in intimate partner violence, women are arrested every day, and criminal justice personnel do their best to try to hold these women accountable and provide treatment to prevent the behavior from reoccurring. While some treatment programs for domestically violent women have been developed, this work is in its early stages, and little is known about the effectiveness of these programs.

One point that is clear, however, is that to develop effective interventions for women who use violence against their partners, applying a "one-size-fits-all" model based on male violence is unlikely to work for most women. Rather, we must understand why women use violence against intimate partners, the context for their violence, and the outcomes for their partners, their children, and the women themselves. Researchers are beginning to develop this understanding. The following sections provide a review of major findings from research on women's use of violence against male intimate partners. The review includes a discussion of the prevalence of women's commission of different types of aggressive behaviors and how that compares to the prevalence of men's commission of such behaviors, ways in which women's violence often differs from men's violence, gender differences in the physical and psychological impact of domestic violence, gender differences in motivations for using violence, and characteristics of women who use violence against male intimate partners.

We begin with a description of a study we conducted that examines women's violence and victimization in intimate relationships.

THE NEW HAVEN STUDY OF WOMEN'S VIOLENCE AND VICTIMIZATION

To develop a knowledge base regarding women's violence, we conducted a study of women's violence and victimization in intimate relationships with male partners funded by the National Institute of Justice.[9] Brochures and fliers were used to recruit a community sample of 412 women from locations such as primary care clinics, churches, shops, libraries, community kiosks, restaurants, grocery stores, and laundromats. The sampling strategy was designed to obtain roughly equivalent numbers of diverse racial and ethnic groups, and was composed of 150 African American women, 150 Latinas, and 112 white women. Women interested in the study were given a brief telephone screen to assess if they met study criteria. To participate in the study, women had to have committed physical aggression against a male partner within the previous six months. Women who met the screening criteria were interviewed individually by female interviewers of the same ethnicity. Latina participants were interviewed by a bilingual and bicultural interviewer and had the option of being interviewed in Spanish. Seventy-four of the 150 Latina participants completed the interview in Spanish. Women reported on their own aggressive behavior toward their partners, as well as the aggression they experienced from their partners.

About Study Participants

Participants ranged in age from 18 to 65 with an average age of 37. Twenty-four percent of participants were married and 43 percent were unmarried and living with their partner at the time of the study. Twenty-six percent were dating but not living together, and 7 percent no longer considered themselves to be together with their partner. The average reported relationship length was 4–5 years, with relationship lengths ranging from six months to more than 20 years. Most of the sample (77 percent) had at least one child. Twenty-eight percent of participants did not complete high school. Forty-one percent had a high school diploma or GED. Twenty-three percent attended some college or vocational training, and 8 percent reported earning a college or advanced degree. Most participants were very poor. Forty-three percent of the sample reported household incomes of less than $10,000 annually, while 28 percent made between $10,000 and $20,000, and 17 percent assessed their household income as between $20,000 and $30,000 a year. Only 12 percent of the sample reported household incomes exceeding $30,000 per year. The majority of women in the sample (64 percent) were unemployed at the time of the study. Twenty percent worked part-time, 14 percent had full-time jobs, and 2 percent were students.

While participants were selected for the study based on their own use of violence, almost all of the women (92 percent) also experienced physical violence from their partners. The extent and seriousness of violence in many of the women's relationships are indicated by the fact that 48 percent reported that the police had been called because of violence. Thirty percent of women in the sample indicated that their partner had been arrested for domestic violence. Fifteen percent of the participants were themselves arrested for domestic violence. Findings from this study will be referred to throughout this chapter.

PREVALENCE OF WOMEN'S PERPETRATION OF DIFFERENT TYPES OF ABUSIVE BEHAVIORS

How prevalent is women's intimate partner violence in the United States, and how does it compare to the prevalence of men's intimate partner violence? The answer to this question varies depending on the type of violence examined. The sections that follow describe gender similarities and differences that have been found in women's and men's physical aggression, sexual coercion, stalking, psychological aggression, and coercive control, as well as injury resulting from intimate partner violence.

Physical Aggression

When physical aggression is the subject of inquiry, studies consistently find as many women self-report perpetrating this behavior as do men; some studies find a higher prevalence of physical aggression committed by women (for a review, see Archer). As mentioned previously, almost all of the studies of physical aggression assess behaviors only, with no reference to the context or consequences of the behaviors. With this limitation in mind, the National Family Violence Survey,[10] a nationally representative study of 6,002 men and women, found that in the past year, 12.4 percent of wives self-reported that they used violence against their husbands compared to 11.6 percent of husbands who self-reported using violence against their wives. Furthermore, 4.8 percent of wives reported using severe violence against their husbands, whereas 3.4 percent of husbands reported using severe violence. Studies with college samples also find that men and women commit similar rates of physical aggression,[11] or that a higher prevalence of women commit physical aggression.[12]

Sexual Coercion

Sexual coercion has been defined as "any situation in which one person uses verbal or physical means to obtain sexual activity against consent (including the administration of drugs or alcohol, with or without the other person's consent)."[13] With only a few exceptions, most studies comparing the prevalence of men's and women's sexually coercive behavior with intimate partners have been conducted with college student populations. Regardless of the population investigated, each of these studies found that a higher percentage of men commit sexually coercive behaviors against partners than do women. The percentage of women who reported perpetrating sexually coercive behaviors in these studies ranged from about 4 to 25 percent, while the prevalence of men who reported perpetrating such acts is double that of women, ranging from 10 to 50 percent. The prevalence of experiences of sexual coercion from partners is higher than reports of perpetration for both sexes, with women reporting much more victimization than men. The percentage of women victimized by sexually coercive behaviors ranged from about 30 to 78 percent, while victimization for males ranged from 19 to 58 percent.[14,15,16,17]

Stalking

He want to know what I'm doing, where I'm going, what friend I'm with, what time I'm coming back ... if he can't get in touch with me, he'll call a hundred times use different names, sit outside the house ... wait to see what kind of car I'm coming in, and see if I'm coming with a guy or ... you know, a woman. (This and all subsequent quotations throughout the chapter are from focus groups conducted with participants in the New Haven study.)

He follows me. And he'll tell me get a ride to where I have to go and he said he'd give me a ride and he's right behind me following me instead of giving me the ride....

Yeah mine follows me too. He'll hide around the corner just to see what
I'm doing.

The best estimates of stalking prevalence come from the National Violence Against Women Survey, a nationally representative survey of 8,000
men and 8,000 women in the United States. Stalking was defined by the
survey as "a course of conduct directed at a specific person that involves
repeated visual or physical proximity, nonconsensual communication, or
verbal, written, or implied threats, or a combination thereof, that would
cause a reasonable person fear."[18] Stalking behaviors may include following or spying on someone, standing outside his or her home or workplace,
making unwanted phone calls, and vandalizing his or her property. The
National Violence Against Women Survey found that the lifetime prevalence of having experienced stalking was 14.2 percent for women and 4.3
percent for men.[19] Among those stalked, 41 percent of women and 28 percent of men were stalked by an intimate partner. Furthermore, women
were 13 times as likely as men to report being very afraid of the stalker,
and the majority of both female and male stalking victims indicated that
the perpetrators of the stalking were male.

The National Violence Against Women Survey assessed experiences
of stalking victimization but did not assess stalking perpetration. Wom-
en's stalking perpetration and victimization were assessed in our New
Haven study. Stalking is often thought of in the context of unrequited
love or obsession, in which the stalker may be merely an acquaintance
of the victim, or in relationships that have ended, in which the stalker
pursues a former intimate. However, stalking behaviors between
women and their partners were very common in the ongoing violent
relationships examined in the New Haven study. Eighty percent of the
women engaged in at least one stalking behavior, and 85 percent experienced stalking from their partner.[20] Of those women who had been
stalked, almost half (46 percent) reported that the stalking made them
"afraid" or "very afraid" of their partners. The stalking behaviors
women most frequently engaged in were vandalizing the partner's
property (52 percent of women did this), making unwanted phone
calls (48 percent), following or spying on the partner (43 percent),
and showing up where the partner was even though she had no
business being there (40 percent). Women reported engaging in less
"monitoring" behaviors than their partners did to them—that is, following or spying, standing outside the partner's home or work, or
showing up at places the partner was. However, women were
equally likely to communicate with their partners when they knew
he did not want them to (through phone calls, letters, and leaving
items for him to find) as their partners. Women also were equally
likely to vandalize their partner's property. In sum, most of the
stalking in the women's relationships was reciprocal. The high rates

of stalking seem to reflect a fundamental lack of trust in these relationships.

Psychological Aggression

Focus group leader: What do wom[e]n do to ... m[e]n that is considered violent or abusive?

Participant: Tend to nag, a lot of gossip ... and tell them that they are a liar and a dog and they are a cheater and you just don't trust them.

Psychological aggression has been defined as "a communication, either verbal or nonverbal, intended to cause psychological pain to another person, or perceived as having that intent,"[21] and as behavior that is demeaning or belittling or that undermines the self-worth of one's partner. Women used about as much psychological aggression as men in the National Family Violence Survey. Seventy-four percent of men and 75 percent of women in this survey reported that they committed at least one psychologically aggressive behavior against their partners during the past year. Equivalent levels of men's and women's psychological aggression also have been found in college samples. Cercone et al.[22] found no significant differences between college men and women in the perpetration of minor (86 versus 89 percent, respectively) or more serious (30 versus 27 percent, respectively) forms of psychological aggression.

Coercive Control

Let's say you're going to the store. Honey, I'm going to the store. He figure what time you left. What took you so long. He's timing you. It shouldn't took you this long, or soon as you like get off from work, you usually get home such and such a time. If you five or 10 minutes late, why?

Coercive control is conceptualized as distinct from psychological aggression, and has been defined as

a pattern of coercion characterized by the use of threats, intimidation, isolation, and emotional abuse, as well as a pattern of control over sexuality and social life, including ... relationships with family and friends; material resources (such as money, food, or transportation); and various facets of everyday life (such as coming and going, shopping, cleaning, and so forth).[23]

The central features of coercive control include isolating the victim from her social network and the micromanagement of daily activities through the use of credible threats of negative consequences for noncompliance. From this perspective, physical and sexual violence are tools used by batterers to achieve coercive control of victims. Coercive control mirrors, in an exaggerated manner, cultural gender stereotypes that stipulate male dominance and female submissiveness. Stark also argues that it is coercive control, more than physical violence, that contributes to the devastating psychological effects of domestic violence on many of its victims, such as depression, anxiety, and posttraumatic stress disorder.[24] One study found that, even after controlling for physical, sexual, and psychological abuse, coercive control was related to posttraumatic stress disorder.[25]

Johnson contends that coercive control is a critical factor that distinguishes different types of relationships in which intimate partner violence occurs.[26] Relationships that are characterized by a pattern of coercive control and severe violence have been referred to as "intimate terrorism"; Johnson has found that the victims in these relationships are almost always female, and the perpetrators are almost always male. "Situational couple violence," in contrast, is defined as "an intermittent response to the occasional conflicts of everyday life, motivated by a need to control in the specific situation but not a more general need to be in charge of the relationship." In these relationships, violence usually does not escalate and is typically confined to a particular conflictual incident. It seems to be equally initiated by men and women.

Injury

While survey studies find that women and men report the perpetration of physical violence at similar rates, women are considerably more likely to be injured in domestic violence situations. For example, Archer's meta-analysis of 82 studies examining physical aggression against intimates found that, averaged across all studies, 62 percent of those who reported being injured by an intimate partner were female. In their study of men and women seeking emergency room care, Phelan et al. found that all of the women, compared to 39 percent of the men, had received an injury from a partner.[27] Because men are usually larger and stronger than their female partners, men are more likely to injure their partners through relatively low-level violence, such as slapping or pushing. Women who have experienced violence from partners also are more likely than male victims to require medical attention for their injuries, and Arias and Corso found that the average cost per person of injuries caused by partner violence was twice as high for women as for men.[28]

WHAT IS DIFFERENT ABOUT WOMEN'S VIOLENCE?

Women's Violence Usually Occurs in the Context of Violence against Them by Their Male Partners

When I started with my husband I was good, but with all the abuse, I started to hit him.

Studies have consistently found that the majority of domestically violent women also have experienced violence from their male partners. Two studies of ethnically diverse, low-income community women—the New Haven study and Temple et al.'s study of African American, Mexican American, and white women in Texas—found a high prevalence of victimization among women who used violence.[29] The Texas study found that 86 percent of those who used violence were also victims, and in the New Haven study, this figure was 92 percent. Similar results have been found with college women. Among the women who reported using violence in the National Family Violence Survey, 64 percent also experienced violence from their male partners. Furthermore, several studies with women who have been arrested for domestic violence found that the number of women reporting violence from their male partners was greater than 90 percent.[30,31,32]

In sum, many domestically violent women—especially those who are involved with the criminal justice system—are not the sole perpetrators of violence. The victimization they have experienced from their male partners is an important contextual factor in understanding their motivations for violence. Some women who have been adjudicated for a domestic violence offense are, in fact, battered women who fought back. They may well be at the same level of risk of serious injury or death as battered women who are seeking shelter.

The Types of Violence Women Commit Differ from Men's Violence

Women's commission of different types of violence, and their experiences of violence from their male partners, was examined in two studies conducted in New Haven, including the study described above, and an earlier study with women who used violence against an intimate male partner. Both studies found the same pattern of results with respect to the types of violence that women and their partners committed. Interestingly, this pattern is remarkably similar to the prevalence studies reported earlier, despite the different methodologies and samples. For example, in the New Haven studies, the percentage of women who reported that they used psychological aggression was equivalent to the percentage of women who reported that their partners were psychologically aggressive toward them. The National Family Violence Survey, using a nationally representative sample of men and women, also found that the same percentage of men and women reported using psychological aggression against their partners. In the New Haven studies, women used higher levels of moderate physical violence than their partners used against them, and about the same level of severe physical violence. Similarly, a meta-analysis that compared men's and women's use of physical aggression against intimates also found that, averaged across all studies analyzed, women self-report very slightly higher rates of physical aggression toward their partners than men. The New Haven studies found that the percentage of women who experienced coercive control was over 1.5 times greater than the percentage of women who were coercively controlling. And, the number of women who were sexually coerced was 2.5 times higher than the number of women who used sexual coercion against their partners. Again, sexual coercion studies of men and women have found that the rate of men who perpetrated sexual coercion was double the rate of women. And, the number of women in the New Haven studies who sustained injuries by their partners was 1.5 times greater than the number of women who injured their partners. This finding can be compared with Archer's meta-analysis, which found that 62 percent of those injured by an intimate partner were female.

The New Haven studies are not the only research that has found this pattern of violence and victimization among women. Similar results were found in Stuart et al.'s study of 87 women participating in a court-mandated domestic violence intervention program. This consistent pattern of results, from studies of women who have used violence as well as surveys with mixed-sex samples, provide plentiful evidence that the types of violence women and men commit differ, even in relationships in which both partners use violence.

Domestic Violence May Affect Men and Women Differently

A mutually violent relationship, as defined in the intimate partner violence literature, is a relationship in which both partners use physical violence. The extent to which one partner may be much more violent than the other, or that one partner's violence may be in self-defense, or that one partner may be using more severe forms of violence than the other (e.g., sexual assault) is obviously not taken into account in this definition.

The evidence presented above suggests that in many relationships that can be classified as mutually violent, women are more likely than men to experience severe and coercive forms of partner violence, such as sexual coercion and coercive control; and women are injured more often and more severely. It is not surprising, then, that relationships that are mutually violent have a more detrimental impact on women's psychological and physical well-being, as compared to men. Utilizing information from the National Comorbidity Survey, Williams and Frieze found that female participants who experienced partner violence reported significantly higher distress and lower marital satisfaction when compared to male participants who experienced partner violence.[33] Similarly, college women experienced lower relationship satisfaction as a function of partner violence, but men did not.[34] And, in an examination of predictors of breakups in a national sample of couples, male violence, but not female violence, predicted relationship dissatisfaction and breaking up.[35]

Studies also find more negative psychiatric effects for women in mutually violent relationships when compared to men. Anderson examined 474 couples reporting mutual violence drawn from the National Survey of Families and Households and found that being in a mutually violent relationship predicted greater depression among both men and women, but the effect was approximately twice as great for women.[36] A similar pattern was observed for drug and alcohol problems. In a longitudinal study, Ehrensaft, Moffitt, and Caspi found that women, compared to men, who were victims of intimate partner violence were more likely to develop psychiatric disorders.[37] Similarly, female victims of intimate partner violence have been found to develop posttraumatic stress disorder at significantly higher rates than male victims.[38] Studies with nationally representative samples have found that, compared to male victims of intimate partner violence, female victims are more likely to take time off from work and to make greater use of mental health and criminal justice system services.

WOMEN'S MOTIVATIONS FOR VIOLENCE

In addition to finding differences in the types of abusive behaviors men and women commit as well as differences in outcomes of partner violence for men and women, studies also indicate that women's motivations for using violent behavior in intimate relationships are often quite different from those of men. Women's motivations for violence have been organized into two types: (1) defensive (or reactive) motives, that is, self-protective violence; and (2) active motives, those that go beyond simply defending oneself and are goal-oriented, such as anger, retaliation, and attempts to control the partner.

DEFENSIVE MOTIVES

Self-Defense

> Sometimes you have to use violence to protect yourself if not, you either sit there and let him beat you to death, or you protect yourself.

Women who engage in intimate partner violence commonly report using violence to defend themselves from their partners, and several studies have found that women cite self-defense as a motivation for violence more frequently than men. Caldwell, Swan, Sullivan, and Snow examined women's motives for using violence in the New Haven study, and found that 77 percent of participants stated that self-defense was a motive for their violence at least some of the time.[39] In Stuart et al.'s sample of women who were arrested for intimate partner violence, women's violence was motivated by self-defense 39 percent of the time.

Fear

> Like me, I'm the type that I'm violent with a man because before you getting me I'm getting you because I'm so scared now. My past relationship that I've seen with violence ... I'm not gonna allow anyone to talk to me or hurt me any type of way.

Numerous studies verify that women are more likely than men to report fear in domestic violence situations. Even among studies of male and female domestic violence defendants who were court-ordered to attend a domestic violence treatment program, women reported greater fear of their partner's violence than did men.[40]

Defense of Children

Focus group leader: What were your reasons for using violence?
Participant: I think if you push the wrong button, I ... probably would hurt you.
Leader: What would be for you pushing the wrong button?
Participant: Pushing a button, OK, 'cause when I was in this relationship for 14 years, this man treated my oldest daughter like garbage.
Leader: So one of the things you would say is treating my kids like garbage.
Participant: I think that would be a button.... But just don't please God don't you ever put your hands on my kids, because I never ever put my hands on my kids in my life.

It has been estimated that 30 to 60 percent of children whose mothers are battered are themselves victims of abuse (see the chapters by Stark and Postmus in volume 2). Children living with an abused mother have been found to be 12 to 14 times more likely to be sexually abused than children whose mothers were not abused.[41] The effects of family violence on children, in terms of both the actual physical abuse of children and the abuse children witness, impact how women behave in violent relationships. Some women behave violently toward their partners to protect their children as well as themselves.

ACTIVE MOTIVES

Control

Focus group leader: What does the woman do ... that might be coercive control?
Participant: Put them on a schedule.
Leader: Put the men on a schedule, in what way?

Participant: Come right home from work. Can't go nowhere, you
                        gotta be at home, or you're gonna say you're gonna be
                        somewhere, you gotta call if you change and don't go
                        there, or they will know where you [are] at every
                        moment—no freedom.

A number of studies show that men are more likely than women to
use violence to regain or maintain control of the relationship or a partner who is challenging their authority. Findings from a study of men
and women court-ordered to attend a domestic violence treatment program indicated that men were more likely to initiate and control violent interactions, whereas women also used violence but were not in
control of the violent interactions with their partners.

However, this does not mean that control motives are absent from
women's violence. Caldwell, Swan, Sullivan, and Snow's analysis of
the New Haven study found that two-thirds of women endorsed wanting to control their partners as a motive for their aggression. Furthermore, these control items were related to women's aggression. Women
who endorsed control items used more physical and psychological
aggression than women who did not endorse these items. In addition,
the earlier New Haven study found that 38 percent of women stated
that they had threatened to use violence at least sometimes to make
their partner do the things they wanted him to do; of those, 53 percent
stated that the threats were effective at least some of the time. Similarly, Stuart et al.'s sample of women arrested for intimate partner violence indicated that the percentage of time they used violence "to get
control over your partner" was 22 percent, "to get your partner to do
something or stop doing something" was 22 percent, and "to make
your partner agree with you" was 17 percent.

Retribution

Well, when I got angry with my husband, I kicked him, I punched him, I
slapped him.

Several studies suggest that retribution for real or perceived wrongdoing
is a common motivator of women's violent behavior. Forty-five percent of
the women in the Swan and Snow study stated that they used violence to
get even with their partners.[42] In Stuart et al.'s sample of women arrested
for intimate partner violence, women indicated that 35 percent of the time
they used violence to retaliate for being emotionally hurt by their partners, while 20 percent of the time the motive was to retaliate for being hit
first. Caldwell, Swan, Sullivan, and Snow found in the New Haven study
that 74 percent of participants reported that retaliation was a motive for
their aggression toward their partners. Furthermore, women who

endorsed retaliation items used more physical and psychological aggression than women who did not endorse these items.

The reasons for men's and women's desires for retribution may differ, with women more frequently using violence in retaliation for being emotionally hurt. For example, among individuals in batterer intervention counseling, 42 percent of women stated they used violence to get back at a partner for hurting them emotionally, compared to 22 percent of men. Women in this study also were more likely than men to state that they used physical violence against their partners to retaliate for previous abuse and to punish them.

CHARACTERISTICS OF WOMEN WHO USE VIOLENCE

This next section examines risk factors and mental health– and substance abuse–related problems that are common among women who use violence.

Childhood Trauma

> I been abused ever since I was little coming up, and I'm still [abused], you know.

Evidence from several studies indicates that rates of childhood trauma and abuse are very high among women who use violence. In the New Haven study, 60 percent of women experienced emotional abuse and neglect, 58 percent were sexually abused, 52 percent were physically abused, and 41 percent were physically neglected as children. High rates of childhood abuse also have been found in studies of women in court-mandated treatment for domestic violence.

Experiences of childhood abuse have been found in several studies to be a risk factor for women's violent and abusive behavior toward others. For example, a longitudinal study of 136 women who were treated at a hospital for sexual abuse as children examined the impact of childhood abuse on the women's adult relationships.[43] The study found that childhood experiences of sexual abuse predicted both women's use of violence against intimate partners and the partners' use of violence against them. Experiences of being hit or beaten by a parent also predicted women's violence against their partners.

Psychological Functioning

> When I got with him I went down, I was depressed, he is always trying to control me, no wonder why I am depressed.

Four psychological conditions have been associated with traumatic experiences in general and domestic violence victimization in particular:

depression, anxiety, substance abuse, and posttraumatic stress disorder.[44,45] The prevalence of all of these conditions is very high among women who use intimate partner violence. The New Haven study found that 69 percent of the participants met criteria for depression on a screening measure. Almost one in three met criteria on a posttraumatic stress disorder screen. Nearly one in five were suffering from alcohol or drug problems, and 24 percent of the participants took psychiatric medication. Similarly, in their study of women participating in an anger management program for intimate partner violence, Dowd et al. found a high prevalence of depression (67 percent), bipolar disorder (18 percent), anxiety issues (9 percent), and substance use problems (67 percent).[46] In addition, 30 percent reported suicide attempts, 20 percent had been hospitalized for psychiatric reasons, and 25 percent had been detoxified.

CONCLUSIONS AND IMPLICATIONS

There is much we still have to learn about women who use violence in their intimate relationships, but some points are becoming clearer from the research conducted thus far. To a great extent, women who are violent are also victims of violence from their male partners. In addition, women are more likely than men to be injured during domestic violence incidents and to suffer more severe injuries. Thus, safety issues are paramount for women who are domestically violent. However, women who are arrested for domestic violence are unlikely to receive victim services, such as a victim advocate who can help them develop a plan for how to stay safe. Based on the evidence reviewed in this chapter, we recommend that services for domestically violent women include an assessment of the safety of the woman, her children, and her partner. Providers should work with women to develop a safety plan and help women learn not to rely on violence in response to their partner's violence toward them but to develop other strategies to prevent future victimization.

The statement that women are "just as violent as men" is an oversimplification, at best. Some types of violence do show gender symmetry (i.e., physical and psychological aggression); others have much higher rates of male perpetration (i.e., sexual coercion and coercive control). Furthermore, the same behavior may have a different impact and meaning when committed by a man against a woman than when committed by a woman against a man. Sex and gender differences contribute to discrepancies in a behavior's impact and interpretation. Biologically, men's greater strength often results in more injury per violent act. Men's greater physical and social power, as well as cultural beliefs about men's strength and women's weakness, may exacerbate the sex difference in the amount of fear produced by a violent partner. Similarly, social constructions of gender regarding male dominance and female submissiveness support men's ability to dominate or isolate female partners. For both biological and social reasons, use of coercive control tactics, such as attempts to restrict a partner's telephone use or to prevent a partner from going out, may be more likely to actually achieve control over the partner when committed by men against female partners than when committed by women against male partners.

In some cases that come to the attention of the criminal justice system, women may be perpetrating as much or more physical violence as their partners, but their partners may be committing other types of abuse that are not always assessed, such as sexual abuse or coercive control. If a woman's physical violence is in response to her partner's attempts to coercively control her, and he has a history of violence toward her, behavior change in both partners will be necessary for the abuse to stop. We recommend that services for domestically violent women include a thorough evaluation of the emotional abuse, coercive control, and physical and sexual abuse that has occurred in the relationship, including both the woman's victimization within her relationship as well as her perpetration of these behaviors. Injuries that the woman has received, and injuries that she has inflicted on her partner, should also be assessed.

Many domestically violent women have psychiatric issues that are related to their victimization, and possibly to their violence as well. An untreated psychiatric disorder will make it difficult for a woman to move toward a safe, nonviolent lifestyle. Our third recommendation, then, is that service providers screen for the most common psychiatric disorders that co-occur with intimate partner violence (depression, anxiety, substance abuse, and posttraumatic stress disorder), and refer for treatment as necessary.

In sum, women who use violence against intimate partners are not "just like men." Because of the many differences between men's and women's violence in the types of violent behaviors, motivations for violence, and impact on partners, interventions based on models of male violence against women may not be effective for many women. Gender-specific interventions tailored to the needs of women who are violent are more likely to be successful in creating behavior change.

AUTHOR NOTE

The research described in this chapter was supported by the National Institute of Justice and the University of South Carolina Research Foundation. Correspondence and reprint requests may be sent to Suzanne Swan, University of South Carolina, Department of Psychology and Women's Studies Program, Columbia, SC, 29208, or swan@sc.edu.

NOTES

1. S. D. Dasgupta, "Just Like Men? A Critical View of Violence by Women," in *Coordinating Community Response to Domestic Violence: Lessons from Duluth and Beyond*, ed. M. F. Shepard and E. L. Pence (Thousand Oaks, CA: Sage, 1990), 195–222.

2. *Thurman et al. v. City of Torrington*, 595 F. Supp. 1521 (D. Conn. 1984).

3. D. Hirschel, E. Buzawa, A. Pattavina, D. Faggiani, and M. Reuland, "Explaining the Prevalence, Context, and Consequences of Dual Arrest in Intimate Partner Cases," NCJ 218355 (Washington, D.C.: U.S. Department of Justice, National Institute of Justice, 2007).

4. S. L. Miller, *Victims as Offenders: The Paradox of Women's Violence in Relationships* (New Brunswick, NJ: Rutgers University Press, 2005).

5. M. P. Johnson, "Conflict and Control: Gender Symmetry and Asymmetry in Domestic Violence," *Violence against Women* 12 (2006): 1003–18.

6. J. Archer, "Sex Differences in Aggression between Heterosexual Partners: A Meta-Analytic Review," *Psychological Bulletin* 126 (2000): 651–80.

7. W. S. Dekeseredy, "Future Directions," *Violence against Women* 12 (2006): 1078–85.

8. S. C. Swan and D. L. Snow, "Behavioral and Psychological Differences among Abused Women Who Use Violence in Intimate Relationships," *Violence against Women* 9 (2003): 75–109.

9. S. C. Swan, D. L. Snow, T. P. Sullivan, L. Gambone, and A. Fields, "Technical Report for 'An Empirical Examination of a Theory of Women's Use of Violence in Intimate Relationships,'" National Institute of Justice, November 28, 2005, http://www.ncjrs.gov/pdffiles1/nij/grants/208611.pdf.

10. M. A. Straus and R. J. Gelles, *Physical Violence in American Families: Risk Factors and Adaptations to Violence in 8,145 Families* (New Brunswick, NJ: Transaction, 1990).

11. J. L. Cercone, S. R. H. Beach, and I. Arias, "Gender Symmetry in Dating Intimate Partner Violence: Does Similar Behavior Imply Similar Constructs?" *Violence and Victims* 20, no. 2 (2005): 207–18.

12. M. A. Straus, "Prevalence of Violence against Dating Partners by Male and Female University Students Worldwide," *Violence against Women* 10 (2004): 790–811.

13. L. E. Adams-Curtis and G. B. Forbes, "College Women's Experiences of Sexual Coercion: A Review of Cultural, Perpetrator, Victim, and Situational Variables," *Trauma, Violence, and Abuse* 5 (2004): 91–122.

14. L. F. O'Sullivan, S. E. Byers, and L. Finkelman, "A Comparison of Male and Female College Students' Experiences of Sexual Coercion," *Psychology of Women Quarterly* 22 (1998): 177–95.

15. M. A. Straus, S. L. Hamby, S. Boney-McCoy, and D. B. Sugarman, "The Revised Conflict Tactics Scale (CTS2)," *Journal of Family Issues* 17 (1996): 283–316.

16. C. Struckman-Johnson, D. Struckman-Johnson, and P. B. Anderson, "Tactics of Sexual Coercion: When Men and Women Won't Take No for an Answer," *Journal of Sex Research* 40, no. 1 (2003): 76–86.

17. C. M. West and S. Rose, "Dating Aggression among Low Income African American Youth: An Examination of Gender Differences and Antagonistic Beliefs," *Violence against Women* 6 (2000): 470–95.

18. P. Tjaden and N. Thoennes, *Stalking in America: Findings from the National Violence against Women Survey*, NCJ 169592 (Washington, D.C.: U.S. Department of Justice, National Institute of Justice, 1998).

19. K. E. Davis, A. L. Coker, and M. Sanderson, "Physical and Mental Health Effects of Being Stalked for Men and Women," *Violence and Victims* 17, no. 4 (2002): 429–43.

20. K. E. Davis, S. C. Swan, L. J. Gambone, D. L. Snow, and T. P. Sullivan, "An Examination of the Function of Women's Stalking Behaviors in Violent Relationships," under review.

21. M. A. Straus and S. Sweet, "Verbal/Symbolic Aggression in Couples: Incidence Rates and Relationships to Personal Characteristics," *Journal of Marriage and the Family* 54, no. 2 (1992): 346–57.

22. J. L. Cercone, S. R. H. Beach, and I. Arias, "Gender Symmetry in Dating Intimate Partner Violence: Does Similar Behavior Imply Similar Constructs?" *Violence and Victims* 20, no. 2 (2005): 207–18.

23. E. Stark and A. Flitcraft, *Women at Risk: Domestic Violence and Women's Health* (Thousand Oaks, CA: Sage, 1996).

24. E. Stark, "Reply to Michael P. Johnson's Conflict and Control: Gender Symmetry and Asymmetry in Domestic Violence," *Violence against Women* 12 (2006): 1019–25.

25. M. A. Dutton, L. Goodman, and R. J. Schmidt, *Development and Validation of a Coercive Control Measure for Intimate Partner Violence: Final Technical Report*, USDOJ Document no. 214438 (Washington, D.C.: U.S. Department of Justice, 2006).

26. M. P. Johnson, "Patriarchal Terrorism and Common Couple Violence: Two Forms of Violence against Women," *Journal of Marriage and the Family* 57 (1995): 283–94.

27. M. B. Phelan, L. K. Hamberger, C. E. Guse, S. Edwards, S. Walczak, and A. Zosel, "Domestic Violence among Male and Female Patients Seeking Emergency Medical Services," *Violence and Victims* 20, no. 2 (2005): 187–206.

28. I. Arias and P. Corso, "Average Cost per Person Victimized by an Intimate Partner of the Opposite Gender: A Comparison of Men and Women," *Violence and Victims* 20 (2005): 379–91.

29. J. R. Temple, R. Weston, and L. L. Marshall, "Physical and Mental Health Outcomes of Women in Nonviolent, Unilaterally Violent, and Mutually Violent Relationships," *Violence & Victims* 20 (2005): 335–59.

30. L. K. Hamberger and C. E. Guse, "Men's and Women's Use of Intimate Partner Violence in Clinical Samples," *Violence against Women* 8 (2002): 1301–31.

31. G. L. Stuart, T. M. Moore, K. C. Gordon, J. C. Hellmuth, S. E. Ramsey, and C. W. Kahler, "Reasons for Intimate Partner Violence Perpetration among Arrested Women," *Violence against Women* 12, no. 7 (2006): 609–21.

32. S. C. Swan and D. L. Snow, "A Typology of Women's Use of Violence in Intimate Relationships," *Violence against Women* 8 (2002): 286–319.

33. I. H. Frieze, *Hurting the One You Love: Violence in Relationships* (Belmont, CA: Wadsworth, 2005).

34. J. Katz, S. Kuffel, and A. Coblentz, "Are There Gender Differences in Sustaining Dating Violence? An Examination of Frequency, Severity, and Relationship Satisfaction," *Journal of Family Violence* 17 (2002): 247–71.

35. A. DeMaris, "Till Discord Do Us Part: The Role of Physical and Verbal Conflict in Union Disruption," *Journal of Marriage and the Family* 62 (2000): 683–92.

36. K. L. Anderson, "Perpetrator or Victim? Relationships between Intimate Partner Violence and Well-Being," *Journal of Marriage and Family* 64 (2002): 851–63.

37. M. K. Ehrensaft, T. E. Moffitt, and A. Caspi, "Is Domestic Violence Followed by an Increased Risk of Psychiatric Disorders among Women but Not among Men? A Longitudinal Cohort Study," *American Journal of Psychiatry* 163 (2006): 885–92.

38. B. S. Dansky, C. A. Byrne, and K. T. Brady, "Intimate Violence and Post-Traumatic Stress Disorder among Individuals with Cocaine Dependence," *American Journal of Drug & Alcohol Abuse* 25 (1999): 257–68.

39. J. E. Caldwell, S. C. Swan, T. P. Sullivan, and D. L. Snow, "Why I Hit Him: Women's Reasons for Intimate Partner Violence," *Journal of Aggression, Maltreatment, and Trauma* (in press).

40. P. Kernsmith, "Exerting Power or Striking Back: A Gendered Comparison of Motivations for Domestic Violence Perpetration," *Violence and Victims* 20, no. 2 (2005): 173–85.

41. L. A. McCloskey, A. J. Figuerdo, and M. P. Koss, "The Effects of Systemic Family Violence on Children's Mental Health," *Child Development* 66 (1995): 1239–61.

42. Swan and Snow, "Behavioral and Psychological Differences."

43. J. A. Siegel, "Aggressive Behavior among Women Sexually Abused as Children," *Violence and Victims* 15 (2000): 235–55.

44. J. Axelrod, H. F. Myers, R. S. Durvasula, G. E. Wyatt, and M. Cheng, "The Impact of Relationship Violence, HIV, and Ethnicity on Adjustment in Women," *Cultural Diversity and Ethnic Minority Psychology* 5 (1999): 263–75.

45. E. B. Foa, M. Cascardi, L. A. Zoellner, and N. Feeny, "Psychological and Environmental Factors Associated with Partner Violence," *Trauma, Violence, & Abuse* 1 (2000): 67–91.

46. L. S. Dowd, P. A. Leisring, and A. Rosenbaum, "Partner Aggressive Women: Characteristics and Treatment Attrition," *Violence and Victims* 20, no. 2 (2005): 219–33.

Chapter 4

Evolution of the Police Response to Domestic Violence

Eve S. Buzawa
David Hirschel

Historically, police have been reluctant to intervene in domestic violence crimes, let alone to make an arrest. This chapter reviews the reasons for their reluctance, why the police response has changed dramatically throughout the United States, current police practices, and what we believe to be the most effective forms of police intervention in domestic violence cases.

THE TRADITIONAL POLICE RESPONSE

Until about 30 years ago, the police as an institution tried to limit their involvement with incidents involving domestic violence. This was not understood as a failure on the part of the police, but merely as reflecting the unspoken assumption that internal family disputes largely fell outside their area of responsibility. The reasons for this attitude and the corresponding failure to act, which are explained in the following pages, were reinforcing and stable for generations.

Before the creation of the first modern police force in metropolitan London in 1829, there were no full-time police. Law and order were maintained by volunteer "constables," and key public and private property was protected by "watchmen." If they failed to maintain public order, the armed forces would be called in at the discretion of the government. In 1829, British Home Secretary Sir Robert Peel established the Metropolitan Police, a paramilitary all-male force headquartered in Scotland Yard. These officers were soon popularly known as "the Bobbies." Their self-described mission was to patrol the streets to maintain "public order," both to deter crime and to apprehend criminals. Their organization was intentionally hierarchical, based on a military structure. However, due to British fears of the police becoming oppressive agents of political control, as had occurred at the time in some countries in continental Europe, the force deliberately avoided intrusive policing and focused almost exclusively on maintaining public order. A little later, a separately trained detective force was established to investigate and "solve" crimes. But their mandate did not extend to entering homes, especially in response to family disputes. Private homes were assumed to be analogous to other forms of private property, farms or factories for instance, which police were expected to protect from invasion (or strikes) but not to enter. This approach was also linked to civil law, which recognized the home as the unassailable province of the husband and father.

Public Order as the Police Mission

From this colorful beginning, police traditions of noninterference in family affairs remained fairly constant over the next 150 years. This remained true even as the police, as an organization of social control, crossed the Atlantic to the United States and became entrusted with enforcing an ever-widening range of criminal laws. Here, too, the priority was maintaining "public order," a reality dramatically illustrated by the use of police alongside state militias in quelling the draft "riots" in major cities during the Civil War and labor unrest throughout the nineteenth century. To understand this role, we need to put police practices in the context of the rapid changes in mores occasioned by urbanization, industrialization, and the growth of markets. The most important of these was a growing emphasis on secularism and Lockean individualism that led the public to reframe the police less as guardians of public morality than as an expression of governmental intrusion, a view that reinforced the belief that they had no role in private disputes. This role was modified somewhat during the Progressive era, when the general tendency toward greater regulation of business and the professionalism of social services led many local police departments to add social workers or social work functions to mediate cases of child abuse or neglect brought to juvenile court. During the Great Depression, police often assisted rental agents in evictions and farm foreclosures, and governmental "welfare" took on a more positive connotation because of the New Deal. But during and after World War II, the previous emphasis on police noninterference returned, largely due to the oft-made contrast publicized during the Cold War between "free" societies where government played a minimal role and totalitarian "police states" such as Nazi Germany and the Soviet Union.

Statutory Limits

Massachusetts and several other states had criminal laws on the books prohibiting wife abuse in the 17th century. But these statutes were almost never enforced, leading the author of a multistate review of nineteenth-century court cases to conclude that it appeared that a husband had virtually unfettered physical (and fiscal) control over his wife and children.[1] This changed somewhat after 1870, when England and many U.S. states passed laws explicitly stating that a husband could be criminally prosecuted for beating his wife. Again, however, these laws were only used in the most extreme cases or in cases where children were being abused as well as a wife. Even with the widespread development of specialized family courts in the early 1900s, when several big-city police departments employed female social workers specializing in domestic violence, most cases of domestic abuse were considered to fall in the realm of acts justifying a civil divorce rather than grounds for criminal charges.

There were also practical statutory limitations on the police's ability to actively intervene. For example, in response to public fears of excessive police powers, virtually all states in the United States enacted laws that codified the English Common Law restriction on police arrest powers in cases of misdemeanor assaults, including domestic violence cases. Unless police officers actually witnessed this type of incident, they could not make a warrantless arrest. Since most domestic violence assaults, regardless of the extent of victim injury or assailant use of weapons, were typically termed misdemeanors, and since few acts of spousal abuse would continue after the officer arrived, arrest was strongly discouraged. In those few instances where the responding officer made an arrest due to a severe injury (or perhaps more likely due to the offender's behavior or demeanor when police arrived), the cases were typically disposed of without a conviction. Thus, in reality, the classic statutory structure in effect restricted the "interference" of the police in the family in all but the most extreme cases.

As a result of these trends, by the 1960s, police believed that their statutorily mandated role in domestic violence cases was peripheral, restricted to providing a perfunctory, service-oriented response rather than to investigating and seeking justice for the victim of a crime. The police mission was to separate the parties, restore order, and leave.

Police Attitudes toward Intervention in Family Disputes

As described above, the history and tradition of the police encouraged a mission to maintain "public order" and respect and protect private property. Individual liberty rights were secondary to that mission, as evidenced by the frequent use of aggressive and now unconstitutional practices to "extract" a confession. Similarly, protection of an

individual victim, unless known to the officer or a person of importance in the community, was not a high priority. That attitude was
manifest most clearly if the victim complained about "private"
conduct.

Organizational imperatives and reward systems also supported a
neglect of domestic violence. These imperatives were reinforced by a
desire to pursue "real police work" instead of "social work." Police
embraced an image of a "crime fighter" who was distinguished from
his peers by acts of heroism and/or "significant arrests." Not inciden-
tally, this image was linked to chances for advancement that emphasized arrests (leading to convictions) for high-profile crimes such as
robbery, stranger assaults, or, later, drugs. Moreover, it has been a
tenet of police science that police officers are typically bored by the
daily grind of police work, crave more "action," and, by temperament
or socialization, dislike intervention in interpersonal conflicts, especially if they involve trying to resolve family disputes of any type.[2]

From the officer's perspective, then, intervening in "domestics" was
a waste of time. The prevailing "knowledge" in police circles was that
victims often were not eager to prosecute to conviction and so would
most likely withdraw a complaint or fail to testify if a case went to
trial. Police believed prosecutors shared this belief, leading them to
expect that domestic violence cases would not be pursued even if an
arrest was made. Officers also surmised that not all victims gave a
complete or honest account of the situation, thus reinforcing their tendencies to be wary and skeptical. This led most police to define their
role in domestic violence cases as "handling the situation" rather than
"enforcing the law."

Informal justice meted out by individual officers was often a substitute for enforcement. A sympathetic officer might resort to beating the
offender, for example, especially in cases where lower status males
were involved, allegedly to prevent reabuse by giving the man a "taste
of his own medicine." This approach was codified in the 1880s by statutes providing for use of the "whipping post" for convicted wife beat-
ers in Maryland, Delaware, and several other states. Though whipping
(typically by the sheriff) was used mainly against blacks, the laws
remained on the books until the early 1970s, though the last record of
its use was in Delaware in 1952.

It has long been accepted in the criminal justice field that police are
cynical toward the public in general and about the potential long-term
impacts of their interventions in particular.[3] This general cynicism is
even worse in cases involving intimate partner violence, where they
believe other agencies should be the primary responders, not law
enforcement. This belief remains widespread.

The social class and race of those encountered in the course of
domestic violence complaints reinforced such cynicism. Much research

has shown that when police confront members of the lower economic classes or minorities of any class, they are more likely to act in a bureaucratic, impersonal, authoritarian fashion and fail to show compassion toward victims. When interviewed, even many officers who wish to perform service tasks state that violence is a "normal part of the lives of the lower class." The implication is that domestic problems and the resulting violence are a logical outgrowth of this environment. Defining such behavior as "normal" in the participants' lives meant that the officers were less willing to intervene aggressively and more inclined to "manage" disputes in a fashion that would avoid more "serious" public breaches of peace. From this perspective, an officer would logically prefer to restore order by sending one person away to "cool off," however temporary the solution, rather than by futilely trying to resolve the underlying conflict or expending the effort required to respond to the situation as a criminal incident.

Police Fears

Historically, police have viewed responding to "domestics" as being particularly dangerous. Many officers have been killed or seriously injured during family violence calls. Anecdotal evidence of unprovoked attacks by offenders or even by "unappreciative" victims is legion in police culture, where "war stories" about how spouse abuse cases are the most dangerous assignments police confront are commonplace. For many years, the FBI reinforced this belief by publishing annual reports showing that "disturbance calls" were among the most common sources of officer death. This conclusion was seriously questioned by a 1988 report sponsored by the National Institute of Justice that found that prior FBI reports had overstated rates of police injury and fatality in domestic cases by three times because they had lumped these cases with other, more dangerous "disturbance" calls such as those including gang fights or bar brawls. When domestic violence cases were separated, the reported risk to officers declined markedly.

Although the danger of violence against an officer in "domestics" has proved to be greatly exaggerated, the belief in the dangerousness of these situations remains part of the folklore that rationalizes police reluctance to make a formal arrest. In one sense, this is understandable since almost no other source of injury is as unpredictable or as personally outrageous as being assaulted when responding to a call for help in a domestic case. Resistance might be expected from an offender, whose "power" in what he may consider to be "his castle" is being externally challenged. However, officers say that when they try to interview the person they came to help, she often "turns" against them or, at best, shows no interest in pressing charges. Although this response is often elicited by the "coldness" that officers must assume if they hope to convince an offender they are serious about sanctions, the response by victims remains one of the more perplexing aspects of this police work.

Training

The police training academy is crucial within the police socialization process. During training, police occupational perspectives are transferred to new recruits and course content is presented in such a way as to ensure their continuance. To the extent police historically received training on domestic violence, it reinforced their role as crime fighters and the ancillary nature of violence within families in police work. Before the 1960s, there typically was little or no specific training on domestic violence. The new officer was trained as a recruit in a virtually all-male "paramilitary" organization with a military-type chain of hierarchical command that emphasized his role as "crime fighter" and upholder of public order. This organizational format was hardly conducive to domestic violence. To the contrary, throughout the 1960s and in some departments for years thereafter, officers were instructed simply to quiet tense situations in relationships, provide advice on social welfare agencies that might provide assistance, and quickly extricate themselves.

A nationwide review of existing police training programs conducted in the late 1970s revealed that the domestic violence component was perfunctory and typically composed of a single 4–8-hour lecture segment under the general rubric of handling "disturbed persons."[4] The content was not restricted to, nor did it even necessarily address, the topic of domestic assault. Instead, it included proper techniques for handling hostage situations, potential suicides, mentally disturbed individuals, violent alcoholics and addicts, and child abuse, with a brief mention of domestic disturbance calls.

To the extent that they were addressed as a separate topic, domestic calls were explained to the recruits as a largely unproductive use of time, ineffective in resolving family problems, and potentially dangerous for the responding officer, the same beliefs that dominated the early period. Recruits were told that the desired outcome was to restore peace and maintain control as a vehicle of restoring the public order and ensuring self-protection. Arrests were actively discouraged as a waste of time. The only exception was if disrespect or threats by an offender or victim indicated that the officer might lose situational control. Recruits were trained that arrest was primarily to assert authority rather than to respond to prior criminal action.

The department's choice of training staff did not usually result in interested or qualified instructors in the field of domestic violence. Except for those relatively few larger departments with dedicated permanent training sections, police academies traditionally used senior line personnel. Frequently, the basis for their selection as trainers was "temporary disability" or other special-duty restrictions, such as having been involved in a prior shooting or other incident requiring a departmental investigation prior to being placed back on active duty. These instructors had little interest in training, generally lacked instructional background, and generally did not possess substantive expertise in, or affinity for, the topic of domestic violence.

As a result, it is not surprising that instruction primarily consisted of an explanation of official policies of nonintervention accompanied by colorful (if not totally accurate) stories drawn from personal experiences. Few, if any, training materials or multimedia aids were available or used, and outside expertise was rarely sought.

Formal in-service training in this area also rarely existed before the early 1980s. During the initial entry period, a recruit relied on the perceptions of relevant teachers such as experienced officers to develop his or her own views toward proper organizational practices and objectives. The trainee, after all, had little relevant experiences to guide his or her behavior during the often-frightening immersion into the reality of policing. The field training process, in which the rookie was assigned to learn under the direction of an experienced officer, usually reinforced prejudices against domestic violence cases. In fact, this experience often served to undermine an academy's instruction in those few cases in which the academy might have attempted to promote a more activist police response. For these reasons, traditional police training failed to provide police officers with any rudimentary skills required for successful domestic violence intervention. In one study based on research conducted in the mid-1980s, 50 percent of the officers in a department were not even aware of the elements of probable cause for domestic violence assault.[5] As James Bannon, former Detroit deputy police chief, observed, "[T]he real reason that police avoid domestic violence situations to the greatest extent possible is because they do not know how to cope with them."[6] In sum, until recently, classic patterns of training reinforced prevailing occupational ideology toward domestic violence. The net effect of such a training process was to enhance the likelihood that officers would attempt to either avoid a formal response or rapidly complete domestic violence calls to devote energy to what they deemed more "appropriate" police work.

Actual Police Behavior

How did statutory restrictions, training, and officer attitudes historically limit the effective action of the police? Traditional law enforcement demands fairly routinized behavior in conformity with police and prosecutors' needs to develop and preserve evidence to prosecute a crime. In contrast, the skill of handling a dynamic and potentially volatile intervention among intimates requires specialized skills, a willingness to expend considerable effort, adaptation to the specific circumstances found at the scene, and a statutory basis to justify actions. Given this contrast between the traditional approach and the unique requirements presented in domestic violence cases, few domestic violence cases were formally addressed by the criminal justice system. Instead, the majority of cases were "screened out" so that police could avoid intervention. In most cases where police actually responded, there was a strong, sometimes overwhelming, bias against making arrests.

Police Screening and Downgrading of Calls

Police departments regularly screen incoming calls either on their direct lines or through an operator screen of the 911 emergency number. This is done to classify and prioritize calls and determine whether an officer must be dispatched immediately. A historic strategy for reducing the need to respond to domestic violence calls has been to screen out domestic violence calls and downgrade their seriousness. While police reports might indicate that an assault took place, the call was classified as a low-priority "domestic dispute" or even as "disturbing the peace," limiting the prospect for "real-time" intervention. Dispatch according to standard operating procedures would occur after repetitive calls and then only when time permitted, often hours later. One study reported that over two-thirds of domestic violence cases were thus "solved" without officers being dispatched to the scene. While formally condemned, this practice was unofficially accepted and quite widespread. The failure to respond effectively to repeat calls was compounded by the fact that until very recently most police information systems did not inform responding officers of an offender's prior history of assault. Because police record systems were neither well organized nor computerized, large departments where the same officers rarely had ongoing contact with the families had little ability to differentiate between first offenders and hardcore recidivists. As a result, no matter how often domestic assault was repeated, big-city departments tended to treat such offenses as isolated occurrences.

It is important to recognize the context of this practice. While the police may be singled out for their failure to protect victims of crime, their failure reflected the then pervasive lack of societal concern for domestic violence. As described earlier, for many decades, and for many people today, domestic violence has been "known" to be a problem of the "lower classes" and minority groups. The result was that no one cared enough to devote scarce police resources to address this problem. The police could—and did—minimize their response to domestic violence victims without fear of adverse consequences.

Consequently, many victims were discouraged from contacting the police, and diverted out of the system. They would be referred to social service agencies or incorrectly told that the police could not provide assistance for "marital" conflicts. Still other victims were discouraged from requesting police assistance in the future and even interpreted police nonaction to be tacit approval for the batterer's behavior.

Why Did Established Practices Change?

As an institution, despite their organization into paramilitary "command-and-control" bureaucracies, police departments are known to be remarkably resistant to change. This is partially due to the inability of command officers to observe officer behavior directly, to ingrain "respect" and deference for officer discretion from commanders who were former line officers themselves, and to training systems where formal academic instruction is limited and in-service training often nonexistent. Experienced officers who might be resistant to change are empowered by strong police unions. Such structural bases for resistance to change are often supplemented and reinforced by a widely recognized feature of the police culture: a highly insular and self-reinforcing organization in which both civilians in general and civilian control over police practices in particular are regarded suspiciously and perhaps with cynicism.

As we've seen, deeply entrenched practices have a tendency to be embedded, and so reproduced in each police cohort by training, organizational expectations, organizational culture, and peer pressure. Interestingly, however, and despite a context that strongly favors the status quo, police practices with respect to domestic violence have indeed changed significantly in most jurisdictions. What caused such a dramatic change?

There are three primary reasons for change: (1) political pressure; (2) fear of liability; and (3) widely published research suggesting that arrest deterred domestic assaults, which made it obvious to most police administrators that a policy of deliberate indifference to domestic violence could no longer be tolerated.

The first political challenges to the police arose from early women's rights groups and the feminist movement. While these groups initially concentrated on the problem of rape and sexual assault, it soon became clear that violence against women was mainly perpetrated by a current or former intimate partner, not by a stranger as depicted in television or countless crime novels. Serious domestic violence, although it certainly victimized both sexes, was appropriately seen as a problem primarily of men beating women. By their policies of noninterference, the virtually all-male police forces at that time were perceived as "condoning" such violence because they seldom responded to these calls, dissuaded victims from filing criminal complaints, and rarely if ever arrested perpetrators. Concerns became even more pronounced as women's groups began to realize that the police were basically arresting all violent criminals they apprehended *except* domestic violence offenders. More radicalized groups felt that this indifference constituted an essential part of the overall societal oppression of women, making the police as an institution at least tacitly complicit in the crime committed.

This discontent with existing police practices did not come in isolation. From the early 1970s onward, women en masse volunteered to assist battered women through the establishment of hundreds of battered women's shelters, making the problem visible to society. In this context, by the late 1970s and early 1980s, the United States had turned markedly more "conservative," both politically and in its willingness to enforce laws against visible crimes that, while on the books, had not been marked by aggressive enforcement. Police were being asked to reprioritize their efforts to eliminate petty street crime, arrest drunk drivers, and stop street-level drug trafficking. Not surprisingly, often highly motivated advocates for battered women demanded that the police become more activist in their approach to domestic violence.

The police response was predictable. Police administrators protested that domestic violence was not primarily a "police problem," and further that they could not realistically make arrests due to legal constraints that prevented arrests for misdemeanor assaults that had not been committed in an officer's presence. In the face of these objections, political pressure mounted. The Pennsylvania Protection from Abuse Act of 1977 was the first specific statute adopted in the recent move toward recriminalization of domestic violence. From this point through the late 1980s, antiquated laws restricting police misdemeanor arrests began to be eliminated. In their place were put comprehensive domestic violence specific statutes stating that it was the policy of that state to have police arrest domestic violence offenders.[7]

Social science research on policing had emphasized rehabilitation. Now, its focus shifted toward the role of the police and their ability to punish and even "deter" crime by rigorously enforcing laws. Writings that had favored "informal social controls" to limit violence or the "rehabilitation" of violent offenders began to receive very critical reviews, with some studies showing that the open-ended sentences geared to rehabilitation resulted in longer prison terms. Some well-respected critics went as far as to say that "nothing worked" to rehabilitate violent offenders.[8]

Against this background, studies published in the 1970s suggested that highly trained and motivated police officers could lower future rates of domestic violence. Police Family Crisis Intervention, which focused on police mediation on the scene, was started by forensic psychiatrist Morton Bard as a demonstration project in New York City in the early 1970s and was rapidly copied by major departments across the country. Even as mainstream a body as the International Association of Chiefs of Police endorsed the major tenets of Police Family Crisis Intervention in 1976. As a result, the crisis response became, if not the "standard police response," at least one that was highly visible and purported to produce far better results than the older model of noninvolvement. Evaluators reported that Crisis Intervention led to a reduction in subsequent calls for help from victims, though whether because abuse had ended or because callers were frustrated or disappointed with the police response was never clear.

If earlier research set the theoretical ground for the expansion of police powers in domestic violence cases, the single most important study was the Minneapolis Domestic Violence Experiment (MDVE), funded by the National Institute of Justice and published in 1984 by criminologist Lawrence Sherman and sociologist Richard Berk. In this study, three alternative police actions were randomly assigned to cases that met the eligibility criteria for inclusion in the experiment: ordering one party to leave to cool down (a basic tactic used in traditional policing of family conflicts), counseling both parties (a very rough analog to the then-existing motif of police crisis intervention), and making an arrest. The authors reported that of the 314 cases studied, recidivism, or the repeat of the crime as measured by rearrest during the following six months, occurred in 10 percent of the cases where the offender was arrested, 19 percent of those where they were "advised of alternatives," and 24 percent of those where they were merely removed.[9]

Despite serious methodological problems, the Minneapolis study, heavily promoted by its primary author, Professor Sherman, received unprecedented national attention and provided the impetus for many agencies to move all the way from indifferent enforcement to "mandating arrest"[10] in domestic violence cases.

A decade later, concern had shifted and many researchers worried that police policy had moved too far, too fast on the basis of too little evidence. A series of "replication studies" was funded to determine whether the MDVE findings would be confirmed by research conducted in other locales. The individual findings of these studies were mixed, but this was believed by some to be the result of differences in the way the studies were conducted in the different sites. Using consistent criteria for including cases and defining failure, Maxwell, Garner, and Fagan found that cases assigned to the arrest response resulted in slightly lower levels of subsequent aggression.[11]

The final and perhaps most significant impetus for the change in police policy was a wave of lawsuits against police departments, many of which were highly publicized. Class actions against recalcitrant police departments began as early as the late 1970s and continued through the early 1990s. Remedies, either by judicial decree or by a compromised agreement, promised that the police would treat domestic violence incidents as seriously as others. The failure to protect domestic violence victims was highlighted in spectacular fashion by the case of Tracy Thurman, a Connecticut woman who was beaten so badly in front of a responding police officer that she became paralyzed on one side of her body. This case resulted in considerable legal liability for the city of Torrington, Connecticut (Tracy was awarded $2.3 million in compensatory damages); promoted substantial national press adverse to police indifference; and even generated a film based loosely on aspects of the actual story (see, e.g., the TV film *A Cry for Help: The Tracy Thurman Story* [1989]).

Current Police Practices

As a result of political pressure incorporated into systemic domestic violence laws, highly publicized research, and the threat of legal liability, the old system of police indifference was no longer viable. From the mid-1980s virtually every police department in the United States adapted one of three approaches. Most were covered by new state statutes mandating the arrest of domestic violence offenders or making arrest the preferred response. The rest encouraged arrest, or allowed the responding police officers to use their discretion about whether to make a domestic violence arrest.

The reality of how police organizations and the officers they employ actually responded to the passage of pro-arrest statutes remains problematic and, at times, unpredictable. Department policies may "read well" in that they express institutional commitment to the law and to politically correct policies. However, inasmuch as these policies are written in part to insulate the department from legal liability or to placate strong political constituencies such as battered women's advocates and their allies, there may be less than normal concern for policy adherence. At times, absolute compliance may not be expected or even desired by department leadership. This can make street-level implementation of any legislation or policy directive problematic and suggests that we focus attention on actual police behavior.

Increased Role of Arrest

It is now generally acknowledged that recent years have seen an overall increase not only in the rate of domestic assault reaching police attention, but also in the likelihood of arrest. To a large extent this can be attributed to the passage of domestic violence reform legislation and changes in department policies. While overall domestic violence arrest rates during the 1970s and 1980s were estimated to be in the range of 7 to 15 percent, current rates on average are estimated to be over 30 percent.[12]

In an examination of police incident data in 2,819 jurisdictions in 19 states, David Hirschel and his colleagues reported that, taking into account such factors as the seriousness of the offense, states mandating or indicating a preference for arrest have higher arrest rates than states with discretionary arrest statutes. It is comforting to know that when statutes mandate a more aggressive response and decrease police discretion, officers respond in an appropriate fashion.

Differential Impact of Arrest

Domestic violence arrest rates have clearly increased since the passage of pro-arrest domestic violence arrest laws and policies. But, two interrelated concerns remain: (1) whether specific groups are being disproportionately targeted for arrest, and (2) whether particular aspects of the incident impact the likelihood of arrest rather than domestic violence per se.

Increased Arrest of Children

Domestic violence laws extend to any assault in a family or a relationship context, including assaults by children. There has been a disproportionate increase in overall juvenile arrest rates over the past decade. With regard to domestic assault in particular, some research has suggested that juvenile offenders are significantly more likely to be arrested than adults, regardless of victim injury, threat, or protective order violation. In addition, there is a growing body of research suggesting that aggressive domestic violence policies have a greater impact upon juvenile female offenders since acts of violence committed by females are far more likely to be minor compared to those perpetrated by males. However, when comparing the relative importance of age and gender, one recent study reported that the differences in arrest rates were primarily attributable to age, not gender. Overall, juveniles were found to be more likely to be arrested compared to adults in similar situations. For both aggravated and simple assault, juvenile females had the highest arrest rates, followed by juvenile males, adult males, and adult females.[13]

Increased Arrest of Women

There has also been a disproportionate increase in the rate of female arrests for domestic assaults in recent years, both as sole offenders and as part of a "dual arrest," the situation that occurs when both parties involved in an incident are arrested. The FBI reported that the male arrest rate for assault fell approximately 5.8 percent between 1994 and 2003, whereas the female arrest rate increased by 30.8 percent.[14] While it may appear that this is evidence of a growing propensity for women to engage in criminal acts, the existing data suggest that there has been little or no change in female rates of assault, while the arrest rate for females has steadily grown. This has been further substantiated by other researchers who report that female violence appears to be of overall less severity than males, though a national study of the police response to domestic violence has indicated that, after taking serious- ness of the offense into account, sex of the offender does not impact the likelihood of arrest.

The traditional image of intimate partner violence is of a male of- fender and a female victim. The extent to which there is gender sym- metry in intimate partner violence constitutes a hotly debated issue. Acknowledging that females use violence in intimate relationships does not mean that they are abusers. It is important to understand the con- text in which violence is used and whether such behavior is offensive or defensive in nature. Police reports indicating role reversals between victim and offender in a series of incidents may be the result of a fail- ure to understand defensive behavior, or identify a primary aggressor, rather than a reflection of reality.

The Role of Race

It appears that patterns of differential enforcement based on race and ethnicity have diminished in recent years. One recent study using a national data set reported that, when the seriousness of the reported incident is held constant, whites were significantly more likely than other racial and ethnic groups to be arrested. This may be a result of victim preferences or other factors, but nonetheless it is noteworthy given the concern about the over arrest of minority males. It should also be emphasized that the focus here is on police arrest practices rather than actual incidence of domestic violence among various racial and ethnic groups. In fact, that same study reported that approximately 27 percent of the incidents involved a black offender, which is far higher than their representation in the general population.

Seriousness of Offense

Most police officers believe they should, and do, arrest when the incident indicates that a serious criminal assault has already occurred. In an examination of 577,862 incidents of assault and intimidation for the year 2000, offense seriousness was the single most important pre- dictor of arrest in mandatory, presumptive, and discretionary arrest jurisdictions.[15]

Police, however, may not place as much focus on cases in which there is simply a strong potential for violence or a history of assaults. These types of incidents involve the most use of police discretion in the decision to arrest. As far back as 1980, a study of officers from 17 departments found that more than 90 percent identified the following factors in their decisions to arrest: (1) commission of a felony, (2) serious victim injury, (3) use of a weapon, (4) violence against the police, and (5) likelihood of future violence. In contrast, prior calls from a household and victim preference were not nearly as important.[16] This has been confirmed by numerous other studies.

Offender Absent upon Police Arrival

A key situational or incident-related factor in the decision to arrest is whether the suspect leaves the scene of the offense. Clearly, in stranger assaults, an actual arrest is more difficult when the offender has left the scene and is unknown to the victim. However, police are not confronted with the difficulty of offender identification in cases of domestic assaults unless the victim and/or witnesses are unable or unwilling to cooperate. By questioning victims and witnesses, the police should be able to easily locate most domestic assault offenders, making this less of a discriminator.

Discrepancies in arrest rates between offenders who are present versus those who are absent at the time of police arrival are an important factor in the police response to domestic violence. Estimates are that more than 50 percent of intimate abusers leave the scene before police arrive. Any distinction in treatment of these offenders not only is often unwarranted in terms of police ability to locate perpetrators but also appears to perversely impact offenders less likely to be "experienced" or repeat offenders. For example, it has been reported that, on average, their victims are far more fearful than those whose offenders remained. In another study, offenders who left the scene were twice as likely to reoffend within the next year as those who stayed.[17] Despite this, many police agencies do not aggressively pursue, or even issue warrants for, offenders who have left the scene. A study of police practices in 25 jurisdictions in four states has indicated that, taking into account such factors as seriousness of offense and offender sex, an offender who has left the scene is four times less likely to be arrested than an offender who remains at the scene.[18] The decreased likelihood of arrest may be due to the additional time required to locate offenders. In addition, officers may assume that once an offender is no longer in the presence of a victim, she is safe.

Who Called the Police?

It is important to consider differences in police response when the victim requests assistance compared to someone else. While it is commonly believed and some research indicates that most calls are initiated by the victim, a recent study in Rhode Island reported that the majority of calls came from someone other than the victim. Police appear to differentiate domestic violence cases based on who initiated the call for service. We would normally expect police to be more responsive if the victim initiated the call. After all, this indicates a degree of cooperation by the victim and a willingness to have the offender arrested. However, research has suggested the reverse, and many studies have reported that the likelihood of arrest actually decreases significantly when the victim initiates the call.

While it is unclear why a victim report is taken less seriously than a call from a neighbor or stranger, it is believed that police may attach less significance to cases where they are contacted by the victim and see them as involving "private" family issues. However, when a bystander calls, the initial police characterization of the call would be as a "disorderly conduct" or a "disturbance," a classic mission for police concerned with public order maintenance. Substantiating this hypothesis, one recent study found that 57 percent of intimate partner domestic violence incidents resulted in an arrest when the victim initiated the call compared to 71 percent when someone else contacted the police.[19]

Presence of Weapons

As expected, when an assailant uses or threatens to use a weapon, the odds of an arrest increase dramatically. Use of weapons has consistently been found to be a factor that officers consider in determining risk to the victim.[20] In fact, it may be reported to be the single most important factor in the police decision to arrest.

However, even in circumstances that would seem obvious, officers' value systems can still be a factor. What is defined as a weapon may depend on the particular characteristics of the victim, offender, and situation, as well as the community where it occurs. For example, a police officer may believe that the use of weapons is prevalent in a neighborhood and therefore may discount waving a broken wine bottle around. Alternatively, when an officer responds to an incident where the victim has broken the law in the past (such as drug offenses, or even violence), the officer may consider use of that same broken bottle as something "she has probably used as well."

Criminal History

There is a growing emphasis on the importance of ascertaining the offender's criminal history, for both domestic violence offenses as well as overall history when determining whether an arrest should be made.

The growing availability and use of technology by law enforcement agencies increasingly allow them to consider this factor in their decision to arrest. However, many police agencies only consider domestic violence history rather than overall criminal history when responding to domestic violence calls. This may underestimate the risk posed by some offenders; research suggests that offenders who are "generally violent" pose a greater overall threat than offenders who limit their violence to domestic violence relationships.

Victim Demeanor

Another factor in the decision to arrest is the officer's overall reaction to the traits and conduct of the victim. If, for example, the officer judges the victim to have a "deviant" lifestyle, such as engaging in drug use, an arrest is less likely to be made. When officers observe a regularly recurring pattern of violence, they may believe it is part of the social fabric of the couple's life. Consequently, they are less likely to believe that any police response, including arrest, will be successful in deterring future violence. Many police officers appear to dichotomize between "normal citizens," similar to themselves, and "deviants," perhaps seen to use excessive alcohol, not to speak fluent English, to belong to minority groups, or to participate in an interracial or same-sex relationship. For these groups, many officers perceive battering as merely a part of overall family pathology and, therefore, not amenable to effective intervention.

This is not unexpected. A necessary component of police decision making is to make rapid value judgments in circumstances in which reality is unclear. In the face of ambiguous facts, research on police responses to rape, sexual assault, and domestic violence has long noted that officers make judgments based on their inherent assumptions regarding proper victim conduct. In such cases, the nature of the relationship between the parties as well as their behavior and demeanor may be considered by police as valid factors in evaluating the criminal behavior of either party. Not only do officers scrutinize the victim's behavior as well as that of the assailant, but also this may affect who is actually identified as "victim" and "offender."

Other victim actions at the scene clearly influence the police. For example, victim "cooperation" with the officer influences arrest decisions. In general, police stereotype domestic violence victims as providing little support or dropping complaints, ostensibly because they tend to reconcile with their abusers. In police parlance, they are perceived as "fickle." Of course, officers know that without victim cooperation, a case dismissal or acquittal at trial for lack of evidence is more likely. They may also believe that if the victim is unwilling to extend the effort to initiate a complaint, the seriousness of the injury may not

warrant disrupting their own schedules. Research on victim cooperation has, until recently, largely measured victim cooperation solely by
their preference for arrest.

Offender Behavior and Demeanor

Research on police use of arrest in situations in which the officer has
discretion regarding whether to arrest has consistently found that
police are guided by their reaction to the offender and his demeanor.
Past domestic violence research suggests that both an offender's criminal history and demeanor dramatically affect the likelihood that he will
be arrested. Key factors include lack of offender civility toward the
police and the use of drugs or alcohol.

Assailant demeanor clearly appears to affect the arrest decision. For
example, it has long been known that an arrest nearly always occurs if
an assailant remains violent in the officer's presence. Perhaps because
of the implied threat to the officer's authority or a lack of respect, an
arrest is likely if the offender is perceived to constitute a direct threat
to the officer even independent of the strength of the case. Hence, if
the potential arrestee appears argumentative, appears still ready to
behave aggressively toward the victim, or otherwise challenges police
authority, an arrest is likely to be made, as much to establish control of
the situation as a response to the incident. It has also been observed
that arrests are quite likely when the suspected abuser is belligerent or
drunk. In one early study, it was found that two-thirds of offenders
who were hostile were arrested, whereas none who were civil toward
the police were arrested.[21]

Normative Ambiguities

Arrest practices are also influenced by normative ambiguities in
family and relationship matters. Research in several Massachusetts
communities suggested that, in some departments, the likelihood of
arrest for domestic assaults involving the use of force is low for those
parties who can provide the police with a plausible rationale for the
incident that involves the offender experiencing a major life event.
There was a reduced probability of an arrest if actual violence was
"explained" by a crisis such as an impending divorce or separation,
the birth or impending birth of a child, a child about to be removed
from the household, or the offender experiencing a serious mental
health problem. By contrast, arrest was used in response to more pe-
destrian excuses for violence involving "everyday conflicts," such as
problems with drinking, fights over money, and child custody issues.[22]
We are concerned that, in some departments, police appear less willing
to protect victims if offenders simply provide a rationale for their

conduct. A significant question is why such distinctions are important. For reasons we discuss later, if such distinctions relate to victim preferences, they might be appropriate; however, if they reflect officers' personal beliefs or their identification with the offender's behavior, then the implications are far more insidious.

The Impact of Victim Preferences on the Arrest Decision

Victim preference has long been termed an important determinant of arrest. In all but mandatory arrest jurisdictions, an informal operational requirement for a domestic assault arrest is the victim's desire for the arrest. Without victim concurrence, most jurisdictions in the recent past had policies or at the least standard operating procedures actively discouraging arrest. Studies have confirmed that the probability of an arrest increases by 25 to 30 percent if the woman agrees to sign a complaint and decreases by a similar amount if she refuses. Not surprisingly, it has been observed that victim preferences historically accounted for the largest variance in arrest rates in every study examined. However, most domestic violence studies have not included this factor in their analyses of police decision making. In addition, the passage of mandatory arrest laws would appear to have eliminated victim preference as a factor to be considered in deciding whether to arrest in those states. However, it appears that officers can still pay attention to victim preference when responding to domestic violence incidents in states with preferred or discretionary arrest laws.

IMPLICATIONS FOR BEST PRACTICES

The increased police responsiveness to domestic violence over the past 30 years represents a major achievement for domestic violence victim advocates. Domestic violence clearly is no longer treated as a family matter but is recognized as a criminal offense that merits police intervention. However, it is also clear that the shift from a historic practice of nonintervention to the current emphasis on arrest may have unanticipated consequences that should be given further attention. As discussed in this chapter, any universal mandate requiring police to arrest in cases of domestic assault is likely to disproportionately impact certain segments of the general population. Women, children, and racial and ethnic minority groups have been differentially impacted by these mandates, though to what extent has yet to be completely determined.

In addition, it is important to remember that the purpose of requiring that the police arrest domestic violence offenders is not only to increase the arrest of batterers, but also to protect victims and prevent reoffending. In their role as "gatekeepers," police are seen as the vehicle by which offenders enter a criminal justice system intended to prevent and deter further offending as well as punish the wrongdoers. Victims may also access additional and much-needed resources through their contact with the criminal justice system. However, further research is needed to determine whether an arrest is actually needed to deter low-risk offenders, and if victims might in fact benefit by sometimes—in specifically defined situations—being empowered to make decisions based on what they perceive to be their best interests. This would allow limited resources to better target high-risk offenders who are likely to reoffend, regardless of whether there is further prosecution and adjudication. We also know that mandating arrest may impact victim reporting of new offenses and, as a result, our ability to ensure their overall safety. Many victims who contact the police do so with the expectation that they ultimately determine whether there is an arrest. It can be argued that the failure to pay attention to victim preferences further disempowers an already victimized individual and makes it less likely that she will call the police if she is revictimized.[23]

For all of these reasons, it is our recommendation that using arrest as the preferred response for domestic assault is preferable to mandating it in any and all situations. We stress, however, the need for ensuring strict police accountability in the context of victim needs and preferences.

NOTES

1. E. Pleck, "Criminal Approaches to Family Violence 1640–1980," in *Crime and Justice: A Review of Research*, vol. 11, ed. L. Ohlin and M. Tonry (Chicago: University of Chicago Press, 1989), 19–58.

2. P. Manning, *Police Work: The Social Organization of Policing* (Prospect Heights, IL: Waveland, 1997); and M. Bard and J. Zacker, "Assaultiveness and Alcohol Use in Family Disputes," *Criminology* 12 (1974): 281–92.

3. V. Kappeler, M. Blumberg, and G. Potter, *The Mythology of Crime and Criminal Justice*, 3rd ed. (Prospect Heights, IL: Waveland, 2000).

4. E. Buzawa, "Traditional Responses to Domestic Disturbances" (paper presented at the Michigan Sociological Association, Detroit, MI, 1978).

5. D. Ford, "The Impact of Police Officers' Attitudes toward Victims on the Disinclination to Arrest Wife Batterers" (paper presented at the Third International Conference for Family Violence Researchers, Durham, NC, July 1987).

6. Bannon, 1974, 4.

7. S. Miller, "The Paradox of Women Arrested for Domestic Violence: Criminal Justice Professionals and Service Providers Respond," *Violence against Women* 7 (2001): 1339–76.

8. D. Lipton, R. Martinson, and J. Wilks, *The Effectiveness of Correctional Treatment* (New York: Praeger, 1975).

9. L. Sherman and R. Berk, "The Specific Deterrent Effects of Arrest for Domestic Assault," *American Sociological Review* 49 (1984): 261–72.

10. U.S. Attorney General's Task Force on Family Violence, *Final Report* (Washington, D.C.: U.S. Government Printing Office, 1984).

11. C. Maxwell, J. Garner, and J. Fagan, *The Effects of Arrest on Intimate Partner Violence: New Evidence from the Spouse Assault Replication Program*, Research in Brief (Washington, D.C.: National Institute of Justice, 2001).

12. E. Buzawa and C. Buzawa, *Domestic Violence: The Criminal Justice Response*, 3rd ed. (Thousand Oaks, CA: Sage, 2003); D. J. Hirschel and E. Buzawa, "Understanding the Context of Dual Arrest with Directions for Future Research," *Violence against Women* 8 (2002): 1449–73; and D. J. Hirschel, E. S. Buzawa, A. Pattavina, D. Faggiani, and M. Reuland, *Explaining the Prevalence, Context and Consequences of Dual Arrest in Intimate Partner Cases*, final report submitted to the U.S. Department of Justice, Grant no. 2001-WT-BX-0501 (Washington, D.C.: U.S. Department of Justice, 2007).

13. E. Buzawa and D. J. Hirschel, "Is There an Arrest Bias against Girls?" in *Girls and Violence: Beyond Denial and Demonization*, ed. M. Chesney Lind and M. Jones (Albany: State University of New York Press, 2008).

14. Federal Bureau of Investigation, *Uniform Crime Report* (Washington, D.C.: Federal Bureau of Investigation, 2004).

15. Hirschel, et al., *Explaining the Prevalence* (2007).

16. Loving, 1980.

17. E. Buzawa and G. Hotaling, "Understanding the Impact of Prior Abuse and Prior Victimization on the Decision to Forgo Criminal Justice Assistance in Domestic Violence Incidents: A Lifecourse Perspective," *Brief Treatment & Crisis Intervention* 7, no. 1 (2007): 55–76.

18. Hirschel, Buzawa, Pattavina, Faggiani, and Reuland, *Explaining the Prevalence*.

19. Ibid.

20. Berk and Sherman, 1998.

21. D. Bayley, "The Tactical Choices of Police Patrol Officers," *Journal of Criminal Justice* 14 (1986): 329–48.

22. E. Buzawa and G. Hotaling, "The Impact of Relationship Status, Gender, and Minor Status in the Police Response to Domestic Assaults," *Victim & Offenders* 1 (2006): 1–38.

23. Buzawa and Hotaling, "Understanding the Impact"; H. Eigenberg, ed., *Women Battering in the United States: Till Death Do Us Part* (Prospect Heights, IL: Waveland, 2001); and K. Ferraro, "Policing Women Battering," *Social Problems* 36 (1989): 61–74.

Chapter 5

The Prosecution of Domestic Violence across Time

Christopher D. Maxwell
Amanda L. Robinson
Andrew R. Klein

Since the early 1900s, the prosecution of domestic violence cases has been a central focus of investment and of procedural and statutory reforms at the local and national levels. States and the federal government, as well as local municipalities in urban as well as rural areas, have enacted laws and ordinances designed to address the perceived weakness in the approaches that prosecutors and court officials have used when family members, particularly female members, have sought protection from violence by their intimate partners. This chapter provides an overview of how these approaches evolved and where we are currently. We particularly focus on the shift from the "diversion" approach used before the 1980s to the criminalization models advanced during the 1990s.

EARLY PROSECUTION AND COURT PRACTICES ACROSS THE UNITED STATES

For as far back as historians have documented, western societies have responded to domestic violence, particularly violence against wives, by using both formal and informal sanctions. The historian, Elizabeth Pleck, describes church and state roles in criminalizing wife abuse during the 1600s in Massachusetts and how charitable organizations and the courts fault child abuse and wife battering during the last quarter of the 1800s.[1] Other historians and legal scholars have similarly documented that the American, British, Canadian, and Australian governments relied on formal responses to address wife abuse during the late nineteenth century. Unfortunately, these prohibitions were neither universal nor routinely enforced. For instance, the North Carolina Supreme Court in 1864 ruled that because a husband is responsible for the acts of his wife, he may use force to control her behavior. Further, North Carolina law prohibited the prosecution of a man for assaulting his wife unless the husband caused permanent injury or his force was excessive or cruel.

However widespread their enactment or enforcement, these responses appear to have done little to control family violence. Alternative ideas about how society should respond to family violence began to take hold in the early twentieth century. This was also a time when the perspective broadened from a focus on wife abuse to a more global concern with all forms of family abuse, including child maltreatment and abandonment. For instance, as early as 1910, Chicago court reformers created separate courts (e.g., the Courts of Domestic Relations) to solely address family issues, particularly the issue of the abandonment of wives. While the courts emphasized the preservation of the family by holding men accountable for the support of their wives, one judge did note that some men are "monsters," and therefore viewed "divorce a great blessing."[2] Following the adoption of these and other similar courts across the United States, in 1917 the National Probation Association recommended that family court judges have a sufficiently long term so that they could "develop a social service program" rather than use sanctions to deal with family matters. More extensive family courts with specialized judges developed during the first 70 years of the twentieth century. Many of these courts addressed all family matters by staffing themselves with "family counselors, social investigators, and other specialized staff" to overcome "a lack of cooperation and exchange of information between courts [that resulted in a] duplication of effort because some families are under investigation or supervision by two or more courts."[3]

Early twentieth-century court reform had indirectly addressed assaultive husbands within the context of women's complaints about nonsupport. But by the 1930s, when economic conditions made women reluctant to leave their partners and reduced the probability they would be supported financially if they did so, women's complaints about their victimization appear to have increased sharply and courts began again to emphasize battering. In response, and in an attempt to address women's victimization without resorting to imprisonment, specialized courts opened in several large U.S. cities. One example was the City of Los Angeles's Children's Court of Conciliation. This court tried alternative "social approaches" to address the underlying problems leading to "domestic strife" rather than using the criminal code that "often resulted in fines and imprisonment for offenders."[4] In the late 1940s, a similarly designed specialized magistrate court was established in New York City that worked with nonprofit organizations to collectively provide assistance to families as an alternative to criminal sanctions. During its first decade, this court processed an estimated 10,000 cases annually.[5] Although seen as progressive at the time for trying something other than criminal sanctions, one court observer later noted that this court lacked sufficient authority to address those incidents "when persuasion fails" and therefore advocated that "family disputes should be taken out of the inferior criminal courts entirely and turned over to a fully equipped domestic relations court with plenary power."[6] Law enforcement was given insufficient resources to address the underlying problem causing the violence, critics pointed out. Instead of recommending more law, another critic argued that communities need to "make referrals to family agencies more frequently, more comprehensively, more imaginatively and more skillfully" to reduce domestic violence recidivism.[7] By the late 1960s, there were 14 other similar programs spread across the country. These programs called for police departments to collaborate with victim and mental health services to provide long-term services (e.g., service beyond an arrest).

Besides New York City, other places also established specialized processes or courts during the 1960s to address domestic violence cases. For instance, the City of Milwaukee established a comprehensive misdemeanor court to adjudicate family violence. To help the assigned judge make more informed decisions, the Milwaukee court reporter would hold pretrial conferences with the parties and then use the gathered information to inform the judge about the nature of the violence and the involved parties and recommend a court disposition. The court's assigned police officer would also help by collecting psychiatric examination records and other information for the judge before the hearings. This court was also among the first to use the "continuance for cause" or what is now commonly referred to as a delayed disposition to manage the parties after the hearing. The "continuance" often included "referral to the probation department" and the "judge's explicit suggestion or promise that the case would be dismissed upon the return date if no additional troubles between the parties came to the court's attention during the interim."[8]

Similarly, the City of Detroit developed their Misdemeanor Complaint Bureau to target misdemeanor assaults between relatives, intimates, or neighbors. Under the supervision of the district attorney, the bureau's detectives were directed to hold informal hearings, to which both parties were allowed to bring witnesses and necessary evidence. The cases were then disposed of by using "lectures," "mediation," or "adjournment with date" practices, or they placed one or both parties on a nonexistent, nonsecured, verbal "peace bond." If the cases could not be addressed, they were then forwarded to the prosecutor's office and disposed of by using probation.

The early research across the United States indicated that even though only a minority of domestic violence cases came to the attention of criminal justice officials, the majority of these cases were dismissed or otherwise disposed of using a number of informal practices. For instance, after accepting the guilty plea, Chicago judges often used one or more methods to dispose of the cases. The judges most frequently lectured the defendant, followed by issuing a "peace bond" and/or referring the party to social services or for psychiatric care. Besides these informal remedial steps, judges often tried to identify the extent of the problem, in part to address concerns about children's safety or to help preserve the family. The least frequent disposition was a fine or a short jail term. For example, a review of Manhattan district court records found that, in 1945, only 300 out of 10,000 domestic-related cases were sent to the probation department.[9]

The most likely cause for the large number of diversion outcomes was prosecution procedures at the time; few jurisdictions had explicit policies codifying how prosecutors should respond to cases of domestic violence. Similar to policy directives for police officers to avoid making arrests in cases of domestic violence, it is likely that many prosecutors adopted a de facto policy of diverting these cases out of the criminal courts. At this time, diversion was preferred because traditional punitive sanctions were thought to be too crude to address the underlying problem. The courts' reluctance to sanction domestic violence may have also arisen from a belief that the law ought not to "invade the domestic forum or go behind the curtain." The right to family privacy has been interpreted to mean the criminal law should be used sparingly when addressing a "domestic dispute." Additionally, courts were reluctant to sanction a husband's abuse of his wife because women were largely consigned to a second-class status in the family and the home, over which the husband was assumed to have ultimate authority.

By the early 1970s, the distinction made between "public" and "private" issues began to dissolve and more sophisticated, legislative schemes addressing domestic violence were introduced. These changes were compelled by women's increasing importance as economic actors in their own right, growing rates of female participation in civic life at all levels, and the emergence of a women's rights movement that focused the public's attention on the nature and extent of arrest and criminal prosecution for intimate partner violence. During the 1970s, it became commonplace for scholars to criticize law enforcement for its failure to report domestic violence offenses, to arrest male offenders, to redress the victimization of women, and to treat violence against intimate partners as severely as violence against nonintimate partners.

Many of the negative assertions were initially expressed in the context of cited testimonials describing the outcome of a specific domestic violence incident, observations made of the police and courts, or comments by law enforcement executives. One such disturbing comment came from James Bannon, a Detroit Police Department commander. At the 1975 American Bar Association Conference, Bannon reported that in 1972 fewer than 300 cases were tried by a court out of 4,900 warrants for domestic assault.[10] Similarly critical assessments came from researchers who reviewed prosecutors' case files. For instance, when Del Martin reviewed data from the San Francisco District Attorney's Office, she found only eight [felony wife beatings] were prosecuted out of the several thousand [family or quasi-family] cases processed by its Bureau of Family Relationships during the fiscal year 1973–1974.[11] This pattern as well as those identified in other similar studies suggested that in many places prosecution was not a remedy typically available for battered women.

Besides the lack of prosecution, researchers on both sides of the Atlantic reported that domestic violence cases often received a different response by criminal justice officials compared to assault and other crimes not committed in a domestic context. For example, an examination of prosecution practices in England and Wales found that, compared to nondomestic violence cases, domestic violence cases were less likely to be prosecuted and, when they were, more defendants were found not guilty.[12] A later British study using a larger sample found routine charge reductions from Sect. 47, "Assault Occasioning Actual Bodily Harm," to Sect. 39, "Common Assault," and high rates of withdrawals in the progression of domestic assault cases.[13] Reviews of similarly designed studies across the United States found that the difference in the rates of prosecution between domestic and nondomestic cases was largely accounted for by the disparity in the level of victim cooperation, an issue to which we will return. Such general indifference toward prosecution along with several alarming incidents painted a fairly bleak picture at the end of the 1970s of how the court system was failing to respond effectively to family violence, particularly violence between intimates.

POST 1970s: THE MOVEMENT TOWARD PRO-PROSECUTION POLICIES

The perceived limitations in responses to the problem of spouse assault mobilized societal institutions to increase the range of formal social controls of batterers and their families. With the seeming failure of the "social worker" model that first developed during this period, states in the late 1970s initiated mechanisms that labeled batterers as criminals and relied on the "get tough" sanction-dominated theories of social control. The most dramatic procedural change was to have the police arrest batterers every time they responded to incidents of violence between intimates. Before arrest could become standard practice; however, the legal and culture roadblocks that had prevented the police from making arrests in the context of intimate violence had to be removed. One step in this direction was the passage of presumptive or mandatory arrest laws by the states and the development of policies by local departments that made arrest standard operating procedure. These legal and administrative changes allowed or proscribed that patrol officers arrest a suspect whenever they had probable cause that even a misdemeanor assault had occurred between two intimate partners that they had not witnessed. Between 1984 (the year that the results from the influential Minneapolis Domestic Violence Experiment showing the advantage of arrest were released) and 1986, there was a 400 percent increase in the number of urban police departments encouraging arrests in incidents of domestic violence. The central aims of these legal remedies were to deter batterers from abusing their intimate partners again by sending a clear message that assaulting an intimate is criminal, and will again cost them if they were to continue hitting their partners.

With the widespread adoption of pro-arrest laws and policies in the 1980s, the general improvements in the relationships between law enforcement agencies and reform advocates, and the dissemination of research showing deterrent effects for arrest, the criticisms of the police response to domestic violence abated and the policies and practices of prosecutors and judges toward intimate partner violence began to receive heightened attention. But reform in the prosecutorial approach to domestic violence occurred much more slowly than the sea change that characterized policing. There are several reasons why this was so.

First, given the subjective nature of prosecution and the independence of popularly elected prosecutors, legislatures have found it more difficult to enact mandatory prosecution laws, in the hopes of reducing prosecutorial discretion, as they have done in many states for police. Moreover, there is a long tradition of prosecutorial autonomy in accepting, modifying, or dropping any case submitted to their office. While states have enacted general victim rights laws, requiring prosecutors to meet with victims about prosecution decisions to charge defendants, none has enacted specific legislation mandating prosecution of domestic violence. The closest a handful of states have come is to require prosecutors to have written policies on domestic violence prosecution. Florida has gone the furthest, requiring the state's attorney general and local prosecutors to adopt a "pro-prosecution policy" for domestic violence, encouraging prosecutors to file even "over the objections of the victim if necessary." The law (Fla. Stat. §741.2901) further requires prosecutors to establish special units or assign prosecutors "to specialize in the prosecution of domestic violence cases ... and receive training in domestic violence issues." Nevertheless, even without widespread legislative mandates, the majority of prosecutors representing larger jurisdictions in the United States had adopted by the mid-1990s some form of a no-drop policy. However, because prosecutors can be replaced by the voters every four years, the consistent implementation of these policies has, no doubt, varied over time.

Even in a country where prosecutors are not elected, such as the United Kingdom, the implementation of policies designed to reduce prosecutorial discretion followed by some years similar policies for the police. In England and Wales, the Crown Prosecution Service (CPS) policy on prosecuting domestic violence states, "Generally, provided we have sufficient evidence, the more serious the offence or the greater the risk of further offences, the more likely we are to prosecute in the public interest—even if victims say they do not wish us to do so."[14] However, this may be difficult to achieve if, at the same time, prosecutors are also instructed (in the same guidance) to always take into account the consequences of prosecution on the victim. This issue highlights the never-ending conundrum facing prosecutors in all jurisdictions of how to balance their responsibility for prosecuting crimes on behalf of the state (in society's interest) versus their concern for the impact of prosecution on particular individuals (the victim's interest). When these two interests conflict, as they often do in cases of domestic violence, it increases the ambiguity confronting prosecutors over the right course of action, increasing their use of discretion.

Second, although there were several early suits against prosecutors for failing to prosecute abusers that were resolved through consent decrees, such class action suits are difficult to win. Given the ambivalence many victims express about testifying against their abusers, and the usual absence of third-party witnesses to domestic assaults that typically occur within the victims' homes, it is difficult to prove that prosecutors are violating the Constitution by discriminating against domestic violence victims in terms of failure to pursue prosecutions.

Third, it is more complicated and difficult for even the most committed and concerned advocates and researchers to monitor and track court prosecutions. Unlike law and order television dramas, most criminal cases are resolved in court corridors rather than courtrooms. Further, in many jurisdictions, prosecution is bifurcated between misdemeanors and felonies with different prosecutors handling different sets of cases or different stages of the same cases. Very few cases actually go to trial before a judge; even fewer go before a jury. Often, except for an exceptional, high-publicity case like the O.J. Simpson prosecution, domestic violence cases are prosecuted out of public view.

The difficulty of tracking prosecution cases is illustrated by work done by an Arizona researcher who attempted to determine domestic violence prosecution rates across that state. What he found was that police and prosecutors failed to adhere to Ariz. Rev. Stat. § 13-3601(H) requiring domestic violence crimes to be designated as such. He even found that the majority of arrests for "aggravated domestic violence" (which actually specifies "domestic violence" in the charge) were not designated as domestic violence, nor were most stalking charges or violations of protective orders, notwithstanding the fact that the vast majority of these charges typically involve relationships qualifying as domestic violence under Arizona law. Further, although police records showed they made 89,960 domestic violence arrests from 2000 to 2002, court records revealed only 45,237 of the cases were disposed of by the fall of 2003. While the remainder may have still been pending, the researcher suggested it was more likely that officials either failed to record their dispositions or actually dropped the charges.[15]

Fourth, and perhaps much more important, successful prosecution of domestic violence cases even among motivated prosecutors is often challenging because relatively few of the cases presented to prosecutors are accompanied by a great deal of evidence, other than the testimony of the victim. Research has found that while responding patrol officers may gather what evidence they can at the scene, most cases are not assigned to a detective to complete an independent or follow-up investigation as they would in more serious capital or felony cases. For example, across Rhode Island in 2002, local and state police responded to over 7,000 domestic violence incidents, arresting perpetrators in more than 65 percent and issuing warrants in another 9 percent of the incidents. While the police reported receiving written statements from victims in 49 percent of the incidents, they only secured physical evidence in 9 percent, and interviewed witnesses other than the victim in only 24 percent of the incidents.[16] In Mecklenburg County, North Carolina, researchers similarly found that the police rarely provided physical evidence to the county's special domestic violence prosecution unit. Photos were available in only 15 percent of cases submitted by patrol officers and only 31 percent of cases submitted by the police department's specialized domestic violence unit assigned the most serious abuse cases. Medical evidence was available in less than 10 percent of the patrol cases and 34 percent of the special unit cases. Third-party witnesses were available in only 16 percent of patrol cases and 19 percent of special unit cases.[17] Similarly, an Ohio domestic violence court study found photos of injuries and damages available in only 14 percent of the cases, police officer testimony in just 7 percent of the cases, and 911 tapes, medical records, or eyewitness testimony in only 6 percent.[18] A British multisite study also found that anything but the most basic type of evidence (i.e., victim or suspect statements) was rare:

statements from other witnesses (28 percent), case exhibits (usually photographs; 27 percent), transcripts or recordings of 999 calls (26 percent), medical statements (19 percent), and forensic evidence (5 percent).[19] It was surmised that, as currently investigated, domestic violence cases provided many lost opportunities for evidence collection.

On the other hand, researchers have yet to demonstrate that physical evidence has an independent, positive relationship with a guilty disposition. In one study, the availability of evidence, including 911 tapes, photographs, medical records, and police testimony, was not associated with the likelihood of a conviction.[20] In several other jurisdictions, another study found, evidence (eyewitnesses, photos, admissions, excited utterances, medical evidence, and physical evidence) was not uniformly the most powerful predictor of prosecutors' decisions to proceed without victims and was not significantly associated with the decision to prosecute at all in one study jurisdiction.[21]

Beyond the challenges faced by the lack of evidence, several U.S. Supreme Court decisions, including *Crawford v. Washington* (541 U.S. 36 (2004)), limit the admissibility of hearsay evidence, which includes the types of victim statements typically captured in police reports. As a result, prosecutors must now rely on the live testimony of victims, who may be uncooperative. Several studies have found that as many as half of all victims do not want their abusers prosecuted, even when they initiated the call to the police. For example, a Chicago misdemeanor court study found that almost a third of victims reported they did not want their abusers to be prosecuted.[22] Another study involving prosecution programs in California, Washington, Oregon, and Nebraska found that half of the victims did not want them prosecuted.[23] In a related study, Massachusetts researchers found only 47 percent wanted their arrested abusers to be prosecuted as charged or wanted more serious charges filed.[24]

A large part of what makes case progression in domestic violence cases unique is the important role given to victim participation. The influence of the victim's willingness to participate in the case cannot be overstated, and there is a well-documented and pronounced relationship between victim participation and the continuation of domestic violence cases. Victims who are reluctant or unwilling to participate in the prosecution are more likely to have their cases dropped or withdrawn. Put another way, prosecutors are unlikely to continue with a case in which the victim does not want to give evidence. This relationship has not seemed to change much over time.

On the other hand, several studies of domestic violence prosecution practices across entire states suggest that the commitment and determination of prosecutors are more important factors in the success or failure in domestic violence prosecutions than victim cooperation or even the availability of other evidence. The *Boston Globe*, for example, reviewed 15,000 domestic violence prosecutions across Massachusetts between 1992 and 1994 handled by the state's 12 county district attorneys' offices for violations of protective orders, a misdemeanor. It found that conviction rates ranged from 25 to 88 percent county to county. The average was 60 percent. Though there were some demographic variations among counties, even in adjacent counties with similar demographics, the rates varied dramatically. District attorneys with lower conviction rates attributed their low rates to lack of victim cooperation, but the newspaper found no evidence that victims behaved differently across county lines.[25]

Similar newspaper examinations in South Carolina for domestic violence prosecutions between 1996 and 2000 and in North Carolina between 1997 and 2002 confirmed the *Globe*'s conclusions. In South Carolina, *The State* reviewed 4,351 felony domestic violence cases prosecuted by regional prosecutors. It too found conviction rates varied dramatically, even among similar districts, from a low of 22 percent to a high of 69 percent. After the state's attorney general criticized the district prosecutors for a generally low rate of prosecution, 46 percent, the statewide average increased the following month to 71 percent.[26] In neighboring North Carolina, the *News and Observer* in Raleigh reviewed 238,000 misdemeanor domestic violence cases prosecuted by 39 district attorneys' offices in that state between 1997 and 2002. Again, conviction rates varied dramatically from a low of 21 percent to a high of 57 percent. The average was 47 percent. The paper concluded that the policies of the individual district attorneys, including the resources they committed to the prosecution of domestic violence, were responsible for the variation in rates.[27]

Other systematic studies and many national and international case examples suggest that domestic violence prosecution rates might be increased through the creation of specialized prosecution programs, often accompanying specialized domestic violence courts. The objectives of these courts are to expedite the victim's safety following an arrest and to ensure the defendant's accountability. A study of specialized domestic violence prosecution programs established in San Diego, California; Everett, Washington; Omaha, Nebraska; and Klamath Falls, Oregon, where prosecutors adopted so-called no-drop domestic violence policies, found prosecutors were able to significantly increase domestic violence conviction rates in all four jurisdictions. Conviction rates increased to 96 percent in San Diego, 85 percent in Omaha, 78 percent in Klamath Falls, and 55 percent in Everett. The latter rate was the lowest because prosecutors maintained a diversion program that removed 22 percent of the cases prosecuted. The dismissal rates fell by more than half in Everett after no drop was instituted, from 79 percent to 29 percent; in Klamath Falls, they dropped from 47 percent to 14 percent.[28] In the Queens Borough of New York City, prosecutors increased convictions from 24 to 60 percent, with research suggesting that much of the increase was the result of increased follow-up with victims and prosecutors' improved linkages with police; for example, prosecutors monitored the same case log that asked whether each of eight evidentiary items was covered in police incident reports, including photos and witness, victim, and suspect statements.[29] An evaluation of the development of two specialized courts in the United Kingdom found that conviction rates increased, ineffective trials were reduced, and victim confidence was increased post implementation.[30]

Prosecutors can take affirmative steps to reduce victim fear and increase cooperation. A three-state study found that victim fear was reduced in sites with specialized prosecution programs, increased victim advocacy, and specialized domestic violence courts.[31] These specialized response programs generally include fast-track scheduling, reducing victim vulnerability pending trial, increasing victim contact pending trial, and using victim-friendly proceedings that remove, as much as possible, victim involvement to proceed with prosecution. These measures are in contrast with jurisdictions where studies indicate some prosecutors treat victims like civil claimants. In a large 45-county study of domestic violence prosecution in upstate New York, researchers found half of the prosecutors required victims to sign complaints before prosecutors would file charges against the alleged abusers.

There is more research on what prosecutors should not do than what they should do to increase prosecutorial success. Specific studies suggest that the more prosecution-related burdens placed on victims, the less likely victims are to cooperate. In Milwaukee, for example, the majority of cases were dismissed where victims were required to attend a charging conference within days of the arrest of their abusers. However, absolved of this responsibility, Milwaukee prosecution rates increased from 20 to 60 percent.[32] In a similar vein, a comparison of protective order violation prosecutions across Massachusetts found a 66 percent dismissal rate where prosecutors routinely provided and encouraged victims to sign waivers of prosecution forms (often in front of defendants) compared to a 33 percent dismissal rate in an abutting county where victims were not provided this alternative.[33]

Some prosecutors are better at maintaining contact with victims than others. An Ohio court study found that the majority of victims never received rudimentary information from prosecutors before trial, including notification of court dates. In almost 90 percent of the court cases, prosecutors never spoke with the victim on the phone and in more than half never met with them before the trial date. When they did meet, it typically was for no more than a few minutes.[34] The importance of prosecutor-victim contact is also underscored by a Toronto study that found if the victim met with a victim-witness representative, their cooperation increased by a factor of 3.3.[35] In the Ohio court study, the strongest predictor of a guilty verdict in domestic violence misdemeanor cases was found to be how many times the prosecutors met with the victim before trial.

A number of studies also suggest that court-based victim advocates may help prosecutors. In the United Kingdom, the implementation of specialized courts throughout England and Wales is premised on evidence that victim advocates are essential for the delivery of improved prosecution and court outcomes. Consequently, specialist courts are not set up without arrangements in place for victims to be supported throughout the process by a victim advocate. Victims appreciated contact with victim advocates or liaisons, reporting a high degree of satisfaction. In a Massachusetts study, for example, 81 percent of victims reported satisfaction with the time they spent with victim advocates; three-quarters (77 percent) said they would talk to the advocate again if a similar incident reoccurred.[36] Chicago domestic violence victims who had contact with victim advocates also reported more satisfaction with the proceedings than those who had no contact. However, the same study reported that victims contacted by advocates were not more likely to come to court. A similar finding was reported in Britain, indicating that even properly supported and informed victims will decide against participating with a criminal case against their former or current partners.

Other prosecution studies have also begun to confirm that jurisdictions with specialized domestic violence prosecution programs generally produce the highest rates of successful prosecution. These specialized programs apparently create their own momentum. They either stimulate or are already linked to courts with expedited domestic violence dockets. As a result of the specialized prosecution in San Diego, for example, processing time for domestic violence cases decreased to 32 days with almost half of the defendants (46 percent) pleading at the arraignment. Similarly, in Everett, Washington, time to trial was 80 days; in Omaha, it was 43 days. Shortened trial times reduce both victims' vulnerability to threats and the chances of their reconciling with abusers pending trial. In both San Diego and Everett, bails were regularly set at $10,000 per domestic violence charge (with no cash alternative in the latter). As a result, for defendants unable to raise bail, the incentive is to plead guilty to get out of jail. Further supporting the contention that prosecutorial determination is a powerful predictor of prosecutorial success, the Ohio court study found the increased time prosecutors spent with victims preparing the case was positively associated with successful prosecutions, whereas high prosecution caseloads were negatively associated with successful outcomes.

A 2005 study of more than 4,000 defendants processed by a domestic violence court in Memphis also demonstrated the benefits of a special domestic violence court. This study found that prosecutors proceeded in 80 percent of cases, and more than two-thirds of defendants pled guilty, were found guilty, or were placed on diversion.[37] Recently, "snapshot" statistics provided by the British CPS similarly showed that conviction rates for domestic violence in domestic violence courts are higher than in other British courts: 71 compared to 59 percent.[38] Specialized courts, therefore, appear to keep more domestic violence cases in the criminal justice system and lead to more sanctions.

It is important to remember, however, that even within domestic violence courts, maintaining victim participation can be a difficult process. One British study found that, even with the support provided to victims from advocates (now known nationally as independent domestic violence advisors, or IDVAs) and the multiagency partnerships within which the courts were embedded, nearly half of victims still chose to retract their complaints.[39] Of the 438 cases processed in a study of seven British domestic violence courts, about half resulted in convictions.[40] The pattern of attrition showed that 87 were lost before the case was listed for trial (41 were withdrawn and 46 were discontinued). The most common reason for pretrial attrition was due to victim retraction (relevant to 69 of 87 cases). A further 101 cases were lost by prosecutors offering "no evidence" at trial. Again, the most common reason was due to victim retraction (59 of 101 cases). In 13 cases the defendants were found not guilty at trial. The overall pattern of attrition, therefore, appears to be due to victims deciding whether to continue with the case or to retract their statements, but not all cases where victims retracted were lost. In 58 cases the victim decided to retract her statement, yet the offender was still convicted. This demonstrates the possibility of prosecutors continuing with cases regardless of victim involvement.

The research on victim retraction highlights the difficulty of using the criminal law and the criminal justice system to address problems between people who have once had, or who continue to have, an intimate relationship. David Ford found that women in Indianapolis called the police to help them manage the violence against them, but after this immediate goal was satisfied, they often disengaged from the system (i.e., dropped the charges against their exes or partners). He viewed victims' decision making as rational and strategic, even when it was at odds with the goals of the criminal justice system.[41]

Research in the United Kingdom and Australia has reinforced Ford's observation, showing that the decision of victims to retract is taken in the context of a range of pressures, many of which derive from the actions or "controlling behaviors" of perpetrators. Factors influencing victims' decisions to engage or withdraw from the criminal justice process include fear of the perpetrator and/or repercussions from his family, her own family, and/or the community; the extent and nature of her injuries; fear of damaging family status and honor; fear of losing children; a lack of information about and fear of criminal and civil processes, particularly for women who do not speak or read English; lack of information about, and delays to, the progress of their case; whether the defendant offers an initial plea of guilty; changes to bail conditions; and immigration status.

IMPACT OF PROSECUTION INITIATIVES ON VICTIMS AND OFFENDERS

Further complicating attempts to understand the actions taken by prosecutors and/or the courts is that these actions must be viewed from the perspectives of many different audiences, each of whom might have different ideas about what should be prioritized in terms of case progression. A prosecutor's success will not necessarily translate into a victim's safe outcome. The court clerk attempting to "speed up the process" and reduce ineffective trials might be at odds with the advocate who needs more time to support the victim so that she does not drop out of the process. Furthermore, problems for victims can result from a range of different court outcomes, and therefore "success" is in the eye of the beholder. As a result, the monitoring of case outcomes cannot tell us whether victims are more empowered, more satisfied, or safer as a result of having their cases prosecuted.

Other factors such as victim safety and satisfaction might represent equally important court performance metrics. For example, a victim may be more interested in receiving continued child support to maintain a roof over her and her children's heads than seeing her abuser prosecuted or imprisoned. Or the victim may have successfully extricated herself from the abusive relationship, and even be in hiding, and have no desire to reinvolve herself with her abuser even in the context of a criminal prosecution.

Victim Safety

Data from 120 victims in the United Kingdom showed that by far the most common response to the question "What do you want to result from this incident?" was "To be safe" (80 percent). However, these victims had different ideas about what type of outcome will be most likely to facilitate their safety. The most common desire expressed by women was for their partners to receive some kind of help, while a desire for a more punitive response by the criminal justice system was less common amongst the victims.[42]

The perspectives of victims serve as a useful reminder that concepts such as "justice" and "fairness" are formulated and perceived in different ways. Consequently, it is difficult to meaningfully assess the performance of prosecutors or courts, as safety is not always achieved when criminal justice outcomes are achieved. What produces a satisfied, safe victim in one case (e.g., custodial sentence) will produce the opposite effect for a different victim or even the same victim at a different point in time. Furthermore, even when a victim's safety has been enhanced, this can have occurred due to myriad reasons, only some of which might be due to actions taken within the court. Because courts do not routinely collect information about *victim safety* as part of the case finalization process, let alone include this as an official performance target, the situation remains that criminal justice performance indicators are used as proxies. For these reasons, it is important to expand our notions of what counts as success in the adjudication of domestic violence cases.

Victim Satisfaction

Notwithstanding the fact that a large minority of victims do not want their abusers prosecuted, studies indicate that the majority express satisfaction with prosecutors and courts after the cases are prosecuted. In the Massachusetts arrest study, for example, only 47 percent wanted their abusers to be prosecuted as charged or wanted more serious charges filed. However, after trial, 53 percent said the court experience gave them a "sense of control," while 37 percent said it motivated them to end the relationship with their abuser and 39 percent said it "made them safer." Most victims (71 percent) who did not want the case to go to court expressed satisfaction after trial.[43] Similarly, a study of four specialized prosecution programs in four different states found that, although 45 percent did not want their cases prosecuted, once they were prosecuted, only 14 percent tried to stop the prosecutors and only 4 percent said they wanted the court to let the defendant go. About three-quarters (72 percent) reported they wanted the defendant jailed and/or ordered into treatment, 64 percent expressed satisfaction with the prosecution, 9 percent were neutral, and 27 percent were dissatisfied. However, most (85 percent) reported that they felt the prosecution was "helpful."[44]

It should be noted that, although victim perceptions of the dangerousness of suspects have been found to be a good predictor of subsequent revictimization, victim preferences of how the case should be prosecuted are not. In the Massachusetts study, for example, those victims who wanted charges dropped were as likely as those who did not want them dropped to be revictimized: 51 percent compared to 48 percent after one year.[45] Similarly, studies in New York found that victim cooperation with prosecutors did not predict recidivism. In other words, if prosecutors proceeded with uncooperative victims, these victims were no more or less likely to be revictimized than victims who cooperated with prosecutors.

Sentencing Convicted Abusers

Not only do domestic violence prosecution rates vary greatly, but so too do the dispositions imposed after a finding or admission of guilt. Several studies from disparate jurisdictions across the country illustrate this point. In Quincy, Massachusetts, where three-quarters (74 percent) of the domestic violence suspects were charged with some form of assault and/or battery, a quarter of the defendants were diverted after a plea to sufficient facts, a quarter were placed on probation, and 14 percent were imprisoned. The remainder defaulted or had their cases filed.[46] In Ohio, of those found guilty, almost 70 percent were incarcerated, with the largest number incarcerated between 30 and 45 days, although 19 percent were incarcerated 150 to 180 days. A little more than 60 percent of those found guilty were placed under probation supervision with the largest number, 31 percent for between 360 and 499 days.[47] In the Brooklyn Misdemeanor Domestic Violence Court study of 9,157 cases in 2002, of those pleading or found guilty, 51 percent received a conditional discharge, 35 percent received jail, 7 percent received probation, 5 percent were ordered to complete community service, and 1 percent was fined.[48] In Milwaukee in the mid-1990s, out of 669 sample cases prosecutors accepted for prosecution, 30 percent were convicted with a jail sentence and a little less than a quarter were sentenced to probation.[49] In Chicago, a little less than a third was given conditional discharges, 24 percent probation or court supervision, and 23 percent jail (including time served pending trial).[50] A study of more than a thousand domestic violence arrests across three states, Connecticut, Idaho, and Virginia, found of those convicted three-quarters were incarcerated, sentenced to probation, and/or fined. A little less than half (46.7 percent) were ordered into either anger management or batterer programs.[51]

A study of domestic violence courts with specialized prosecutors in three different states found that the conditions of probation were much broader than, in comparison, jurisdictions without domestic violence specialization. These conditions included drug and alcohol abstinence and testing, batterer intervention programs that lasted longer and were more expensive than in comparison courts, more no-contact orders, attendance at fatherhood programs or women's groups (for female offenders), more mental health evaluations, mandatory employment, and restrictions on weapons.[52] Studies of four jurisdictions with specialized prosecution programs in as many states found incarceration rates ranged from 20 to 76 percent. Most also were placed on probation conditioned upon no victim contact and batterer treatment.[53] In at least one state, imprisonment of domestic violence felons has mushroomed over the last decade and a half. The number of domestic violence offenders sent to Ohio prisons increased ninefold between 1991 and 2005.[54]

Many of the domestic violence dispositional studies suggest that domestic violence sentences generally differ from standard sentencing patterns. Surprisingly, they often do not reflect defendants' prior criminal history, suggesting that prosecutors and/or judges may disregard prior records that are not domestic violence related. In the Ohio study, for example, researchers found no correlation between offenders' prior criminal histories and sentence severity. Similarly and surprisingly, the Toledo, Ohio, study found defendants with prior felony convictions were the least likely to be prosecuted and sentenced. In contrast, in both Quincy, Massachusetts, and Rhode Island, prior criminal history was significantly associated with severity of sentences.

A multiyear statewide examination of prosecution of domestic violence cases in Arizona compared similar charges designated as domestic violence and those not so designated. First, it found that conviction rates in domestic violence cases were 34 percent, significantly lower than the comparable conviction rate for the non–domestic violence prosecutions, which averaged 41 percent. Second, in regard to sentencing, men convicted of domestic violence–designated assault crimes were less likely to be incarcerated than men arrested for equivalent assaults that were not designated domestic violence, 49 percent compared to 62 percent for those convicted of misdemeanors and 70 percent compared to 74 percent for those convicted of felonies. The study also found that domestic violence sentencing rates varied significantly by county, ranging from only 6 percent incarcerated for domestic violence assaults in one county to 75 percent in another.

Reoffending

Should prosecution of domestic violence be encouraged? It appears that prosecuting abusers without regard to the specific risk they pose, unlike arresting domestic violence defendants, will not consistently deter further criminal abuse A number of studies have found that the abusers who are low risk (e.g., those with few prior incidents, less serious violence, or no prior drug use) are unlikely to reabuse in the short term, whether prosecuted or not. Alternatively, without the imposition of significant sanctions that include incarceration, those who are at high risk for reoffending are likely to reabuse regardless of the outcome of their prosecution. For example, a study of a large number of arrests in three states, Connecticut, Idaho, and Virginia, found that those who were prosecuted and convicted for domestic violence were more likely to be rearrested than offenders who were not convicted.

However, in this study, those prosecuted and convicted were significantly more likely to be higher risk offenders as measured by their prior criminal history records.[55]

A number of studies have found prosecution might reduce subsequent arrests and violence. However, the key to reduced reabuse may not be whether the case is prosecuted or not, but the disposition imposed by the court following the prosecution. For example, a Toledo, Ohio, misdemeanor court study found conviction was significantly associated with reduced rearrests for domestic violence one year following court disposition, even when controlling for batterers' prior history of domestic violence arrests, age, gender, education, employment, and marital status. The specific disposition, however, mattered. The more intrusive sentences, including jail, work release, electronic monitoring, and/or probation, significantly reduced rearrest for domestic violence over the less intrusive sentences of fines or suspended sentences without probation. The difference was statistically significant, with rearrests at 23 percent for defendants with more intrusive dispositions compared to 66 percent for those with less.[56] Another study of 683 defendants in Hamilton County (Cincinnati), Ohio, arrested for misdemeanor domestic violence also confirmed that sentence severity was significantly associated with reduced recidivism, especially for unmarried defendants, although in this study the actual sentence length (number of days in jail) was not found to be significant.[57]

Similar research looking at the cumulative effects of arrest followed by prosecution and court dispositions, including those with batterer treatment, has found modest reductions in reabuse to be associated with greater postarrest criminal justice involvement.[58] Research using almost 2,000 domestic violence defendants in Alexandria, Virginia, found, for example, that those most likely to reoffend were repeat offenders with a prior criminal history who had not been sentenced to incarceration for the study arrest, leading researchers to recommend jail sentences for domestic violence defendants with any prior criminal history.[59] By contrast, the Ohio felony study had mixed results. While jail sentences were significantly related to lower odds of subsequent misdemeanor or felony intimate assaults after two years, prison sentences were not. While the likelihood of these new charges was 9 percent less for those jailed compared to those placed on probation, it was only 2 percent lower for those imprisoned compared to those placed on probation.[60]

A major reexamination of the Ohio study involving more than 3,000 suspects arrested for domestic violence found prosecution is associated with less repeat offending for domestic violence over two years, as are their conviction and sentencing to probation. However, the sentencing of abusers to batterer treatment alone was not associated with less repeat offending, nor was sentencing to jail (although the number sentenced to jail was small). Based on the findings, the researchers concluded that the weight of the evidence "slightly shifts" toward a more positive assessment of domestic violence prosecution. They noted that many of the prior studies showing no deterrent effect of domestic violence prosecution may have reflected limitations of the research and sample size, not limitations of prosecution per se.

FUTURE DIRECTIONS IN THE PROSECUTION OF DOMESTIC VIOLENCE

Despite the increased attention and focus, the use of criminal sanctions beyond arrest to deter and incapacitate intimate violence offenders remains controversial. Since the early 1990s, scholars and others have found a range of reasons to criticize efforts by criminal justice officials and advocates to increase domestic violence prosecution rates. Some have complained that the system is now biased in favor of female victims, depriving alleged male abusers of their constitutional rights, especially against specious claims of abuse made by women seeking beneficial divorce settlements. Others have worried that the intervention of police and courts disempowers women, forcing them to cooperate, often to their peril, with a system that does not necessarily have their best interests at heart. Still others have felt that these two arguments are ironic given that many jurisdictions have yet to increase their prosecution of domestic violence cases. In 2005, for example, a South Carolina legislator castigated women for wanting "to punish the men," yet he noted that they "continue to go back around men who abuse them." At the time, South Carolina had one of the weakest sanctions for domestic violence in the country coupled with an extremely low prosecution rate. Even after the legislator's comment provoked an uproar that resulted in increased penalties, South Carolina law mandates only a year's incarceration for a third offense (S.C. Code Ann. §16-25-20). By contrast, Massachusetts law provides for a sentence of up to 2.5 years for a first offense of domestic battery.

Others are concerned that prosecution of domestic violence is, by definition, reactive, requiring the abuse to have occurred in the first place. Emphasis should be placed on prevention and treatment, rather than prosecution, using approaches such as therapeutic jurisprudence and restorative justice that are more widely used with drug and alcohol crimes and juvenile offenders. For instance, the therapeutic jurisprudence model uses the notion of quality processes that take into account the individual concerns of victims and the outcomes that matter to them (namely, for the violence to stop). This approach is also viewed as a useful lens through which criminal justice practice can be evaluated, as it asserts that the law should promote the well-being—even the empowerment—of people with whom it comes into contact.

Victim empowerment is a concept that could provide a more meaningful indication of the performance of institutions in contact with victims
of domestic violence, as it brings attention to the victim's own power
and her own actions to improve her life and keep herself and any children safer. The law may be seen as a victim power resource or as a
mechanism by which some of society's most vulnerable are doubly victimized: the key is to not only steer away from the latter, but also
measure and prioritize the former. Restorative justice similarly suggests
that "healing and restorative approaches may be an effective alternative" to a criminal justice response to domestic violence, especially
from the perspective of victims.

Unfortunately, for a small minority of victims, alternative interventions come too late. For example, between January 2003 and 2007, a
Florida victim called the sheriff's deputies on her husband more than
20 times, took out a succession of protective orders against him, and
fled to a shelter. The victim, a mail-order bride from Russia, was fearful she would be deported. She was dependent on her husband
because she spoke broken English and came to the United States with
no job or family here. A review of the sheriff's and state attorney's
office investigative files shows that authorities rarely took any but the
most basic steps to investigate the abuse that could have put the husband behind bars. The prosecutors pursued only one case because the
victim asked that the charges be dropped even though Florida law says
state attorneys should prosecute even over the objection of the victim.
The state attorney's office even declined to prosecute a restraining
order violation the husband admitted to. The husband was only
arrested three times on charges related to domestic violence, even
though his wife called deputies nearly two dozen times to report abuse
or violations of a restraining order. She told police that her husband
fired a gun in front of her and threatened to shoot her and feed her to
the alligators. When he stalked her at her church, he was issued a
warning for trespass. Twice when she took her son to the Regional
Medical Center in Port Charlotte with injuries, medical workers called
authorities because they suspected child abuse, but the sheriff's reports
show that deputies did not believe there was enough evidence to pursue charges even though the Department of Children and Families recommended counseling and periodic home visits after the second
hospital visit.

In 2007, her husband murdered her. After her murder, the state
attorney's office in Port Charlotte blamed the victim for being "uncooperative." While it could have proceeded without the victim, a
spokesperson said it was office policy not to. For his part, the Charlotte
County sheriff admitted, "We're not perfect." Accordingly, providing a
truly holistic response to victims of domestic violence must still include
the criminal justice system and beyond. Therefore, further research is

needed to continue to improve and monitor the potential impact of locating the primary government response to domestic violence within, rather than outside of, the criminal justice system while still availing parties of necessary and appropriate health and social services.

NOTES

1. E. Pleck, *Domestic Tyranny: The Making of American Social Policy against Family Violence from Colonial Times to the Present* (Champaign: University of Illinois Press, 2004).

2. W. N. Gemmill, "Chicago court of domestic relations." *The Annals of the American Academy of Political and Social Science*, 52 (1914): 115–123.

3. Chute, "Divorce and the Family Court," 51.

4. G. R. Ferguson, "An Experimental Psychiatric Clinic in a Family Court: With Diagnostic Impressions," *International Journal of Social Psychiatry* 4 (1958): 108.

5. Ferguson, "An Experimental Psychiatric Clinic," 109.

6. M. Ploscowe, "The Inferior Criminal Courts in Action," *Annals of the American Academy of Political and Social Science* 287 (1953): 9–10.

7. R. I. Parnas, "The Response of Some Relevant Community Resources to Intra-Family Violence," *Indiana Law Journal* 44, no. 2 (1969): 159–81.

8. R. I. Parnas, "Judicial Response to Intra-Family Violence," *Minnesota Law Review* 54 (1970): 616.

9. Parnas, "Judicial Response to Intra-Family Violence."

10. J. Bannon (commander, Detroit Police Department), "Law Enforcement Problems with Intra-Family Violence," in *American Bar Association Conference* (Montreal, Canada: American Bar Association, 1975).

11. D. Martin, *Battered Wives*, 110. Courtesy of Volcano Press, www.volcanopress.com

12. A. Sanders, "The Limits to Diversion from Prosecution," *British Journal of Criminology* 28, no. 4 (Autumn 1988): 513–32.

13. A. Cretney and G. Davis, "Prosecution Domestic Assault: Victims Failing Courts or Courts Failing Victims?" *Howard Journal* 36, no. 2 (May 1997): 146–57.

14. Crown Prosecution Service, *CPS Policy on Prosecuting Cases of Domestic Violence*, CPS Policy Directorate, February 2005, http://www.cps.gov.uk/publications/docs/DomesticViolencePolicy.pdf.

15. D. Wells, *Domestic Violence Prosecutions: Inequalities by Gender and Race Perpetrated in Arizona* (Tempe: Arizona State University, 2003).

16. A. Klein et al., *A Statewide Profile of Older Women Abuse and the Criminal Justice Response*, Final Report Submitted to the National Institute of Justice for Grant no. 2006-WG-BX-0009 (Washington, D.C.: U.S. Department of Justice, 2008).

17. P. C. Friday et al., *Evaluating the Impact of a Specialized Domestic Violence Police Unit*, Final Report Submitted to the National Institute of Justice for Grant no. 2004-WG-BX-0004, NCJ 215916, May (Charlotte: University of North Carolina at Charlotte, 2006).

18. J. Belknap et al., "To Go or Not to Go: Preliminary Findings on Battered Women's Decisions Regarding Court Cases," in *Women Battering in the United States: Till Death Do Us Part*, ed. H. M. Eigenberg (Prospect Heights, IL: Waveland, 2000), 319–26.

19. A. L. Robinson, *Measuring What Matters in Specialist Domestic*, working paper no. 102 (Cardiff, Wales: School of Social Science, Cardiff University, 2008).

20. Belknap et al., "To Go or Not to Go."

21. B. E. Smith et al., *Evaluation of Efforts to Implement No-Drop Policies: Two Central Values in Conflict*, Final Report Submitted to the National Institute of Justice for Grant no. 1998-WT-VX-0029, NCJ 187772, March (Washington, D.C.: American Bar Association, 2001).

22. C. Hartley and L. Frohmann, *Cook County Target Abuser Call (TAC): An Evaluation of a Specialized Domestic Violence Court*, Final Report Submitted to the National Institute of Justice for Grant no. 2000-WT-VX-0003, NCJ 202945, August (Iowa City: University of Iowa, 2003).

23. Smith et al., *Evaluation of Efforts*.

24. E. Buzawa et al., *Response to Domestic Violence in a Pro-Active Court Setting*, Final Report Submitted to the National Institute of Justice for Grant no. 1998-WT-NX-0027, NCJ 181427 (Lowell: University of Massachusetts, 1999).

25. A. Bass, P. Nealon, and D. Armstrong, "The War on Domestic Abuse," *Boston Globe*, September 25, 1994, 1, 21.

26. R. Brundrett, R. Roberts, and C. Leblanc, "S. C. Dismisses 54% of Worst Domestic Violence Cases," *The (Charlotte, NC) State*, May 20, 2001, 1.

27. A. Bible and A. Weigl, "Cries of Abuse Unheeded, Assaults Ride to Murders," *(Raleigh, N.C.) News and Observer*, May 18, 2003, 1.

28. Smith et al., *Evaluation of Efforts*.

29. N. Miller, *Queens County, New York, Arrest Policies Project: A Process Evaluation*, Research Supported by Grant no. 1998-WE-VX-0012 Award by the National Institute of Justice, NCJ 201886 (Washington, D.C.: U.S. Department of Justice, 2003).

30. C. Vallely et al., *Evaluation of Domestic Violence Pilot Sites at Caerphilly (Gwent) and Croydon 2004/05*, DV Project Team, Equality and Diversity Unit, Crown Prosecution Service, June 2005, http://www.cps.gov.uk/publications/reports, 72.

31. Adele Harrell et al., *Final Report on the Evaluation of the Judicial Oversight Demonstration, The Impact of JOD in Dorchester and Washtenaw County*, vol. 1 (Washington, D.C.: Urban Institute, 2007).

32. R. C. Davis and B. E. Smith, "Domestic Violence Reforms: Empty Promises or Fulfilled Expectations?" *Crime & Delinquency* 41, no. 4 (October 1995): 541–52.

33. Bass, Nealon, and Armstrong, "The War on Domestic Abuse."

34. Belknap et al., "To Go or Not to Go."

35. M. Dawson and R. Dinovitzer, "Victim Cooperation and the Prosecution of Domestic Violence in a Specialized Court," *Justice Quarterly* 18, no. 3 (September 2001): 593–622.

36. Buzawa et al., *Response to Domestic Violence*.

37. K. Henning and L. Feder, "Criminal Prosecution of Domestic Violence Offenses: An Investigation of Factors Predictive of Court Outcome," *Criminal Justice and Behavior* 32, no. 6 (2005): 612–42.

38. Crown Prosecution Service, *More Domestic Violence Offenders Convicted*, June 29, 2006, Crown Prosecution Service, http://www.cps.gov.uk/news/pressreleases/archive/2006/139_06.html.

39. Robinson and Cook, "Understanding Victim Retraction in Cases of Domestic Violence: Specialist Courts, Government Policy, and Victim-Centered Justice."

40. Robinson, *Measuring What Matters*.

41. D. A. Ford, "Prosecution as a Victim Power Resource: A Note on Empowering Women in Violent Conjugal Relationships," *Law & Society Review* 25, no. 2 (1991): 313–34.

42. A. L. Robinson, *The Cardiff Women's Safety Unit* (Cardiff, Wales: School of Social Sciences, Cardiff University, 2005).

43. Buzawa et al., *Response to Domestic Violence*.

44. Smith et al., *Evaluation of Efforts*.

45. Buzawa et al., *Response to Domestic Violence*.

46. Ibid.

47. Belknap et al., "To Go or Not to Go."

48. A. B. Cissner and N. K. Puffett, *Do Batterer Program Length or Approach Affect Completion or Re-Arrest Rates?* Research Supported by the Office on Violence against Women, under Grant no. 97-WE-VX-0128, September 16 (Washington, D.C.: U.S. Department of Justice, Center for Court Innovations, 2006), http://www.courtinnovation.org/_uploads/documents/IDCC%20DCAP%20final%20.pdf.

49. R. C. Davis, B. E. Smith, and L. B. Nickles, "The Deterrent Effect of Prosecuting Domestic Violence Misdemeanors," *Crime & Delinquency* 3, no. 44 (July 1998): 434–42.

50. Hartley and Frohmann, *Cook County Target Abuser Call (TAC)*.

51. David Hirschel et al., *Explaining the Prevalence, Context, and Consequences of Dual Arrest in Intimate Partner Cases*, Final Report Submitted to the National Institute of Justice for Grant no. 2001-WT-BX-0501, NCJ 218355, April (Lowell: University of Massachusetts, 2007).

52. Harrell et al., *Final Report*.

53. Smith et al., *Evaluation of Efforts*.

54. J. D. Wooldredge, "Convicting and Incarcerating Felony Offenders of Intimate Assault and the Odds of New Assault Charges," *Journal of Criminal Justice* 35, no. 401 (2007): 379–89.

55. Hirschel et al., *Explaining the Prevalence*.

56. Ventura and Davis, *Domestic Violence: Court Cases Conviction and Recidivism in Toledo*.

57. A. Thistlethwaite, J. Wooldredge, and D. Gibbs, "Severity of Dispositions and Domestic Violence Recidivism," *Crime & Delinquency* 44, no. 3 (1998): 388–98.

58. C. M. Murphy, P. H. Musser, and K. I. Maton, "Coordinated Community Intervention for Domestic Abusers: Intervention System Involvement and Criminal Recidivism," *Journal of Family Violence* 13, no. 3 (September 1998): 263–84.

59. S. J. Orchowsky, *Evaluation of a Coordinated Community Response to Domestic Violence: The Alexandria Domestic Violence Intervention Project*, Final Report Submitted to the National Institute of Justice for Grant no. 1995-WT-NX-0004, NCJ 179974 (Richmond, VA: Applied Research Associates, 1999).

60. Wooldredge, "Convicting and Incarcerating Felony Offenders."

Chapter 6

Offenders and the Criminal Justice System

Andrew Klein

Is criminal justice intervention effective? The answer to this question depends upon the particular abuser, what is considered abuse, what time period is being considered, how effectiveness and reabuse are determined, and whether or not the reabuse is confined to the abuser's original victim or extends to future intimates. This chapter will provide an overview of the extent of abuse, particularly with respect to sex differences in abusive behavior; outline what is known about characteristics of domestic violence offenders who reach the attention of the criminal justice system; and assess the efficacy of criminal justice at preventing reabuse.

HARM INFLICTED BY BATTERERS

Some people believe that male abuse is exaggerated and that females abuse their current or former partners as often as do males. They argue that the abuse data from police and courts are distorted by a feminist bias and do not reflect the abuse that is actually occurring. While few seriously argue that responding police officers are card-carrying feminists out to combat patriarchy in American society by arresting only males, proponents of the view that there is sex equity in abuse suggest that males are embarrassed to ask for help, that males are afraid they will not be believed, or that the level of abuse by females is not sufficient to cause men undue alarm.

According to the latest 2004 National Crime Victimization Survey (NCVS), over the decade from 1993 to 2004, the average annual

domestic violence rate per 1,000 population (age 12 or older) for intimate partners and/or relatives was 8.6 for females and 2.5 for males.
About a third of the victims reported they were physically attacked;
two-thirds were threatened with attack or death. About half of the
female victims suffered an injury, but less than 5 percent were seriously injured. A little over 3 percent were sexually assaulted. Fewer
male victims, a third, reported injuries, less than 5 percent serious.
Those who were separated (or divorced) experienced more nonfatal
domestic violence than those who were together.[1]

An earlier National Violence Against Women Survey (NVAWS) conducted between 1995 and 1996 found greater annual victimization rates
per year for intimate partner violence: 13 per 1,000 women (age 18 and
older) for physical assaults, 2 per 1,000 for rape, and 9 per 1,000 for
physical assault against male victims.[2]

A large percentage of women who experience abuse is subject to
"systemic abuse" and are likely to suffer physical attacks, with and
without weapons, and strangulation, with a quarter also experiencing
sexual assaults and almost half experiencing stalking.[3] A study of dating violence similarly found substantial overlap between physical and
sexual victimization.[4]

In addition, female homicide by intimate partners is a significant
cause for concern. According to the Supplementary Homicide Reports
(SHR) of the FBI's Uniform Crime Reporting Program (UCR) in 2004,
1,596 females and 385 males were killed by their intimate partners. The
number of men killed has dropped by 71 percent since 1976, while the
number of women killed has only dropped by 27 percent. The number
of white females killed has declined the least: only 5 percent. Intimate
homicides constituted 11 percent of all homicides between 1976 and
2004, 30 percent of all female murders, and 3 percent of all male murders. Unlike nonfatal domestic violence, most intimate homicides (54
percent) involve spouses or ex-spouses, although intimate homicides
for unmarried couples are catching up to parity.

In addition, my research in Rhode Island suggests that the vast majority of stalking incidents reported may not involve physical assaults.
However, in the majority of cases, the victims reported that they had
been previously physically assaulted by their stalkers. In other words,
while the act of stalking could be characterized as nonviolent, the
stalkers were, in fact, violent individuals. As a result, their stalking created genuine victim fear of bodily injury or death or a level of emotional distress required to meet the definition of criminal under the
state's stalking statute.[5]

More often than not, stalkers are charged with lesser offenses such
as harassment, threats, or violation of protective or no-contact orders.
In other words, the level of abuse reported *to* police may be substantially greater than that reported *by* police. As a result, stalking arrests

are extremely rare. In Florida, in 2005, for example, police arrested 64,000 persons for domestic violence, including only 383 for stalking. According to the NVAWS estimates, based on 2000 state census data, there were almost 88,000 persons stalked that year in the Sunshine State.

Notwithstanding the above discussion, this chapter will discuss the "typical" abuser who is brought to the attention of the criminal justice and court agencies and subsequently reported by these agencies. As a result, this discussion does not address the many persons who may engage in minor or isolated acts of physical and related abuse, either offensively or defensively, including most women who readily admit in phone surveys to having struck their male partners at some time or other. It does include seemingly less serious abusers reported by police who may be guilty of more serious abuse such as stalking, but who are reported by police or courts for reduced offenses or lesser abusive behavior.

TYPICAL BATTERERS BROUGHT TO THE ATTENTION OF AUTHORITIES

The typical abuser brought to the attention of criminal justice or court agencies is the result of either a 911 call to police or a victim filing a petition to secure a court protective or restraining order. They are usually males who purportedly abused a current or former female intimate partner. Whether or not this population of abusers and their victims represent actual abusers and victims in the community is beyond the scope of this chapter. However, in at least some jurisdictions, domestic violence actually reported to police matches what victims reveal to interviewers in national crime victim surveys.

Most "official reports" of domestic violence come from victims. Most calls that police receive are from victims. Except for cases involving juvenile victims, all petitions for protective or restraining orders are filed by victims. Victims do not generally call police or petition courts for orders the first time they are abused. As a result, by the time most alleged abusers are reported to criminal justice and court agencies, they have engaged in multiple intimate victimizations and/or more severe abuse.

The majority of abusers are already known to law enforcement because they have been arrested before, although not necessarily for prior domestic violence. This includes both males arrested for abuse and those brought to courts for protective or restraining orders. In fact, a Massachusetts study found purported male abusers brought to court for civil restraining orders by their female victims were *more* likely to have a criminal history than those brought to court arrested for abuse by police.[6] Many reported abusers have records indicating alcohol or drug abuse, although most do not suffer from mental illness. On average, abusers have had plenty of time to build up criminal histories because their average age, when brought to the attention of either police or courts for abuse, is around 32 years.

Perpetrators that come to the attention of the criminal justice system are overwhelmingly male. An analysis of Massachusetts computerized restraining order files over five years revealed that 86 percent of the orders were taken out against male abusers.[7] Arrest studies from California to North Carolina have found the same percentage to be males among those arrested by police for abuse.[8,9] A Cincinnati court study also found 86.5 percent of 2,670 misdemeanor domestic violence court defendants to be male.[10] Similarly, a 2000 National Incident-Based Reporting System multistate study found 81 percent of abuse suspects were male and their victims female.[11]

Studies of jurisdictions with higher numbers of female suspects and male victims usually include higher numbers of nonintimate family violence cases. Often lumped together under the heading of "domestic violence," nonintimate family abuse is more likely to include female abusers than intimate partner abuse. A study in Rhode Island, for example, documented that the vast majority of abuse against women aged 59 years and younger reported to police across that state was committed by current or former male intimates. However, after age 60, the majority was committed by family members, adult children, and grandchildren. Further, although the majority of these abusers were male, the percent of female abusers rose sharply.[12]

Most studies find that the majority of perpetrators are between the ages of 18 and 35 with a median age of about 33 years, although they range in age from 13 to 81. A large west coast study of abusers subject to police incident reports or protective orders found 33 percent were between 20 and 29 years old, and slightly more, 33.4 percent, were between 30 and 39 years old.[13]

As mentioned, the majority of domestic violence perpetrators that come to the attention of criminal justice or court authorities have a criminal history for a variety of nonviolent and violent offenses, against males as well as females, domestic and nondomestic. A study of intimate partner arrests in Connecticut, Idaho, and Virginia of more than a thousand cases, for example, found that almost 70 percent (69.2 percent) had a prior record, 41.8 percent for a violent crime.[14] The rates vary, of course, upon the jurisdiction and the varying arrest rates of that jurisdiction. Studies have documented prior arrest rates for abusers to be as low as 49 percent for a prior arrest within five years in Portland, Oregon,[15] to 89 percent for at least one prior misdemeanor arrest for abusers arraigned in a Toledo, Ohio, municipal court.[16] Not only did most of the abusers brought to the Toledo court for domestic violence have an arrest history, but also the average number of prior arrests was 14. Similarly, both a Massachusetts abuser arrest study and a Cook County (Chicago) misdemeanor court study observed that the vast majority of abusers had arrest records, averaging from five to 13 prior arrests for a variety of crimes.[17,18]

One could conclude that abusers arrested by police are more likely to be those offenders who have a criminal history. In other words, police don't arrest offenders who only commit minor acts of domestic assault but are otherwise law abiding, but instead arrest offenders they recognize as violent or criminal, in general. However, this does not appear to be the case. First of all, many states have mandatory arrest provisions in their statutes depriving police of discretion in arresting alleged abusers. More critically, the high correlation between domestic violence and general criminal history also holds true for abusers brought to civil court for protective orders by their victims. These men also typically have prior arrest histories similar to those brought to court for an abuse arrest. In fact, despite claims that protective orders are typically filed by men or women seeking a leg up in divorce settlements, studies indicate that subjects of court protective orders resemble those abusers brought to court for abuse-related arrests.

Abusers also generally resemble the drug and alcohol abuse histories of criminals. Most dramatically, a medical team accompanied Memphis police during successive night shifts and documented that almost all of the assailants arrested during these shifts for abuse used drugs or alcohol on the day of the assault, and nearly half were described by families as daily substance abusers for the prior month.[19] While other studies have not been as dramatic, most document substantial substance abuse. For example, a California arrest study found alcohol and/or drugs were involved in 38 percent of the domestic violence incident arrests while a large Seattle arrest and protective order study found alcohol and/or drug use was reported in almost a quarter of the incidents.[20,21]

Interviews with more than 400 North Carolina female victims who called police for misdemeanor domestic assaults found abuser drunkenness was the most consistent predictor of a call to police. According to the victims, almost a quarter (23.0 percent) of the abusers "very often" or "almost always" got drunk when they drank, more than half (55 percent) were binge drinkers, a little over a quarter used cocaine at least once a month, and more than a third (39.0 percent) smoked marijuana. Further, almost two-thirds were drinking at the incident, having consumed an average of almost seven drinks and resulting in more than half (58 percent) being drunk.[22]

In New Mexico, domestic violence fatality reviews are conducted out of the coroner's office. As a result, drug screens are reported for victims and perpetrators who commit suicide, about a third of the perpetrators. The coroner reports that alcohol and drugs were present in

65 percent of 46 domestic violence homicides between 1993 and 1996, 43 percent alcohol and 22 percent drugs.[23]

Both batterer and alcohol treatment studies similarly reveal a consistent, high correlation between alcohol abuse and domestic violence. Studies, for example, have found that the odds of any male-to-female aggression were 8 to 11 times higher on days abusers drank than days they had not.[24] This is not to suggest that alcohol and drug abuse cause abusers to abuse. Correlation is not causation.

In addition, after reading of a particular heinous domestic homicide, it may appear reasonable to conclude that such perpetrators suffer from mental illness; in fact, most abusers do not. Batterers are no more likely to be mentally ill than the general population. Although various researchers have attempted to classify abusers, ranging from "dependent" to "dysphoric/borderline" and "generally avoidance and antisocial," attempts to utilize these classifications to predict risk of reabuse have proven unhelpful.

Nonetheless, it is evident that abusers differ. There is no one "type" that defines all abusers. While some offenders, for example, may appear to responding police officers as emotionally overwrought, others may appear calm and collected, labeled by two researchers as "pitbulls" versus "cobras."[25] Other research suggests that batterers can be classified as low, moderate, and high and that, contrary to common beliefs, batterers remain within these categories.[26] Similarly, in the treatment literature a multistate study of four batterer intervention programs consistently found that approximately a quarter of court-referred batterers are high-level, chronic abusers unlikely to respond to treatment.[27]

While, statutorily, domestic violence crimes are often defined by the relationship of the parties involved as opposed to the nature of the incident itself, abuse is not dependent upon the state of the relationship of the abuser and his victim. Deprived of their victim, many abusers will go on to abuse another intimate partner or family member. Others may abuse multiple intimate partners and family members simultaneously.[28] As a result, in trying to assess the risk presented by a specific abuser for reabuse, victim characteristics have generally been found to be irrelevant. In other words, the abuse is dependent upon the abuser, not the victim.

A Rhode Island probation study, for example, found that in a one-year period, more than a quarter (28 percent) of abusers on probation who were rearrested for a new crime of domestic violence abused a different partner or family member.[29] Another Massachusetts study of persons arrested for violating a civil restraining order found that almost half (43 percent) had *two or more* victims over six years,[30] confirming an earlier state study that found 25 percent of individuals who had protective orders taken out against them in 1992 had up to eight new orders taken out against them by as many victims during the subsequent six years.[31]

Studies have generally found that abusers who go on to abuse new partners are not substantially different from those who reabuse the same partner, with the exceptions that they tend to be younger and not married to their partners.[32]

NATURE OF REPORTED ABUSE

Although most statutes define domestic violence and abuse broadly, at least two-thirds of domestic violence reported to police is for assaults. Similarly, assaults form the basis for most requests for protective or restraining orders.

Most assaults are charged as misdemeanors because they do not cause severe physical injuries requiring medical attention. This is not to say, however, that these incidents do not cause severe distress and trauma to their victims. If you are beaten by a stranger, you at least go home to the safety and security of your house. If you are beaten by an intimate, you often go home to that intimate. Even if you live apart, your abuser has ready access and knows where you are likely to be, night or day. Further, as discussed previously, police and prosecutors may routinely reduce charges.

A number of states enhance misdemeanor domestic violence offenses if they are repeated, making second or third offenses a felony. An increasing number of states have also made stalking a felony, even for a first offense. Others enhance charge levels based on special victim status, including whether the victim is pregnant or elderly or has a protective order against her assailant. Notwithstanding these statutes, by the time most domestic violence cases are resolved in court, if they end up in convictions, the convictions are for misdemeanors.

In a seminal study of one of the early specialized probation domestic violence supervision programs, researchers found the specialized supervision made a statistically significant difference in terms of reduced recidivism, but only for those abuser probationers who were first or second offenders. It was not associated with reduced recidivism for repeat offenders. Ironically, as the researchers noted, if the prosecutors had strictly adhered to the state's domestic violence enhancement statute and prosecuted the abusers as the repeat offenders they actually were, almost none would have been eligible to have been on probation in the first place![33]

Finally, although abusers are generally charged with discrete incidents, except for stalking (which by definition consists of a course of conduct or series of acts), most victims of domestic violence experience systemic abuse. They are likely to suffer physical attacks, with and without weapons, and strangulation, with others also experiencing sexual assaults, and even more experiencing stalking.[34] A study of dating violence similarly found substantial overlap between physical and sexual victimization.[35] These physical acts may also be accompanied by threats, harassment, and other criminal behaviors that may not be charged or even cited in police incident reports because they are considered lesser included offenses. Obviously, if an abuser breaks a victim's jaw once, his mere threat to do so again may constitute a terroristic threat to the victim, but be more readily overlooked or dismissed by police or others.

REABUSE

Once Reported, How Likely Are Alleged Abusers to Do It Again?

Since we are dealing with reported cases of abuse, one would suspect that the answer would depend, in large part, on what authorities do once they have received reports of abuse. If reported to police, are the alleged abusers then arrested? If arrested, are they successfully prosecuted? If prosecuted, are they sentenced to probation or jail or ordered into treatment? If ordered into treatment, do they go? If reported by victims seeking court protective or restraining orders, do judges issue the requested orders against the alleged abusers? If issued, do the orders bar contact? Require abusers to stay away from their victims? Enter treatment? If issued, are the orders enforced by police and the courts?

Unfortunately, the majority of studies from disparate jurisdictions across the country concur. Typically, these interventions don't matter much. None of these possible interventions has been found consistently to deter a significant portion of abusers from doing it again. Multiple studies suggest that the deterrence effect of police arrest,[36] prosecution,[37] batterer intervention programs,[38] probation supervision,[39] or issuance of protective orders[40] has only a modest deterrent effect at most. Further, these studies only track the batterers for a relatively short time period, six months to several years at most, limiting the opportunity for abusers to reabuse.

The few studies where interventions have been found to work are those that have the most serious sanctions. For example, a demonstration domestic violence court in Milwaukee, amply funded by the Office on Violence Against Women, halved reabuse simply because its abusers were less available to reabuse. As a result of tight judicial monitoring, enforcement of release conditions, and high rate of probation revocations, the demonstration court abusers spent 13,902 days jailed compared to the 1,059 days predemonstration court abusers spent jailed. In other words, those sentenced by the demonstration domestic violence court had less time on the streets to reabuse.[41]

A Rhode Island specialized probation supervision program was also found to significantly deter abuse and rearrests. While the abuser probationers were not more likely to be incarcerated, they were more intensely supervised, their victims were contacted, and their conditions were more rigidly enforced, resulting in significantly more court reviews. However, the program only worked for the minority of abusers who had never been sentenced for abuse before and had minimal prior records for any crimes.[42]

We are not suggesting that all reported abusers reabuse in the short or longer term. Many offenders are *not* going to reabuse, whether or not the above interventions occur. Studies have consistently found that between a quarter and a half of reported abusers reabuse, many relatively quickly. Some begin the day after an arrest is made or a no-contact order is imposed against them.[43] Further, these reabuse numbers are generally based on "official" reports of reabuse. If asked, victims consistently report more reabuse.

Many jurisdictions have lower reported rates of reabuse. A study of more than a thousand female victims in Florida, New York City, and Los Angeles, for example, found only 4 to 6 percent of their abusers were arrested for reabuse within one year.[44] However, these lower reported reabuse rates reflect lack of police response not lack of reabuse. When questioned, 31 percent of the study victims reported that they had been reassaulted, half of whom reported being strangled, burned, beaten up, or seriously injured. Similarly, a Bronx Domestic Violence Court study documented that while only 15 percent of convicted abusers were rearrested after one year, 48 percent of the victims revealed reabuse to interviewers.[45]

Abusers who reabuse often do so quickly. This may be one reason for the relative ineffectiveness of criminal justice interventions. In two separate court studies, for example, it was documented that the majority of abusers rearrested for new abuse committed the new abuse while their original abuse cases were still pending.[46]

Similarly, a probation study found that the largest portion of the 40 percent of defendants supervised for domestic violence who were rearrested for new domestic violence within the year were arrested before their cases were assigned to a probation officer and/or were able to enroll in a state-mandated batterer intervention program.[47]

However, efforts to examine reabuse and/or recidivism immediately following arrest, prosecution, probationary supervision, and/or imprisonment may not necessarily reflect long-term prognosis for abuse or criminal conduct during the subsequent decade. While most abusers may desist from being rearrested for abuse, or other offenses, and victims may not file new restraining orders against them for the first year, during the course of the next decade, the majority of abusers may be arrested for new crimes and be arrested or brought to civil court for new abuse.

A case from Quincy, Massachusetts demonstrates the difficulties confronting the criminal justice system in their efforts to keep track of repeat abusers, often to the benefit of the abusers in court. The police arrested the abuser in 1995 for violating a protective order, trespassing, and assault with a knife against his girlfriend. While that case was pending, he was arrested again for threatening the same victim, violating the order again, and another assault. While both of these cases were pending, he was returned to court five days later for trespassing and violating the order a third time. While these cases were pending, he was returned to court twice more over the next month for more threats and assault and battery, respectively. He was arrested for violating the order once more before finally being sentenced to six months in jail with 18 months suspended for all of the pending cases, wrapped up as one. He eventually served the full sentence after his probation was revoked on a technical (noncrime) violation.[48]

There are other abusers who seemingly abstain from new abuse for years before they are reported for reabuse. Short-term reabuse studies fail to capture a number of batterers who eventually reabuse; however, we lack many studies that help us understand long-term patterns of abuse. In one study of men arrested for domestic abuse, mostly assaults, along the south shore of Massachusetts, 32.2 percent were rearrested for reabusing the same or different victim or had a new restraining order taken out by the same or different victim within a year of their arrest.[49] Within 10 years, a follow-up study revealed that number had increased to 60 percent, almost doubling the reported reabuse.[50] Since victim surveys initially indicated that approximately half of the new offenses were not reported, it is likely that the figure of 60 percent is lower than the true reabuse rate.

Another reason why short-term reabuse rates may not reveal true abuser reabuse proclivities is that it often takes several years before those who abused *new* victims were reported as reabusers. In one study, almost 20 percent of those who went on to reabuse new victims, for example, were not reported to police or courts for their new abuse for five years.[51]

Returning to the case example from Quincy, Massachusetts, that same defendant refrained from new abuse after his multiple 1995 cases. However, after a pause of seven years, he resumed his abusive behavior. The defendant was arrested for abuse again in 2002 for violating another protective order. While that case was pending, he was arrested for another order violation in another court against a different victim. The second court disposed of its case first. Although this represented the abuser's sixth violation of a protective order, he was given a suspended sentence. The next day, the first court jailed him for 60 days on his fifth order violation. Although incarcerated, he received less time for his fifth violation than he had for his fourth.[52]

Studies to date have not found significant differences between serial abusers, defined as abusers who go from one victim to the next, and those who reabuse the same victim. The one exception, as mentioned previously, is that serial abusers tend to be younger and not married to their victims.[53] At least one study has also found the serial abusers had greater prior criminal records for alcohol and drug crime.[54] The only real difference between serial and same-victim reabusers may just boil down to access to convenient victims.

Which Batterers Are Most Likely to Reabuse?

There are a few basic factors that are associated with reabuse. Victim characteristics are *not* among them, suggesting abuse has to do with him (the typical abuser), not her (the typical victim). The abuse incident itself is also *not* usually associated with likelihood of reabuse. It doesn't matter whether the victim is physically assaulted and seriously injured or merely threatened with injury.

What matters most are abuser age and criminal history.[55] Younger abusers are more likely to reabuse than those who are older, and abusers who have criminal histories are more likely to reabuse than those without or with more limited criminal histories. Criminologists recognize that these same variables predict reoffending in general, suggesting the overall link between abuse and criminality. A record of just *one* prior arrest, for any offense, not just domestic violence, means the abuser is significantly more likely to reabuse than an abuser with no records.[56] If an abuser brought to court for a protective or restraining order has just one prior arrest for a drug or alcohol offense, such as possession of drugs or drunk driving, he is twice as likely to reabuse during two years compared to an abuser with no prior record for a drug or alcohol offense.[57] Of course, past reports of abuse, reported to either police or courts through protective or restraining order petitions, are also significantly associated with increased likelihood of reabuse.

Not surprisingly, it appears that chronic abusers resemble career criminals, neither of whom sticks to one type of criminal behavior. Very few abusers restrict their criminal activity to abuse only. The research suggests that, for most abusers, their abuse and general criminal careers are intertwined. While reabuse rates do not constitute a fixed percent of all abuser arrests, the more an abuser is rearrested, the more likely he is to be arrested for reabuse. The reverse also appears to be true. Those with the greatest abuse histories, as indicated by domestic violence–related arrests or prior civil restraining orders filed against them, are also the most likely to have the most numerous subsequent nonabuse arrests.

However, the research suggests that chronic abusers may differ from other career criminals in regard to the effects of aging and marriage.

Like most career criminals, abuser age, including age at study arrest and age at first offense, and being married negatively correlate with subsequent arrests for nondomestic abuse offenses. While age negatively correlates with rearrests for abuse, martial status does not. This suggests that married abusers as they get older may be significantly more likely to stop committing crimes outside, but not inside, the family. In other words, whereas age and marriage have been found as major factors in ending criminal careers,[58] marriage seems to offset the effects of aging in terms of association with new abuse compared to new nonabuse offenses. This suggests that marriage may not be "the safest place for women and children," as suggested by proponents of marriage promotion advocates.[59] As these abuser-criminals age, they simply continue their criminal behavior within their families.

A recent study of reported domestic violence across the state of Rhode Island of women aged 50 years and older found that women aged 60 years or older were significantly less likely to be abused by an intimate partner than younger women, with one exception. If the 60 or older women were married, their intimate abuse rates were the same as those of the younger women in the study, specifically those between 50 and 59.[60] Some examples from the study illustrate the finding.

The 21-year-old stepdaughter of an elderly 72-year-old white Hispanic woman called police in October at 6:42 P.M. to report an assault on her mother by her 72-year-old Hispanic stepfather, who was living with them. When police arrived, they found both mother and daughter crying. The daughter told them that her stepfather had tried to stab her mother, punched her in the face, and threatened to kill her. The mother had blood coming from her lips and blood on her shirt. She had a large cut on the palm side of her right hand sustained when she tried to grab the knife she was being threatened with. The daughter said her stepfather was still in the house, probably still armed and maybe in the basement.

Police observed drops of blood on the floor and inside of the downstairs door. They found the suspect sitting on the bed in a bedroom downstairs. He spoke no English. He was patted down for weapons, but none was found. The weapon used was later found in the kitchen drawer.

When a Spanish-speaking officer was brought in to interview the suspect, it was learned that the daughter also was assaulted by the suspect when she tried to separate him from her mother. The suspect admitted to punching his wife twice and assaulting her with the knife. He told the Spanish-speaking officer that he said to his wife as he held the knife, "This is what you need." The police noted that the defendant had been drinking. The mother was transported to a hospital by the Fire Department. The stepfather was charged with a felony assault and two misdemeanor domestic assaults. On June 16, 2003, the defendant pled no contest and was given a 10-year sentence.

In a second case, in August, 2002, at approximately 7:15 P.M., an upset, 76-year-old elderly white woman called police to report an assault by her 76-year-old husband, with whom she lived in the family home owned by the couple. Police arrived quickly, greeted by the alleged victim. The husband was not present. The victim told the police that her husband and she had argued. The argument had turned violent when the husband grabbed her left forearm and applied pressure, leaving a visible bruise. Then, after grabbing her neck and strangling her, he left the scene in his car. The victim proceeded to lock the door to prevent his reentry. He soon returned and tried to reenter, breaking the glass in the door in an attempt to get in. He then took off again and drove to a neighboring town.

The responding officer observed a bruise to the victim's left forearm and took a photo. An officer also took 35 mm pictures of the broken glass in the door and called the neighboring police department to take the suspect into custody, which was done. Apparently, the strangulation left no visible marks at that time, and no photos were taken of the victim's neck. Officers noted no weapons were used, nor were either victim or abuser under the influence of alcohol or drugs. Officers checked the state's protective order file to find that none was in effect concerning the involved couple. Police informed the victim how to obtain a temporary protective order. The victim provided police with a written statement and identified the suspect to police.

After being apprehended, the husband was charged with domestic assault as well as domestic disorderly, a lesser offense. Police also notified the Department of Elder Affairs. The next month, the prosecutor had the charges dismissed in court.

Perhaps because marriage does not deter abuse careers, unlike other criminal careers, the average criminal career of chronic abusers is longer than that of typical career criminals. In the Quincy longitudinal study of abusers, for example, the average abuse career was found to be 16.5 years with at least 10 percent still active at the time of the study (committing their last abuse crime within a year of the last study record check). However, their full abuse careers were probably underassessed because domestic violence arrests were not common before the mid-1980s and restraining orders were not recorded in Massachusetts until 1992. As a result, early abuse incidents are not included, which, if they occurred, would have added years to these abuse careers.[61]

Adult criminal careers, by contrast, have been found to typically span five years. However, as Blumstein points out, this average "hides major differences across offenders." While the residual career length is five years for 18-year-old index offenders, it is 10 years for index offenders who are still active in their 30s and it does not begin to decline for active offenders until their 40s. Those active in their 30s display the lowest termination rates and the longest residual careers.

Victims are generally good predictors of their likelihood of being abused, although they tend to be too optimistic. Those who report being uncertain about their abusers, for example, are more likely to be reassaulted than those who feel themselves to be unsafe. Researchers explain that the latter are more apt to take precautions that the former fail to take.[62] Those victims who feel the intervention of police and courts were too tepid to protect them also prove correct. At least one study found such victims were more likely to be reabused than those who were satisfied with the state's response.[63]

LETHAL REABUSE

The discussion so far has focused on nonlethal abuse. During first half decade of the twenty-first century, a little over 9,000 males and females were murdered by their intimate partners, according to the FBI. These numbers are down significantly since the FBI first tracked intimate partner homicides in the mid-1970s. From 1976 through 1980, there were almost 16,500 intimate homicides. In other words, intimate homicides have been reduced almost in half.

However, the decline has been far more dramatic for male than female victims. During the above periods, the number of male intimates murdered has dropped more than 70 percent, while female intimate homicides have dropped only a little more than 20 percent. As a result, while there was almost parity between male and female intimate homicide victims in the 1970s, currently more than three-quarters of intimate homicide victims are female.

Male and female intimate homicide victims differ dramatically for reasons besides gender. The male victims of intimate homicides are more likely to have abused the women who then killed them. By contrast, the killing of female intimates is more likely to be the culmination of repeated and escalating abuse by their male intimates.

In terms of lethal abuse, it appears the dramatic national response to domestic violence since the 1970s, the enactment and reform of state and federal laws to further criminalize abuse, increasing the arrest and prosecution of abusers, and providing additional funds for shelters and other victim services have more significantly increased the safety of abusive males than that of their victims. This is evidenced by the latest FBI reports, which report that while homicides of male intimates continued to decline between 2004 and 2005, from 344 to 329, female intimate deaths actually increased from 1,155 to 1,188.

Which Abusers Are Most Likely to Kill?

Predictions of lethality are more difficult than predictions of reabuse because, fortunately, lethal abuse is rarer. However, one risk factor that stands out clearly is abuser access to firearms. Just having firearms in the households of abusers increase the odds of lethal abuse more than six to one.[64] Women who are threatened or assaulted with firearms or other weapons are 20 times more likely to be murdered than other abused women.[65]

While Congress has enacted federal laws in the mid-1980s barring court-restrained and criminally convicted abusers from possessing firearms, so far, the laws appear to have had limited effect. Enforcement and prosecution have proven rare. A study of currently incarcerated male intimate murderers, for example, found that almost two-thirds of them used firearms that were prohibited them under the federal law.

The research also closely links stalking with femicide, finding intimate partner stalkers to be "startlingly" violent. The only group found to be more violent, in fact, was predator rapists who stalked their victims in order to rape them.[66]

No one has studied lethal batterers to determine if they are likely to kill again, probably because no one assumed it was an issue. However, anecdotal evidence collected by the *National Bulletin on Domestic Violence Prevention*, a national newsletter, finds an alarming number of repeat murders by abusers. Often authorities fail to correctly identify the first intimate homicide until after the abuser has been convicted of a second—or third—offense.

Studies of intimate homicides typically focus on partner murders. However, many intimate homicides involve multiple deaths. The *Washington State Domestic Violence Fatality Review* reports, for example, that between January 1, 1997, and June 30, 2004, male abusers also killed 21 children, 32 victim friends or family members, 19 new boyfriends of victims, one victim coworker, and three law enforcement officers. Additionally, 93 of the male murderers then committed suicide, and nine were killed by responding police officers.[67]

Stopping Batterers

The evidence appears compelling. While sociologists may argue about the relative aggressiveness of females and males, the police and courts and, less frequently, coroners are typically confronted by an abuser who is male and in his twenties or thirties. Once identified by police or courts and despite current criminal justice interventions, he is eventually likely to reabuse the same or a different female victim. Despite the many advances and reforms since the 1970s in the criminal justice response to domestic violence, this batterer is also almost as likely to kill his female partner.

The reason why typical criminal justice and related interventions fail to deter repeat abuse is that abusers are typically treated as perpetual "first offenders." These offenders are viewed as unlikely to reoffend, because officials discount prior criminal histories that are not abuse related. While half of state domestic violence statutes provide for enhanced punishments of repeat abusers, the offenses are limited to domestic violence–related charges. Even then, prosecutors frequently are willing plead down enhanced charges so that repeat abusers evade enhanced punishments.

Following is a typical example from Rhode Island, which has an enhancement statute that mandates 10 days of incarceration for second domestic violence offenses (any crime involving intimates) and one year of incarceration for third domestic violence offenses, making the offense a felony. The abuser, age 21, was placed on probation for a domestic assault in December 2001 against the mother of their child. That was subsequently converted to a suspended sentence when he was charged with another domestic assault the following September. On the new domestic assault, he was given another suspended sentence. As a result of the revocation, he had two convictions on his record so that when he was arrested for another domestic assault in July 2003, he was charged as a third-time offender and the case was transferred to superior court, the state's felony court. Notwithstanding the felony charges, on April 15, 2004, the charge was reduced to simple assault and the defendant was given another one-year suspended sentence.

In Utah, the state legislature actually intervened to ameliorate sentences for abusers. It specifically amended its domestic assault law to allow courts to convict assaultive abusers for "domestic disorderly" instead so that they would not lose their right to possess firearms pursuant to federal firearm prohibitions.

But probably the major reason for the lack of effective criminal justice intervention to stop repeat batterers is that the criminal justice system is stuck. It is stuck on batterer intervention programs, developed in the last century to provide prosecutors and judges a place to put convicted batterers. Without a program in which to place them, courts were reluctant to take on this additional criminal caseload because they refused to utilize their traditional correctional resources of probation and prison. Consequently, advocates developed batterer intervention programs.

The problem is that while these programs were immediately and enthusiastically adopted by the criminal justice system, they have had little success with batterers, who have proven largely resistant to program teachings. These programs have been extensively studied but found to have, at best, a very modest positive effect that was limited to the least serious abusers. Yet the criminal justice system remains committed to these programs, ignoring alternatives that might prove more effective at stopping batterers from reabusing their victims.

Rhode Island state law, for example, like the laws in many other states, requires judges to send anyone convicted of domestic violence to a state-certified batterer program. As a result, in the probation study cited earlier, it was not uncommon to uncover cases of batterers who have been through the same certified program up to six times over the last dozen years. Didn't Einstein supposedly say the definition of insanity is doing the same thing over and over, expecting different results?

While there is wide disagreement over why men batter intimate partners, it is doubtful that repeat batterers, at least, do so in error, lacking an understanding or appreciation of the harmful effects of their behavior on their intimates and family. At a minimum, they batter because their violence and abuse work, achieving its desired effect, at least in the short term. The criminal justice system must adjust its interventions to ensure that battering no longer "works" for the batterer, and that its immediate priority is the protection of batterers' victims. This will require a significant increase in criminal justice and correctional resources, including the increased capacity for the incarceration of repeat batterers. Unless and until the true danger of the "typical" abuser identified by the criminal justice system is appreciated, this is unlikely to happen.

NOTES

1. S. Catalano, *Intimate Partner Violence in the United States* (Washington, D.C.: U.S. Department of Justice, Bureau of Justice Statistics, 2006), http://www.ojp.usdoj.gov/bjs.

2. P. Tjaden and N. Thoennes, *Extent, Nature, and Consequences of Intimate Partner Violence: Findings from the National Violence against Women Survey*, 93-IJ-CX-0012, NCJ 181867 (Washington, D.C.: U.S. Department of Justice, National Institute of Justice, 2000).

3. R. Macmillan and C. Kruttdschnitt, *Patterns of Violence against Women: Risk Factors and Consequences*, 2002-IJ-CX-0011, NCJ 208346 (Washington, D.C.: U.S. Department of Justice, National Institute of Justice, 2005).

4. J. White and P. Smith, *A Longitudinal Perspective on Physical and Sexual Intimate Partner Violence against Women*, NCJ199708 (Washington, D.C.: U.S. Department of Justice, National Institute of Justice, 2004).

5. P. Tjaden and N. Thoennes, *Stalking: Its Role in Serious Domestic Violence Cases*, 97-WT-VX-0002, 187446 (Washington, D.C.: U.S. Department of Justice, National Institute of Justice, 2001).

6. D. Cochran, S. Adams, and P. O'Brien, "From Chaos to Clarity in Understanding Domestic Violence," *Domestic Violence Report* 3, no. 5 (June–July 1998).

7. S. Adams, *Serial Batterers* (Boston: Office of the Commissioner of Probation, 1999).

8. M. Wordes, *Creating a Structured Decision-Making Model for Police Intervention in Intimate Partner Violence*, 96-IJ-CX-0098, NCJ 182781 (Washington, D.C.:U.S. Department of Justice, National Institute of Justice, 2000).

9. P. Friday, V. Lord, M. Exum, and J. Hartman, *Evaluating the Impact of a Specialized Domestic Violence Police Unit*, 2004-WG-BX-0004, NCJ 215916 (Washington, D.C.: U.S. Department of Justice, National Institute of Justice, 2006).

10. J. Belknap, D. Graham, J. Hartman, V. Lippen, G. Allen, and J. Sutherland, *Factors Related to Domestic Violence Court Dispositions in a Large Urban Area: The Role of Victim/Witness Reluctance and Other Variables, Executive Summary*, 96-WT-NX-0004 NCJ 184112 (Washington, D.C.: U.S. Department of Justice, National Institute of Justice, 2000).

11. D. Hirschel, E. Buzawa, A. Pattavina, D. Faggiana, and M. Ruelan, *Explaining the Prevalence, Context, and Consequences of Dual Arrest in Intimate Partner Cases*, 2001-WT-BX-0501, NCJ 218355 (Washington, D.C.: U.S. Department of Justice, National Institute of Justice, 2007).

12. A. Klein, T. Tobin, A. Salomon, and J. Dubois, *A Statewide Profile of Older Women Abuse and the Criminal Justice Response*, 2006-WG-BX-0009 (Washington, D.C.: U.S. Department of Justice, National Institute of Justice, 2008).

13. V. Holt, M. Kernic, M. Wolf, and F. Rivara, "Do Protection Orders Affect the Likelihood of Future Partner Violence and Injury?" *American Journal of Preventive Medicine* 24, no. 1 (2003): 16–21.

14. Hirschel, Buzawa, Pattavina, Faggiana, and Ruelan, *Explaining the Prevalence*.

15. A. Jolin, W. Feyerherm, R. Fountain, and S. Friedman, *Beyond Arrest: The Portland, Oregon Domestic Violence Experiment, Final Report*, 95-IJ-CX-0054, NCJ 179968 (Washington, D.C.: U.S. Department of Justice, National Institute of Justice, 1998).

16. L. Ventura and G. Davis, *Domestic Violence: Court Case Conviction and Recidivism in Toledo* (Toledo, OH: University of Toledo Urban Affairs Center, October 2004).

17. E. Buzawa, G. Hotaling, A. Klein, and J. Byrnes, *Response to Domestic Violence in a Pro-Active Court Setting, Final Report*, 95-IJ-CX-0027, NCJ 181427 (Washington, D.C.: U.S. Department of Justice, National Institute of Justice, 1999).

18. C. Hartley and L. Frohmann, *Cook County Target Abuser Call (TAC): An Evaluation of a Specialized Domestic Violence Court*, 2000-WT-VX-0003, NCJ 202944 (Washington, D.C.: U.S. Department of Justice, National Institute of Justice, 2003).

19. D. Brookoff, *Drugs, Alcohol, and Domestic Violence in Memphis, Research Review*, NCJ 000172, October (Washington, D.C.: U.S. Department of Justice, National Institute of Justice, 1997).

20. Wordes, *Creating a Structured Decision-Making Model*.

21. Holt, Kernic, Wolf, and Rivara, "Do Protection Orders Affect the Likelihood"; and V. Holt, M. Kernic, T. Lumley, M. Wolf, and F. Rivara, "Civil Protection Orders and Risk of Subsequent Police-Reported Violence," *Journal of American Medical Association* 288, no. 5 (2002): 598–94.

22. I. Hutchison, *The Influence of Alcohol and Drugs on Women's Utilization of the Police for Domestic Violence*, NCJ 179277, 97-IJ-CX-0047 (Washington, D.C.: U.S. Department of Justice, National Institute of Justice, 1999).

23. L. Olson, C. Crandall, and D. Broudy, *Getting Away with Murder: A Report of the New Mexico Female Intimate Partner Violence Death Review Team* (Albuquerque, NM: Center for Injury Prevention Research and Education, University of New Mexico School of Medicine, 1998).

24. W. Fals-Stewart, "The Occurrence of Partner Physical Aggression on Days of Alcohol Consumption: A Longitudinal Diary Study," *Journal of Consulting Psychology* 71, no. 1 (2003): 41–52.

25. N. Jacobson and J. Gottman, *When Men Batter Women* (New York: Simon & Schuster, 1998).

26. M. Cavanaugh and R. Gelles, "The Utility of Male Domestic Violence Typologies," *Journal of Interpersonal Violence* 20, no. 2 (2005): 155–66.

27. E. Gondolf, "The Program Effects of Batterer Programs in Three Cities," *Violence and Victims* 16 (2001): 693–704; E. Gondolf, *Results of a Multi-Site Evaluation of Batterer Intervention Systems* (Indiana, PA: Mid-Atlantic Addiction Training Institute, 1997); and E. Gondolf, "A 30-Month Follow-Up of Court Referred Batterers in Four Cities," *International Journal of Offender Therapy and Comparative Criminology* 44, no. 1 (2000): 111–28.

28. D. Cochran, S. Adams, and P. O'Brien, "From Chaos to Clarity in Understanding Domestic Violence," *Domestic Violence Report* 3, no. 5 (June–July 1998).

29. A. Klein, D. Wilson, A. Crowe, and M. DeMichele, *An Evaluation of Rhode Island's Specialized Supervision of Domestic Violence Probationers*, final report to NIJ on Grant 2002-WG-BX-0011 (Cambridge, MA: BOTEC Analysis Corporation and American Probation and Parole Association, 2005).

30. S. Bocko, C. Cicchetti, L. Lempicki, and A. Powell, *Restraining Order Violators, Corrective Programming and Recidivism*, November (Boston: Office of the Commissioner of Probation, 2004).

31. S. Adams, *Serial Batterers* (Boston: Office of the Commissioner of Probation, 1999).

32. Adams, *Serial Batterers*; and Klein, Wilson, Crowe, and DeMichele, *An Evaluation of Rhode Island's Specialized Supervision.*

33. A. Klein and A. Crowe, "Findings from and Outcome Examination of Rhode Island's Specialized Domestic Violence Probation Supervision Program," *Violence against Women* 14, no. 2 (2008): 226–46.

34. Macmillan and Kruttdschnitt, *Patterns of Violence against Women.*

35. White and Smith, *A Longitudinal Perspective.*

36. C. Maxwell, J. Garner, and J. Fagan, *The Effects of Arrest on Intimate Partner Violence: New Evidence from the Spouse Assault Replication Program*, National Institute of Justice Research in Brief, NCJ 188199, June (Washington, D.C.: U.S. Department of Justice, National Institute of Justice, 2001).

37. R. Davis, B. Smith, and L. Nickles, "The Deterrent Effect of Prosecuting Domestic Violence Misdemeanors," *Crime & Delinquency* 44, no. 3 (1998): 434–43.

38. J. Babcock, C. Green, and C. Robie, "Does Batterer Treatment Work? A Meta-Analytic Review of Domestic Violence Outcome Research," *Journal of Family Psychology* 13 (2003): 46–59.

39. M. Gross, E. Cramer, J. Forte, J. Gordon, T. Kunkel, and L. Morrissey, "Court Sentencing Options and Recidivism among Domestic Violence Offenders," *Domestic Violence Report* 5, no. 4 (2000).

40. A. Klein, "Reabuse in a Population of Court Restrained Batterers," in *Do Arrest and Restraining Orders Work?* ed. E. Buzawa and C. Buzawa (Thousand Oaks, CA: Sage, 1996), 192–214.

41. A. Harrell, M. Schaffer, C. DeStefano, and J. Castro, *The Evaluation of Milwaukee's Judicial Oversight Demonstration, Final Research Report*, 99-WT-VX-K005 (Washington, D.C.: U.S Department of Justice, Urban Institute, 2006), http://www.urban.org/publications/411315.html.

42. Klein, Wilson, Crowe, and DeMichele, *An Evaluation of Rhode Island's Specialized Supervision.*

43. See, e.g., Wordes, *Creating a Structured Decision-Making Model*; L. Bennett, C. Stoops, C. Call, and H. Flett, "Program Completion and Re-arrest in a Batterer Intervention System," *Research on Social Work Practice* 17, no. 42 (2007): 42–54; Klein, Wilson, Crowe, and DeMichele, *An Evaluation of Rhode Island's Specialized Supervision*; and E. Aldarondo, "Evaluating the Efficacy of Interventions with Men Who Batter," in *Programs for Men Who Batter*, ed. E. Aldarondo and F. Mederos (Kingston, NJ: Civic Research Institute, 2002), 3–12.

44. J. Roehl, C. O'Sullivan, D. Webster, and J. Campbell, *Intimate Partner Violence Risk Assessment Validation Study: The RAVE Study-Practitioner Summary and Recommendations: Validation of Tools for Assessing Risk from Violent Intimate Partners*, 2000-WT-VX-0011, NCJ 209731 (Washington, D.C.: U.S. Department of Justice, National Institute of Justice, 2005).

45. M. Rempel, M. Labriola, and R. Davis, "Does Judicial Monitoring Deter Domestic Violence Recidivism?" *Violence against Victims* 14, no. 2 (2008): 185–207, http://www.courtinnovation.org/publicationsall.html.

46. Buzawa, Hotaling, Klein, and Byrnes, *Response to Domestic Violence*; L. Newmark, M. Rempel, M. Diffily, and K. Kane, *Specialized Felony Domestic Violence Court: Lessons on Implementation and Impacts from the Kings County Experience*, 97-WT-VX-0005, NCJ 191861 and NCJ 199723 (Washington, D.C.: U.S. Department of Justice, National Institute of Justice, 2001, 2005).

47. Klein, Wilson, Crowe, and DeMichele, *An Evaluation of Rhode Island's Specialized Supervision*.

48. D. Wilson and A. Klein, *A Longitudinal Study of a Cohort of Batterers Arraigned in a Massachusetts District Court 1995–2004*, 2004-WB-GX-0011, NCJ 215346 (Washington, D.C.: U.S. Department of Justice, National Institute of Justice, 2006).

49. Buzawa, Hotaling, Klein, and Byrnes, *Response to Domestic Violence*.

50. A. Klein and T. Tobin, "Longitudinal Study of Arrested Batterers, 1995–2005: Career Criminals," *Violence against Women* 14, no. 2 (2008): 136–57.

51. D. Adams, *Why Do They Kill? Men Who Murder Their Intimate Partners* (Nashville, TN: Vanderbilt University Press, 2007).

52. Wilson and Klein, *A Longitudinal Study*.

53. Klein, Wilson, Crowe, and DeMichele, *An Evaluation of Rhode Island's Specialized Supervision*.

54. Buzawa, Hotaling, Klein, and Byrnes, *Response to Domestic Violence*.

55. See, e.g., A. Klein, *The Criminal Justice Response to Domestic Violence* (Belmont, CA: Thomson/Wadsworth, 2004).

56. See, e.g., Hirschel, Buzawa, Pattavina, Faggiana, and Ruelan, *Explaining the Prevalence*.

57. Klein, "Reabuse in a Population."

58. J. Laub, D. Nagin, and R. Sampson, "Trajectories of Change in Criminal Offending: Good Marriages and the Desistance Process," *American Sociological Review* 63, no. 2 (1998): 225–38.

59. R. Rector, O. Fagan, and K. Johnson, *Marriage: Still the Safest Place for Women and Children*, Backgrounder no. 1732, March (Washington, D.C.: Heritage Foundation, 2004).

60. A. Klein, T. Tobin, A. Salomon, and J. Dubois, *A Statewide Profile of Abuse of Older Women and the Criminal Justice Response*, 2006-WG-BX-0009 (Washington, D.C.: U.S. Department of Justice, National Institute of Justice, 2008).

61. Klein and Tobin, "Longitudinal Study of Arrested Batterers".

62. D. Heckert and E. Gondolf, "Battered Women's Perceptions of Risk versus Risk Factors and Instruments in Predicting Repeat Reassault," *Journal of Interpersonal Violence* 19, no. 7 (2004): 778–800.

63. Buzawa, Hotaling, Klein, and Byrnes, *Response to Domestic Violence*.

64. L. Paulkossi, "Surveillance for Homicide among Intimate Partners: United States, 1991–1998," *Morbidity and Mortality Weekly Surveillance Summaries* 5 (October 2001): 1–16.

65. J. Campbell, D. Webster, D. Koziol-McLain, R. Block, D. Campbell, M. Curry, F. Gary, J. McFarlane, C. Sachs, P. Sharps, Y. Urich, and S. Wilt, "Assessing Risk Factors for Intimate Partner Homicide," *National Institute of Justice Journal* 250 (2003): 14–19.

66. P. Mullen, M. Pathe, R. Purcell, and G. Stuart, *Stalkers and Their Victims* (London: Cambridge University Press, 2000); and J. Meloy, "Stalking and Violence," in *Stalking and Psychosexual Obsession: Psychological Perspectives for Prevention, Policing, and Treatment*, ed. J. Boon and L. Sheridan (West Sussex, UK: John Wiley, 2002).

67. Washington State Coalition against Domestic Violence, *Findings and Recommendations from the Washington State Domestic Violence Fatality Review* (Seattle: Washington State Coalition against Domestic Violence, 2004).

Chapter 7

Abusers' Narratives Following Arrest and Prosecution for Domestic Violence

Keith Guzik

OVERVIEW

Presumptive arrest and prosecution policies combat intimate partner abuse by encouraging state interventions against abusers. In addition to ensuring victim safety, these policies are intended to change batterers by holding them accountable for their behavior. This chapter considers the power of presumptive arrest and prosecution to change abusers by sharing the stories of people arrested and prosecuted for domestic violence. More specifically, it examines how abusers experience arrest and prosecution, how they view their violence following contact with the police and courts, and how their lives change as a result. In each case, abusers' stories provide grounds for skepticism about aggressive criminal justice policies. Sadly, abusers understand their punishments as unjust sanctions motivated by the biases of legal authorities rather than their own abusive behavior. Men continue to evade responsibility for their violence, often depicting themselves as the true victims of abusive intimate relationships. Finally, batterers focus on personal losses and the acquisition of stigmas when discussing changes in their lives. In sum, aggressive arrest and prosecution policies result in abusers seeing themselves as victims of external social forces rather than as having responsibility for their actions.

Presumptive arrest and prosecution policies in domestic violence cases have been adopted by police departments and state's attorney's offices across the country. Presumptive, or mandatory, arrest policies encourage the police to make arrests when probable cause of physical violence exists, while presumptive, or no-drop, prosecution policies have state's attorneys prosecute domestic violence cases regardless of victims' willingness to testify. The differences in terminology owe to the language of the statutes themselves. For instance, mandatory arrest policies dictate that officers "must" arrest when probable cause exists, while presumptive arrest policies dictate that they "should" arrest. The term used here is "presumptive arrest," since the jurisdiction in which the interviews discussed in this chapter were conducted followed presumptive policies. Together with orders of protection and batterer intervention programs, these policies represent key elements in the state's response to intimate partner abuse.

Presumptive arrest and prosecution are controversial among battered women's advocates. Supporters argue that these measures are needed to provide battered women the same legal protections afforded other victims of violent crime and to relieve them of difficult decisions regarding the prosecution of their cases. Critics argue that these policies further disempower women by removing their ability to make decisions and aggravate other extant problems associated with our criminal justice system.

Research on presumptive policies has generally paid less attention to their effects on abusers. Arresting and prosecuting domestic batterers are intended to disrupt men's ability to rationalize and normalize violence against women. At the societal level, punishing batterers conveys the message that violence against women is not acceptable. At the individual level, punishment complicates the batterer's ability to simply explain away his violence by denying its existence or blaming it on the victim.

This chapter examines the effects of presumptive policies on abusers by sharing the stories of 30 persons interviewed following their arrest and prosecution for domestic violence (see Table 7.1 for a list of the research participants). The chapter discusses three questions significant for understanding the impact of presumptive policies: *how do abusers experience arrest and prosecution, how do abusers describe their violence following arrest and prosecution,* and *what changes do abusers experience following arrest and prosecution?* Overall, batterers' stories provide reason to be pessimistic about the power of aggressive arrest and prosecution policies. Rather than coming to assume responsibility for their actions, offenders instead develop a perception of victimization. In general, the people interviewed believed that they had been mistreated by the police and courts, that they were the victims in their intimate relationships, and that they had lost key dimensions of their selves as a result of their legal encounters. While such claims might simply be dismissed as the defensive posturing of a group of people finally being held

Table 7.1.
Pseudonyms and Sociodemographic Characteristics

Name	Sex	Age	Race	Employment	Marital Status
1. Ann	F	43	European-American	Unemployed	Single
2. Betty	F	42	African-American	Unemployed	Cohabitating
3. Adam	M	47	Latino	Custodian	Married
4. Bob	M	35	European-American	Disability	Single
5. Chris	M	46	African-American	Unemployed	Cohabitating
6. Dave	M	38	European-American	Disability	Single
7. Eric	M	21	European-American	Painter	Cohabitating
8. Frank	M	31	European-American	Carpenter	Single
9. Gary	M	22	European-American	Gas Station	Cohabitating
10. Henry	M	53	African-American	Unemployed	Single
11. Isaac	M	24	African-American	Unemployed	Single
12. John	M	25*	African-American	Fast Food	Cohabitating
13. Kevin	M	24	African-American	Fast Food	Cohabitating
14. Larry	M	58	European-American	Disability	Cohabitating
15. Mike	M	36	African-American	Cook	Cohabitating
16. Nic	M	29	Latino	Public Works	Married
17. Oscar	M	43	African-American	Construction	Married
18. Pete	M	45*	European-American	Employed	Married
19. Quinn	M	32*	European-American	Construction	Separated
20. Ralph	M	28*	African-American	Factory	Single
21. Steve	M	43	African-American	Hotel	Married
22. Tom	M	20	African-American	Gas Station	Cohabitating
23. Victor	M	23	African-American	Unemployed	Single
24. Walter	M	32	African-American	Employed	Single
25. Aaron	M	26	African-American	Unemployed	Single
26. Brett	M	38	African-American	Factory; Teacher's Aide	Single
27. Carl	M	42	European-American	Cook; Real Estate	Single
28. Doug	M	41	European-American	Mechanic; Real Estate	Separated, Cohabitating
29. Ed	M	25	African-American	Unemployed	Single
30. Carrie	F	21	European-American	Unemployed	Married

These numbers reflect an estimate of the person's approximate age.

accountable for their criminality, they are more accurately read as expressions of the multiple subject positions—not only gender, but also race, class, and so on—that abusers occupy in society, and through which they make sense of their legal experiences. We should concern ourselves with tailoring policies that can go further in having abusers recognize their responsibility for violence as such understandings cloud the recognition needed to realize behavioral change.

HOW DO ABUSERS EXPERIENCE ARREST AND PROSECUTION?

Arresting and prosecuting batterers are intended to teach them a lesson. Following arrest and prosecution, some do come to understand their actions as wrong. For the most part, however, the lessons learned from punishment are different. Rather than triggering inward reflections by abusers on the wrongness of their behavior, arrests and prosecutions trigger outward reflections on the wrongness of legal authorities' actions. Overwhelmingly, respondents in my research believed that they had been mistreated by the police and courts.

In the case of the police, for instance, participants described some aspect of their interactions with the police as unjust. Usually, they claimed that the police did a poor job of investigating their cases. To provide a few examples:

> In the police report, they said I backtracked my story, but I never remember telling them a story. To me, when I read the police report, that kind of in my mind gave the appearance that I was guilty, that I had changed my story. But I never changed my story. (Dave)

> So they [the police] come up and I was getting out of the car. They said I had alcohol on my breath. This was at 9 a.m. At 9 a.m.! He said, "Well, I don't know if it's from last night or if you got it on your clothes." I said, "Maybe that's the case, but I have not been drinking." So, they started going on the alcohol charge! They were going to get me for a DUI. *Did they give you a field sobriety test?* No, nothing. But of course they put in the police report to make it look even worse. (Ann)

> I still think the courthouse, as a matter of fact, the policemen too, they should, when they come on a domestic case, a domestic feud, period, to someone's home, they should look in that more deeper. (Henry)

> They don't investigate them like they should. The officers don't. So the state's attorney gets what the officers give him. Like the officer never goes out and does a reinvestigation, you know, to see if her story is going to match up.... So, they feel like what they give them at that time is good enough and they give it to the state's attorney and the state's attorney goes off of that. You know, it's all lies, it doesn't matter. (Ed)

These quotes highlight different dimensions of police investigations that suspects found unfair. Dave and Ann believed the police misrepresented them in order to make them look guiltier. Henry and Ed, meanwhile, touched upon themes of procedural justice in claiming that the police did not investigate their cases properly. Interestingly, they are not saying that the police had no right getting involved in their personal affairs. Having had prior contact with the law, they actually would have preferred more, rather than less, police attention to their cases.

In terms of the court, most of the respondents cited elements of its handling of cases that struck them as unjust. Many complained that the court system, and by extension the legal system, was impersonal and insensitive to their concerns. Walter, for instance, bemoaned that in court, "There's no consideration for the other person," and the money and time from work they lose by attending court dates. In addition, many respondents described the court as a close-knit group of professionals who were uninterested in the lives of individual defendants. Frank noted, "I have to come to the conclusion that they all sit around in a bar and have nachos and chips and trade each other lives. 'I give you this guy for that guy, and you let him off; now I will give you this guy.'"

In addition to identifying *how* they believed legal authorities mistreated them, respondents also offered rationales for *why* they were treated this way. For instance, male respondents typically believed they were victims of gender bias at the hands of either individual officers or laws designed to protect women. With regard to the former, men often noted that officers seemed to have "talked to the lady more and tried to get more information from her" (John). With regard to the latter, the participants described the law as "all just women's agenda" (Peter) and "strictly for a woman" (Walter).

While claims of gender bias by men arrested for domestic violence have been noted in the past, what proved surprising in talking to this group of men was that some actually accepted the premise that domestic violence laws favor women:

Who doesn't protect a woman? You know what I mean? And Mary, she's a very cute girl. At the same time, she's smaller than me. I'm 5'7", 155, she's 5'3", 125. She's female; I'm male. So, yeah. So, of course the cops inside are pushing and pushing her, "Tell us." (Nic)

I believe he handled the situation very fairly. It wasn't ... it could have been probably handled different, like you know, trying to get both sides of the story. But I guess, that's how life is. I mean, I feel that they look at a woman as very weak because that call owns you and you ain't got to do nothing. And they assume, they take it from there. (Aaron)

I think it sucks. I don't think it's no good. I know, I understand. I like to give a female the benefit of the doubt too. I don't agree with jumping on females. I'm totally against that. And I raised my kids, I have a 15-year-old son who's going to be 16, and I got a 14 year old, who just turned 14, and I teach them, if they touch anyone, I got two girls, if they touch their sisters, I'm on their ass. I don't care if the girls are right or wrong. You know, I don't like that. But, I feel like the law is wrong when they always take the female's side no matter what. (Steve)

These are mixed messages, to be sure. These men felt victimized by the law. But at the same time, they believed that society needs to protect women, since they are weaker than men. Nic could understand why the police would want to protect his wife, who, beyond being petite, is also pretty. Aaron too could not fault the police for not listening to both sides of the story, since it is natural to see women as weak. Steve, for his part, felt so strongly against being violent against women that he was violent against his sons when they mistreated their sisters. So, he too could understand the desire to protect women. Of course, that the police "always take the female's side no matter what" is wrong, especially if he is the one apprehended. At the very least, these responses demonstrate the varied meanings that the practice of domestic violence law can take for individual abusers.

Despite the primacy of gender as a framework for claiming injustice, respondents also interpreted their experiences through other, nonprivileged group identities. For instance, African American participants in my research commonly perceived race as a factor in the police's handling of their cases.

> They arrested me. And, I don't know, one of the officers, he was just really smug towards me. He just [had] an air of prejudice about himself. It was like they totally disregarded anything I had said. I mean, it was just the way he was looking at me and just laughing at me the whole time. (Chris)

> This black officer was telling me, "Hey, I understand, just go ahead and get your clothes and all and leave." But this white officer came, he said, "No." He said, "Put those handcuffs back on him," just like that ... I knew the white officer who told him to put that handcuffs back on me. The only reason I knew him ... I don't know him, I just knew of him because I'd seen his picture on the TV and I heard a lot of conflict about what he help did. (Henry)

Chris noted the presence of the officer as prejudicial, while Henry specified a particular interaction, favorable treatment by a black officer and unfavorable treatment by a white officer, as evidence that he had been unfairly treated due to his race. In Henry's case, his personal experience with the local police was woven together with that of his community. The white officer's picture had been on TV, and he was known in the African American community to treat people unfairly. For African American men then with prior contact with the police, their arrest for domestic battery represented not a just punishment for being abusive, but an unjust punishment levied by racist police officers.

Other respondents interpreted the criminal justice system's handling of their cases in terms of money. Quinn, a former cop, believed that domestic violence cases simply serve to enrich the state and lawyers.

"It's all status and money," he noted; "I mean, there are guys out there who deserve to be arrested. But there's a lot of guys being arrested who don't deserve to be, couples who are trying to work things out. But it's about money. They want their money."

Others repeated these sentiments. Ann and Peter, for example, focused on the costs associated with completing their sentences:

> You're thrown into these classes, you know, a lot of people can't afford them, and they're expensive.... I don't think that they [the state] take it seriously because to them it's all a moneymaker. You know, do this class, do that, you know, everything is about money. (Ann)

> And the courts, they just kick you while you're down. Make you pay fines, for evaluation, for classes, but you gotta work to be able to pay them. This deal, my attorney says if I don't take this deal and I lose the trial, it'll be even worse. So, I have to take this. They just take your money. (Peter)

Such comments echo those of people who stand "up against" the law[1] and interpret their legal experiences in terms of resources. These respondents, for whom hiring a defense attorney, appearing in court, and abiding by their sentences represented significant costs, believed the criminal justice system punished them not to stop their abusive behavior, but to get their money. In the process, their sense of injustice takes shape.

Finally, some respondents believed their past criminal records prejudiced the authorities' handling of their cases. Ann believed her involvement in past domestic violence cases automatically identified her to the police as the aggressor in her current case. She explained, "I had a couple of priors to that with domestics, but once you're pegged in Plainsville, you're pretty well screwed." Dave interpreted the state's decision to charge him after his latest domestic violence arrest as motivated by his criminal record: "My record is what hurts me more than the crime that I actually did." Again, these respondents, like the others citing unjust treatment by the police and courts, believed that they were punished not for what they did, but for who they were.

HOW DO ABUSERS DESCRIBE THEIR VIOLENCE FOLLOWING ARREST AND PROSECUTION?

Feminist researchers in the past have established a link between the stories abusive partners use to describe their behavior and their violent selves. Men describe their violence by denying it, minimizing its severity or harm, excusing its occurrence, and/or justifying its occurrence. In *denials*, batterers simply deny that any abuse or violence took place ("I didn't touch her"). In *minimizations*, abusers admit that violence took place, but minimize either its seriousness ("I just pushed her") or the harm resulting from it ("No one got hurt"). In *excuses*, men admit that violence took place, and do not question its seriousness, but reduce their culpability by blaming the episode on being under the influence of alcohol, drugs, or strong, uncontrollable emotions ("I was drunk and I hit her"). In *justifications*, batterers admit their violence, do not question its seriousness, but rationalize it as a justified response to provocations from their partners ("She was pushing my buttons"). In doing so, they insulate themselves from taking responsibility for their actions.

Arresting and prosecuting domestic batterers are intended to disrupt men's ability to rationalize violence against women. When asked to describe the events that led to their arrests, however, the individuals interviewed continued to deny, minimize, excuse, and justify their abusive conduct.

Interestingly, in addition to these descriptions, respondents frequently offered another type of story to depict their violence. These are *self-defense stories*. In the self-defense story, the narrator admits to having engaged in violence. However, he describes his actions as a response to physical aggression initiated by the partner. To the extent that violence is characterized as a response to the actions of the intimate partner, the self-defense story resembles a justification, where the abuser explains that he is violent in answer to provocations from his partner. Yet the self-defense story is distinct as the partner is not only verbally provoking or pushing buttons, but also actually engaging in physical violence that the man perceives and portrays as threatening.

Some examples help demonstrate the difference between these two story types. In his interview, Steve explained that he got into an argument with his girlfriend after she brought up the topic of his wife and the possibility of him leaving her. Eventually, he explained, the argument became physical after she spat in his face:

> I've been messing with my girlfriend for about three to four years. OK. And she start to talk about, you know, I wasn't ever going to leave my wife and I'm not never going to be with her, and that's what started the argument.... So we're sitting there and we're talking, we're arguing. So all of a sudden she slaps me. I asked her not to, you know, don't put her hands on me. So, I sit there 20 minutes after we started arguing and she spits on me. OK. So when she spit on me, that's when I grab her by the hair.

This is a typical justification story. The offender explains that the partner does something to him, in this case bringing up an uncomfortable topic and spitting on him, that he interprets as antagonizing and meriting a physical response. It is telling that his partner did become physically aggressive with him ("all of a sudden she slaps me"), but this action did not prompt a physical response from him. Rather, he noted, it was being spat upon that made him violent.

In contrast to this justification story is that of Carl, who went to his ex-girlfriend's apartment, upset that she had gone out by herself and had not been returning his phone calls:

> I went over to my girlfriend's house. She was in bed, and we were discussing some things. I walked to the foot of the bed, and I noticed that she didn't have any underwear on. I bent over the bed, and I said, "Look, you don't even have any underwear on." I don't remember exactly what was said, but that's why I was bending over the bed. At that time, she turned and put her hands down on the bed, gritted her teeth, and just came up and kicked me right across the face. She then leaned up and started toward me. When she did that, I swung at her to get her away from me ... all I did was stop her from coming at me.

In this description, the respondent presented his violence as a response to a physical assault by his partner. He centered his description on her actions and the threats they posed. All he did "was stop her from coming at" him, and he overlooked his own psychological abuse in the scene, where he insulted his partner by implying that she was indecent because of the way she was dressed.

Surprisingly, *self-defense* stories were the second most common description of violence offered by respondents, following denials. In these descriptions, the same basic pattern is repeated. An argument arises, the partner attacks, and the respondent is left to defend himself:

> I was lying in bed, listening to music. My friend came in and she turned the music off. I got up and turned it back on and asked her what was her problem. When I turned around to face her, she pushed me on the bed. And when I went to stand up, she just grabbed me by my neck and started scratching me. And I grabbed her and held her real close to me to stop her from hurting me any further, and she bit me extremely hard. So, I pushed her away from me, and I'm not sure if she fell over a box or whatever in the room, but she got up and she ran into the front room and called 911. (Chris)

> She came home ready to argue because she's like "I couldn't get out of work. My boss said if I don't show up tomorrow, then I'm going to get in trouble." And I was like "Well, what do you want me to do?" So we throw down then. We argued. It escalated. There was a lot of things getting thrown around with her throwing my bag around. So, you know, our neighbors hear all the banging and everything. She's throwing my bag, and I would push her off me. I was trying to get out the door. They heard the back door slamming. She was slamming the door, like "No, we're going to argue about this," and I'd move out of the way. I never really hit her.... I mean, one time, I had to, she was all over me. She

was ripping at my coat and stuff, and I picked her up and I pushed her over to the couch. (Nic)

What happened was we were driving. I stopped and picked her up. She had a beer. I quit drinking over six years ago. I wasn't going to give away my transportation license, so I quit drinking. Her four year old was between us, and I'm like "Okay, whatever." So I take her there and let her have a beer in the truck. We weren't going very far. We were going out to the park to have a picnic. She snagged my phone, and I went to reach for my phone, and she went ballistic in the truck. She had boots on, kicking everything. So, I held her over against the door and pulled over the truck. She got out and kicked the hell out of my truck. I went to the police. (Doug)

Although distinct from the other types of descriptions presented by batterers, the self-defense story mirrors denials, minimizations, excuses, and justifications in that it allows the batterer to separate himself from the violence he participated in. He was violent, but only in reaction to an outside threat to his well-being. Blame, as in the justification story, lies squarely on the partner, who in these cases has become violent against him. At first glance, then, this review of batterers' descriptions of their violent behavior provides strong evidence that they do not come to accept responsibility for their abuse following their contact with the criminal justice system.

Respondents' narratives also illuminate how these men see themselves and their partners through violence. Previous studies have found that men construct and affirm masculine and feminine subjectivities *through* their descriptions of violence. Abusive men "depict their violence as rational, effective, and explosive," all positive traits associated with masculinity, whereas they describe their partners' violence as "hysterical, trivial, and ineffectual," which tap into and reinforce negative stereotypes of women.[2] Further, in absolving themselves of responsibility for violence, batterers often present their partners as demanding women who "wind them up" or "provoke" them to be violent.[3]

Respondents' narratives bear these ideas out. Men frequently described themselves as "angry," "pissed-off," tough guys during their violent episodes while portraying their partners as "controlling" or "demanding" women who initiated the conflict that led to violence. Nevertheless, batterers' descriptions of violence also paint a more complex picture of the relation between violence and gender.

First, the types of masculine and feminine subjects appearing in batterers' accounts of violence are numerous. Men affirmed themselves not only as strong, lethal, no-bullshit guys in enacting violence, but as other masculine subjects as well.

For instance, in describing his violation of an order of protection against his ex-girlfriend, which fell within a pattern of highly abusive behavior, including the eventual kidnapping of the woman, Frank affirmed his identity as a caring father. He noted,

> So I went to the drug store and, "Lo and Behold!" right across the street there is my son with his mom, waiting at the bus stop. So I stopped the truck ... yeah, I wasn't expecting them ... it might have run through my mind that they might be there. Well, I got to stop at the drug store. I don't know what I was thinking. So, I stopped the truck there, and I stayed on my side of the street, and I just waved because I haven't seen him. You know, I manage to see my kid everyday. I pick him up from school everyday. I am part of his life. I am part of his social environment and everything. I am his dad.

In this account, Frank let slip out that his "chance" encounter with his ex-girlfriend ("Lo and Behold!") might actually have been planned on his part ("it might have run through my mind that they might be there"). Regardless, his stalking and violation of the court order intended to protect her were justified on the basis of being a father ("I pick him up from school everyday.... I am his dad").

In other stories, men affirmed themselves as breadwinners, another positive masculine subject, through their violence. Eric, for example, punched his girlfriend and looked to initiate sex with her after she did not come home after a night out with friends. In narrating the scene, however, he explained that he was upset because she had spent the money he had given her to pay household bills:

> I was paying all the bills and everything on my own. I was giving her everything. Really she didn't have to do nothing. Just be there for me. And what happened that morning, I wouldn't never put my hands on her but that was, I was screwed, you know what I'm saying, all my bills wasn't paid, how I'm gonna explain this?

Eric's attempt to reframe the conflict as one primarily concerning finances faltered to the extent that he let out that he had expected his girlfriend to fulfill a traditional feminine gender role for him, to stay at home and "be there" for him, which he believes involves doing "nothing." This notwithstanding, he presented himself through his violence as a responsible, hardworking breadwinner who was concerned about the household's finances.

Not all presentations of the masculine self in violence are positive. Some men affirmed themselves as drunks and alcoholics in their stories. Larry, who elsewhere in his interview reports harassing his girlfriend for fun, described the conflict that led to his violence as follows:

> She didn't really want to put this [calling the cops] on me. But at the time, when you're mad and you're fighting, you know, you blow up. And I don't blame her. I mean, we were both drinking that night and I

wish I'd never drunk. I shouldn't even be drinking because I'm an alco-
holic and two alcoholics don't get along with alcohol and stuff.

It is worth noting that Larry's violence in this episode left his partner with
severe injuries, including a large bruise under her left eye and a severely
swollen nose. Larry does not blame her, however, nor does he blame himself. Rather, he is simply a drunk who never should have drank that night.

What is important to note in these descriptions is not merely the
multiple masculine subjects men affirm through violence. Rather, it is
that in each case the men affirmed a masculine subject that possesses a
certain license for violence. The father has historically possessed the
authority to be violent against his family for the sake of discipline and
order. While this license for violence has diminished, thanks in large
part to the activism of battered women's and child welfare advocates,
Frank still presented his abuse toward his ex-girlfriend as a justified
demonstration of his love for his child. Likewise, the breadwinner, having provided for his household, has earned the right to be violent if his
partner loses the money and leaves him "screwed." Even the drunk,
though certainly not an appealing masculine subject, provides a cover
for violence, as he is understood to not have the ability to control himself. For these men, then, the concern was not just to present themselves as tough, strong men, but also to present themselves with
gender identities possessing the authority to be violent.

This multiplicity of violent masculine subjectivities in men's stories
is mirrored by a multiplicity of feminine subjectivities against whom
violence is justified. As noted in past research, the "controlling" partner who pushes buttons and provokes violence is one such feminine
subject. Another appearing frequently in men's narratives is the promiscuous, cheating partner:

> The thing about this girl is she just has this thing where she goes and
> finds another little boy. She thinks it's cool to bring him over to the
> house and says, "I'm going to go out drinking with this guy." That don't
> sit right, right there. (Bob)

> It's a terrible feeling, you know? Because, number one, when you think a
> person really love you and right just betrays you with another human. It
> hurts. It really do. (Aaron)

> If you have a girlfriend and she's going out with other guys and taking
> your money while she's doing it, and she's waking you up while you're
> trying to sleep.... I work nights and she called me during the day that
> day to go and buy her a tire and go put it on her car in the middle of
> my night so that she could go out that night with another guy. Are you
> just going to ignore that? (Carl)

Similar to the controlling partner, the promiscuous partner incites men to
violence. However, what the partners were guilty of was not annoying

men, but hurting them ("It hurts") and their masculine pride. Such immoral betrayals provided these men justification for violence ("That don't sit right," and "Are you just going to ignore that?").

As these points demonstrate, if men's descriptions of violence reinforce a patriarchal gender system, there is a certain multiplicity of gendered subjects within this system. More centrally, when describing and affirming their selves in their violence, abusers chose identities that possess a sanction for violence. Likewise, when describing their partners through their violence, they presented stereotypical, negative depictions of women whom the men understood to be deserving of abuse.

HOW DO ABUSERS CHANGE FOLLOWING ARREST AND PROSECUTION?

The failure of abusers to assume responsibility for their actions demonstrates the limits of presumptive arrest and prosecution to realize change. Nevertheless, we might hope that these policies, even if failing to change batterers' beliefs, change behaviors. Ultimately, this question is beyond the scope of this chapter, as only partners can verify whether a person has ceased being abusive. Still, respondents' views of change are important in order to gain a fuller perspective on the impact of criminal justice interventions upon them.

When asked about how their lives have changed following contact with the police and courts, respondents offered a host of answers. Here, I have grouped these responses into three general categories: religiosity, loss, and stigma.

Religiosity

One change noted by some men was becoming closer to their faith as a result of their contact with the criminal justice system. In each case, this change was connected to spending extended amounts of time incarcerated. Unable to bond out following their arrests, and exposed to prolonged periods of material and spatial deprivation, these respondents established a new relationship to religion. As Isaac noted, reflecting on his time in jail, "I'll just say I pray more now. I just pray more."

The connection between jail and religiosity represents a more general element of incarceration culture.[4] "They call it 'Christianity in jail,'" Aaron explained in his interview. "Christianity in jail—that's the only time you pick up a bible." Despite the dismissive tone, respondents' increased religiosity in jail plays a central role in their definition of self and the reasons for their detention. Aaron said later of his time in jail, "I did a lot of reading. It [reading the bible] basically helps me. It help me. It help me sit down and realize who I am. What's my reason for being here, you know."

Reflection on oneself and one's actions in the solitude of jail is, of course, an intended effect of incarceration. Through such effort, the offender should come to repent his crime. However, such reflection does not necessarily lead to a critical self-appraisal of one's criminal conduct. Instead, through the embrace of religion, it recasts the reasons for detention in spiritual, rather than criminal, terms. Chris noted in his interview that

> I've come to the conclusion that I had turned my back against God. And so now God turned his back against me. I feel like I'm being punished for living in the sinful ways that I have, living with women without being married to them. I had drank with some of them. And I had tried smoking marijuana with some of them.

Rather than viewing his detention as a punishment for unlawful abusive behavior *against* his intimate partner, Chris came while in jail to understand it as a punishment sanctioned by God for sinful behavior *with* intimate partners out of wedlock. In the process, the meaning of punishment for him was (re)defined.

For these men who believed that they were innocent of any statutory crime and are victims of an unjust legal system, religion offered a moral template for interpreting their actions that supersedes the laws dictated by government authorities. The notion that they had been punished for some higher purpose became a defining characteristic of their legal encounter. Like Chris, Aaron noted that his punishment was a sign from God. And, like Chris, the crime committed was not abusive behavior against a woman, but immoral living against God with a woman. "My God," he said, "want me to sit down and acknowledge him more. Get a closer relationship instead of using this materialistic money and woman." Kevin, too, explained that "what I did in the past," in terms of sinful living, "came back on me." As such, "This domestic dispute is just a piece of the puzzle. I think I was locked up for another reason, just to read through what's really going on around me."

The shift to a deeper religiosity on the part of intimate abusers provides further evidence that arrest and prosecution fail to increase their responsibility for violence. Although few in number, these respondents found the cultural resources to redefine the legal system's identification of their behavior as criminal in new ways that distanced them from violence. As such, the experiences of these men underscore the unpredictable outcomes resulting from the government's exercise of power against intimate abuse.

Loss

A more common change that abusers reported was loss. Respondents described experiencing loss in different aspects of their lives following their encounters with the police and courts. For some, the loss was financial. Tom, for instance, lost the job he had just begun after he failed to appear at work following his night in jail. "I didn't go back to work on that next day or anything because I was kind of messed up," he explained. "So I called up and told them that I wasn't going to be able [to] come in. And they said they needed me to come in that day, and if I wouldn't come in, then don't come back at all." Doug similarly emphasized the financial costs involved in taking his case to trial. "Financially, it's been devastating," he said. "Financially, it sucks, man. There's several thousand dollars that I had put up in the state's hands for no reason." In citing that there was "no reason" to have needed to spend money on his case, Doug reaffirmed his belief that the case against him was a sham.

Others noted loss in terms of family and intimate relationships. Brett focused on his partner's decision to leave him, depicting it as a hurtful void in his life:

> It [the criminal case] nearly destroyed my family. We no longer live together. She's living with another guy now. She threw it away. Those few months apart, we couldn't talk, we couldn't communicate. It destroyed my whole life. I'm hurt. I'm mad. It's just hard for me, man, and there's no way to fix it.

Brett blamed both the no-contact order imposed during his case ("we couldn't talk, we couldn't communicate") as well as his ex-girlfriend's own lack of commitment to their relationship ("She threw it away") for the loss he felt. Seeing his "life" destroyed, Brett assumed a fatalistic stance, claiming there's "no way to fix" the pain he suffered.

In addition to the loss of persons in their lives, respondents reported the loss of trust in personal relationships. In some cases, this loss of trust involved relationships that remained active after the resolution of respondents' criminal cases. Steve, for instance, who was violent against a girlfriend he was seeing outside of his marriage, lost the trust of his wife. "My wife still don't trust me," he says. "When she see my cell phone ring ... normally, I mean, I had this phone for about 10 years, and my phone ring, she would never touch it. Now, when it rings, she grabs it like I got an answering service. She just don't trust me."

More commonly, loss of trust was described by respondents whose partners had reported their abuse to the police. These men interpreted their partners' calls for help as acts of betrayal since they trusted their partners to suffer through their abusive behavior. As a result, their trust in their partners was affected. Victor related that his experience with the criminal justice system was "affecting me a lot with the trust" he has for his partner, who appeared on the day of his trial to testify against him. His girlfriend ultimately did not testify against him.

However, rather than interpreting her refusal to cooperate with the state as a show of faith in him and the relationship, he still understood it as a betrayal.

For Doug and Chris, the loss of trust extended to personal relationships in general:

> I don't have any trust anymore for anybody. That's what it's done to me. I lost all that. I lost my balls. She was the one person, I mean, I could have murdered somebody or something like that, and if I told her, she would never say a word. (Doug)

> My faith and trust in women are really down now. I mean, I'm the type of person, if you treat me nice, then I'm going to think you're a nice person. I see now that it takes time to really get to know a person. I just can't take your word for it. (Chris)

For Doug, the fact that a trusted partner, whom he thought could be trusted with knowledge of his abusive self ("I could have murdered somebody ... she would never say a word"), refused to endure his abuse any longer means that he cannot trust anyone any longer. The loss of trust involved a loss of masculinity as well ("I lost my balls"), a response conveying how Doug interpreted trusting a partner with his abusive self as a particularly masculine characteristic. Chris, in the same way, interpreted his partner's contacting the police as a betrayal. As a result, his trust in women has been lost, and he noted that he will take more time in the future to evaluate partners before putting his faith in them.

These findings concerning the losses that batterers experience through their contact with the criminal justice system add greater insight into the variable costs of arrest and prosecution for abusers. Those with jobs (Tom) and financial resources (Doug) risk losing them as a result of time missed from work and the expenses required to retain an attorney. However, even those unemployed and unmarried abusers with "nothing to lose," such as Victor and Chris, in fact lose much in losing trust in their partners. It is of significance that they are no longer confident that their abuse can simply be hidden away from public view.

Stigma

In addition to these "losses," many respondents expressed concern with what they had gained through their experiences with the criminal justice system: a stigmatized identity[5] as a criminal and "wife beater." Respondents' narratives revealed that their legal encounters left them with stigmatized identities that contaminate different everyday social interactions.

For example, job searches force respondents to identify themselves as convicted criminals, which hinders their ability to secure employment and other financial services. Carrie, for example, was working at a large retail store when she was arrested for abusing her boyfriend. Promised a promotion before the arrest, she found that the promotion never materialized. She explained, "[T]hey treated me differently after I called them and let them know I was arrested. (They were) treating me, you know, as if 'Okay, well, if she sticks with this overnight position, then maybe she'll just quit and we won't have to fire her.'" Identifying for herself the stigmatized identity, Carrie understood it to harm her ability to locate subsequent employment. "They treat you differently," she reported. "They pretty much treat you like you're a criminal even though it could be for something small. So, it's really hard to find employment right now."

Other respondents related similar problems. Chris wanted to get life insurance to save his family "the burden of burying me and all that," but the insurance company told him that "because I have felonies with violence, I can't get life insurance." John noted that people "look at me differently" at work since his arrest. Carl mentioned his conviction affecting job applications. "I've had to fill out a job application since then and had to put 'yes' where it says, 'Have you ever been convicted of a misdemeanor or felony?'" Doug, meanwhile, "was doing specialty work, 160 bucks an hour, specialty welding at the [local] car plant," a side job he would often get through a friend of a friend. After his arrest, he noted that "I don't get that no more."

While the stigma affecting respondents in these interactions is that of being a criminal, the stigma impacting them in other interactions is that of being a domestic batterer. Carl explained, "I feel like I'm marked as a wife beater or a hothead and I go out and get into bar fights and stuff like that." Steve, for his part, described the shift in the way his friends perceive him:

> My friends, a couple of them call me Mr. Goodbar. Mr. Goodbar, don't do shit wrong. I would crack on their asses when they have a fucking domestic, you know. I'd be the main one calling them a dumb fuck. My friends tell you about me, he's a good guy, no problems, no violence, and when he hears about it, he's the first one to try to make the motherfucker feel bad. So then, after all these years, now I have a domestic. It's a big change. They look at you like "You ain't shit."

Here, Steve related undergoing a fundamental transformation in his social identity at work. At one time viewing himself as the primary person who would stigmatize men arrested for domestic violence ("I would crack on their asses when they have a fucking domestic"), he now reported being the one stigmatized ("They look at you like 'You ain't shit'''"). In the process, he has lost his identity as a good person ("Mr. Goodbar") in the eyes of his peers.

The stigma of being a batterer affects intimate relationships as well. Aaron described a date with a woman who knew he had been convicted of domestic violence. Trying to get close to her, the woman became apprehensive. "I was trying to hug her, and she's like 'Aaron!' I'm like, 'What's wrong!?! I ain't going to hit you! I wouldn't do that." Through the public exposure of his intimate abuse, Aaron's future relationships with intimate partners have been affected.

When offenders learn that others now relate differently to them as a result of their domestic violence arrests, respondents reported making efforts to conceal their stigmatized identities in order "to pass" as "normal" citizens, friends, and intimate partners. In effect, having had their intimate abuse revealed, batterers work to reprivatize the violence through various acts of deception. Mike did not mention his criminal history to potential employers when he attempted to find work after his legal encounter. He explained, "I've just gotten lucky [that] a couple jobs have not [done background checks]. A friend of a friend that I knew at the farm supply shop hooked me up with a guy at a flooring surfaces job. So they really didn't really do a background check. They just went off the word of this guy I knew for a long time and I got a job."

Aaron and Carl hid their batterer stigmas from potential intimate partners. Aaron, who above described one woman being afraid of him after learning of his domestic violence conviction, noted that now, "I don't tell them, because I think they'll look at me different." Carl echoed this response: "I'm certainly not going to tell a new girlfriend that I've been arrested for hitting my other girlfriend. I suppose that's not something that I'm happy with. I wouldn't feel right in a relationship not telling her, but I don't think I would ... she'll look at me in a different light." These men simply have chosen to keep these elements of their identities hidden out of fear that their stigmas will endanger the possibilities of future intimacy.

These attempts to present the self as nonviolent are important to consider in assessing the efficacy of presumptive arrest and prosecution. On the one hand, like the increased religiosity reported by respondents, they provide further indications that the abusers participating in this study did not come to claim responsibility for their abuse. This surely counts as a shortcoming of these policies. On the other hand, like the findings on loss, they evidence negative aftereffects from arrest and prosecution that increase the costs of committing intimate abuse. Having had their private intimate violence publicly exposed to friends and other relations, these respondents face the burden of stigmatization in their private and public lives. Again, batterers who were employed either lost or risked losing their jobs and experienced difficulty in locating new ones. And those with seemingly "nothing to lose" in fact could be seen to be losing or at risk of losing much. This included not only the possibility of locating employment or securing vital financial services such as life insurance, but also the possibility of future intimate relationships as well as social acceptance as good persons. In response, abusers seek to reprivatize their violence and (re)define their selves in order to resist contamination from stigmatized batterer identities and "pass" as normal, nonviolent citizens and intimate partners.

DISCUSSION

The narratives in this chapter demonstrate that presumptive arrest and prosecution do not result in batterers accepting responsibility for their violence. Following contact with the police and courts, not only do abusers continue to deny, minimize, justify, excuse, and defend their actions, but also they actually come to see themselves as the true victims of these incidents. To the extent that these findings run counter to what advocates of aggressive criminal justice policies had hoped, one wonders from where this sense of victimization in offenders comes.

On the one hand, the stories of victimization provided by men have something to do with the changing nature of gender relations in society. If we take the men's narratives of the events that led to their arrest, look beyond their normative assessments of women, and consider for a moment who the women described as crazed, controlling, and cheating are and what they are doing, one gets a sense of this transformation. These are women who often own or rent the apartments the men are living in; have lives outside of their intimate relationships and are unwilling to settle down with these men; are willing to contact the police when their partners become abusive; and are apparently willing to fight back when their partners become abusive. These are not the nagging wives and partners described so often by men in other studies of batterers. These are strong, independent, empowered women willing to use different resources in order to negotiate their situations of abuse and to pursue their self-interest. To the extent that these women do not match the traditional, stereotypical depictions of self-sacrificing women, they strike the men as crazy and manipulative. And men, in turn, feel threatened and/or hurt.

On the other hand, men's stories of victimization are not simply products of changing gender relations in society. Rather, respondents' narratives reveal that their relation to violence and claims of victimization also arise in conjunction with the same criminal justice system that is supposed to teach them a lesson. That is, pro-arrest policing and no-drop prosecution policies themselves play a role in men's sense of victimization. There are three general ways in which this happens.

First, at the most basic level, presumptive policies fail to have men assume responsibility for violence because they are contained within an adversarial system of criminal justice that teaches suspects that it is to their benefit to deny their criminal behavior. One of the respondents, Bob, made this point explicit in his discussion of the police's response to the scene.

> So, I go out there and he's asking questions. He says, "Hey, you tried grabbing her?" You know, me, I've got to deny this, you know, because if I even admit to grabbing her I'm going to jail. I said, "I don't know what the hell you talking about." This, that, and the other. All of a sudden, I'm denying it and saying, "I didn't rough her up or nothing."

Believing that he would be arrested for an admission of physical contact, Bob chose to deny any sort of contact with the victim at all. Many men participating in the study, who like Bob had prior contact with the criminal justice system, made the same point. Nic, for instance, explained, "So the cops outside are like 'What have you got to say for yourself?' I'm like 'Nothing.' I'm thinking, I don't want to get arrested. I don't want her to get arrested. You know, that leaves the kids ending up going, getting her grandfather called, or who knows." Dave, likewise, noted that "her version of the story is that I grabbed her by the back of the neck. And then my version was, well, I didn't say anything to the police."

At the point of contact with the criminal justice system, then, these men separated themselves from their violence. Further, while men's initial denials and distancing from violence represented responses to the immediate threat of being arrested, their continued evasions of responsibility during their interviews revealed that this distancing continues beyond the initial police encounter. That is, rather than later reworking their stories of violence to tell some version of the truth that they felt disinclined to share with the police, the respondents instead came to rework their experiences and memories to fit a story that is presentable and defendable before the police and courts.

Second, opposition to the law emerges from the diverse subject positions of domestic violence suspects. While the intimate abuser, domestic batterer, or wife beater has emerged as a unified subject in the popular imagination, persons who commit intimate abuse encompass a diverse population of varying social, racial, and ethnic backgrounds. This study found that respondents use those factors to define their legal experiences of injustice.

Tom's mother, who lives in a major city, explained to him "how those cops are down there" in more rural Centralia County, where the research was conducted. "They would love to lock a Black man up, especially he don't got no record." Henry also believed he was the victim of racism because the officer arresting him had been at the center of a local controversy concerning the police's mistreatment of African Americans. Carrie, for her part, explained to me why she felt her probation sentence was "all just about money":

> I know that it was in the paper they wanted to rebuild the clock of the courthouse or whatever. Ever since then the police are doing different stuff, you know, as far as trying to make more money. Like last week they stopped, oh, three hundred and something people on the corner of Columbia and Neal doing ... I'm not sure what it's called, public safety search or something. *That's an African American neighborhood?* Yeah. And basically what they were doing was checking to see if you have your seatbelt on, checking to see if you have a driver's license and insurance. And if you don't have it, they ended up arresting 60 people just that day.

In this setting, where the court was restoring its iconic clock tower and the police were stepping up a public order campaign specifically in a black neighborhood, Carrie's own experience with the law took on a new meaning.

Third, the failure of presumptive policies to change abusers is related to police and judicial practices. Authorities use of power to gain control over suspects affects their understanding of their punishment and violence. For instance, when describing their interactions with the police and guards in jail, respondents often noted that these officers explained to them that state domestic violence law requires law enforcement officers to make an arrest whenever a domestic violence call is made:

> Of course, on a domestic, the man [police officer] said if they get called, there has to be an arrest made. (Nic)

> He's [the arresting officer] basically telling me that a woman can call and say harassment because, you know, they got laws like that. You know, you work with a woman, you be like "It's nice what you're wearing today"—harassment. (Victor)

Each of these ideas is false. But in my field research of domestic violence policing, I frequently observed police officers and jail guards using such comments, referred to in policing as "verbal judo," in order to make suspects more compliant with police investigations or detention procedures. Interestingly, the way in which such comments achieve compliance is by sending the message to individual suspects that nothing they did is necessarily wrong, but that departmental pro-arrest policy or state domestic violence law is simply strict.

Another example of this dynamic concerns defense attorneys' use of negative depictions of the court system in order to effect "client control," or trust with clients that can be used to influence their decision making:

> She's [the public defender] real cool. She's real down to earth.... She's a white lady. She said if the jurors would be mostly white, they might take

the white girl's side over your story. It's my word against hers.... So, and she told me the judge is a prick. (Ed)

I had three charges against me, and two of them were dropped. In my opinion, they all should have been, but they wanted me to plead guilty to domestic battery. Even after I did it, I thought about appealing. Even though I said yes, I don't think I'm guilty of it. It was happening during the changeover of state's attorney—Nolan was on his way out and the new girl was coming in. She was a female and she was going to crack down on domestic violence. My attorney just thought that maybe it was best for me to do this and get it over with. (Carl)

Such comments are central to legal practice. And, in these two cases, as in many of the respondents' cases, such comments influenced men's decision to plea-bargain their cases. Nevertheless, however effective these comments are in realizing client control, they also come to have a separate meaning for domestic battery suspects. These suspects readily claimed their innocence. But faced with an unjust state and system of justice, they were forced to accept plea bargains that promised lesser punishments than a conviction by jury or bench trial. In the process, their distance from their violence was maintained while their sense of victimization was heightened.

As noted in the introduction to this chapter, domestic violence law seeks to provide women protection from the violence of their abusive partners as well as alter the violent subjectivities of abusive men. With regard to this latter goal, we have seen that men exposed to presumptive arrest and prosecution tend to continue evading responsibility for their violence while developing a sense of victimization at the hands of their partners as well as the criminal justice system.

In conclusion, these findings lend added weight to the increasing calls to consider alternatives to the current criminal justice system's handling of domestic violence cases. This should not entail abandoning the significant gains that have thus far been won with the criminal justice system. The alliance with the justice system represents a significant achievement in providing protection to victims of domestic violence and sending the message to society that domestic violence is morally wrong. In pushing for alternatives then, we might refine, rather than replace, the current system of domestic violence law and seek to employ practices and approaches—restorative justice being the most frequently mentioned option—that prioritize empowering victims and ensuring abuser responsibility.

NOTES

1. See P. Ewick and S. Silbey, *The Common Place of Law: Stories of Popular Legal Consciousness* (Chicago: University of Chicago Press, 1998). In this seminal book on people's experience of the law, Ewick and Silbey offer three types of legal consciousness that people enact in legal encounters: "law as something *before* which they stand, *with* which they engage, and *against* which they

struggle" (p. 47). Persons standing "before the law" envision law as a sphere set apart from their daily world and inhabited by impartial, fair-minded professionals whose conduct is bound by clearly defined rules and procedures. Those standing "with the law" view it as a rule-bound game that is constituent of their daily lives and necessary for the resolution of conflicts and pursuit of self-interest. Those standing "against the law" understand it as an arbitrary system of power in which "might makes right." To the extent that those "against the law" experience it as an intrusion upon their daily lives, they confront law through acts of resistance that circumvent its dictates and operation.

2. K. Anderson and D. Umberson, "Gendering Violence: Masculinity and Power in Men's Accounts of Domestic Violence," *Gender and Society* 15, no. 3 (2001): 358–80.

3. R. Dobash and R. Dobash, "Violent Men and Violence Contexts," in *Rethinking Violence against Women*, ed. R. Dobash and R. Dobash (Thousand Oaks, CA: Sage, 1998).

4. The connection between incarceration and religiosity is generally understudied, especially considering the extent to which the United States relies on incarceration as a punitive practice. See O. Ballesteros, *Behind Jail Bars* (New York: Philosophical Library, 1979), for some general reflections on this connection.

5. See E. Goffman, *Asylums: Essays on the Social Situation of Mental Patients and Other Inmates* (Chicago: Aldine, 1961). In this collection of essays, Goffman defines stigma as a "deeply discrediting" attribute (3).

BIBLIOGRAPHY

Anderson, K., and D. Umberson, "Gendering Violence: Masculinity and Power in Men's Accounts of Domestic Violence," *Gender and Society* 15, no. 3 (2001): 358–80.

Coker, D., "Race, Poverty, and the Crime-Centered Response to Domestic Violence: A Comment on Linda Mills's Insult to Injury: Rethinking Our Response to Intimate Abuse," in *Violence Against Women* 10, no. 11 (2004): 1331–53.

Eisikovits, Z., and E. Buchbinder, *Locked in a Violent Embrace: Understanding and Intervening in Domestic Violence* (Thousand Oaks, CA: Sage, 2000).

Hanna, C., "No Right to Choose: Mandated Victim Participation in Domestic Violence Prosecutions," *Harvard Law Review* 109 (1996).

Mills, L., *Insult to Injury: Rethinking Our Responses to Intimate Abuse* (Princeton, NJ: Princeton University Press, 2003).

Chapter 8

Programs for Men Who Batter

Daniel G. Saunders

Programs for abusive men began soon after shelter and other crisis services for battered women opened in the 1970s. This chapter describes the history of these programs, how they operate, barriers to their success, the major controversies surrounding them, and some promising new directions in which these programs are heading. It also addresses the important question: are these programs effective in ending abuse? The reader will be given tips for assessing the quality of outcome research in order to help answer this question.

HISTORY

Programs for men who batter are rooted in the feminist movement of the 1970s. Pro-feminist men played a central role in their development. These men often had friends and colleagues in the battered women's movement who helped raise their awareness of domestic violence. In some cases, battered women's advocates urged these men to begin abuser programs. However, many advocates were opposed to working with men who batter. In 1982, Susan Schechter observed:[1] "When women discuss the role of men in the movement, they frequently turn to the question: should the shelter movement help violent men? In community speaking engagements, shelter workers are continuously asked, 'So what are you doing to change men? These men will be back on the streets beating the next woman if you don't help them'. These challenges, though logical on one level, frustrate and anger many women. The movement's too-limited resources are being used to keep shelter doors open—barely. Women have taken major responsibility, often in the face of hostile opposition, for helping battered women.

Now an unsavory burden is suggested that would resubmerge women in the very sexist tradition that they are challenging; women, not men, are being asked to nurture the male perpetrators of violence."

Some were concerned that essential resources would be diverted from services for victims. Others believed that programs for abusers would minimize the criminal nature of abuse or reduce the perception that fundamental social change was needed to end domestic violence. In addition, there was skepticism that programs could change entrenched behaviors and beliefs in a population resistant to change.

Many advocates changed their perspective when they realized survivors often returned to their abusive partners and wanted their partners to change through counseling. Or, if couples separated, they saw that abusers often found another partner to abuse. Advocates also learned that funding for abuser programs did not threaten shelter funding because the funds came from clients, criminal justice agencies, or other sources not designated for shelters. The first programs for men who batter were housed in pro-feminist men's collectives, such as EMERGE in Boston and RAVEN in St. Louis, or in nonprofit family service agencies, usually with close ties to shelters. Some shelters eventually opened their own abuser programs, which is one way they could closely monitor these programs. Programs later were developed, administered, and supported through the judicial system and in the military. A small number, developed more recently, are located in prisons and jails.

There are now over 2,500 intervention programs in the United States. According to a recent survey, approximately 15 percent are part of a shelter program. Approximately half are private for-profit, 43 percent are private not-for-profit, and a small percentage are governmental.[2] The setting does not seem to make a difference in the approach that is used. Surprisingly, one study found that shelter-run programs focused less on patriarchal norms than other programs. In a recent survey of programs in many different countries, programs were most likely to be located in victim advocacy or psychological counseling programs. Five percent were in criminal justice settings, and 4 percent were in men's programs.

PROGRAM FORMATS AND METHODS

Men's groups are the most common format being used. Couples counseling, usually in groups, is offered in approximately 15 percent of the programs in the United States, with about one in five men being offered couples counseling in these programs. Compared to individual counseling, which few programs offer, the group format is believed to have several advantages. It can provide opportunities for feedback and confrontation from one's peers and allows for more realistic role-play situations. Groups can also be a more efficient way to treat the large number of men needing services. Concerns have recently been raised that a group format may produce negative outcomes. Men may reinforce each other's negative views of women and support each other's pro-violence attitudes. Some authors also point to the variations among abusers and the ways in which an individualized approach can tailor treatment for more effective outcomes. Programs tend to be labeled according to their major orientation, but these labels do not reflect the rich blending of orientations and methods they usually offer. The "smorgasbord" of approaches usually proceeds through three main phases: (1) expanding the meaning of "abuse" beyond physical abuse, (2) helping the men accept more responsibility for their behavior, and (3) teaching them reactions and behaviors that take the place of aggression.

The methods used can be placed along several dimensions according to the assumptions made about domestic violence:

- *Skills training*. This method is based on social learning assumptions about the behavioral deficits and behavioral excesses of offenders. Group leaders model positive behaviors through role plays, followed by the role-play rehearsal of new behaviors by group members. The goal is to enhance relationship skills in order to replace abusive and other negative behaviors.

- *Cognitive restructuring*. This approach assumes that faulty patterns of thinking lead to negative emotions, which in turn lead to abusive behavior. Restructuring of these thoughts is likely to reduce anger and the fear and hurt that often underlie it. More broadly, these approaches can also help men become aware of belief systems developed in childhood, including beliefs about gender roles and male entitlement.

- *Sex role resocialization*. The focus here is on helping the men consider the negative effects of constricted male roles and the benefits of gender equality. Male dominance is viewed as the result of rigid socialization into the male role.

- *Awareness of control tactics*. These methods build awareness of control tactics used to gain or maintain dominance over one's partner and are represented most fully in the "Duluth model." The meaning of domestic violence is expanded to include many forms of abuse: isolation, demeaning language, control of finances, and other means of control. The need for power and control is seen as the underlying motive for these forms of abuse. The impact of the abuse on the victims is emphasized.

- *Family systems*. A family systems perspective can be applied to men's group work through the analysis of family dynamics and communication patterns and by bringing new insights and skills to the men in the group. There is no single set of assumptions underlying these approaches, but a frequent assumption is that couples unwittingly engage in repeated cycles of interaction that may culminate in abuse.

- *Trauma therapy*. This approach rests on the assumption that the men need to resolve their childhood traumas, in particular those from witnessing parental violence and being physically abused by parents. One assumption is that abusers cannot empathize well with others because they are cut off from their own traumatic experiences.

The first four approaches—skills training, cognitive restructuring, sex role resocialization, and awareness of control tactics—are the ones most commonly integrated in the same program. For example, the EMERGE program combines awareness of abusive behaviors with cognitive restructuring. The widespread and influential Duluth model—named after the city in which it was developed—emphasizes awareness of violent and nonviolent control tactics and, to a lesser extent, the learning of new skills. Here is an excerpt of dialogue from one group session:

Facilitator: Bob, you're saying you wouldn't "let" your wife go to work because that was your job only?

Bob: Well, that's how I grew up. My dad worked, and my mom stayed home. If a guy can't support his family, I've always thought there was something wrong with him.

Mark: Don't you think all of us grew up doing what our fathers did? Don't you think it works both ways? Women grew up thinking that way too.

Facilitator: I just don't think these things happen out of the blue. Why is it set up like that? That men go out to work, and women work in the home without pay?

Pete: It's that way in order to keep order.

Facilitator: Order?

Pete: Well, some roles have to be set in order to keep things from falling apart.

Facilitator: But if men's work or role is to make money and women's work or role is without pay, what does that do? [After several more exchanges John responds.]

John: We get to make family decisions. (p. 70)[3]

Family systems approaches are the most controversial. Critics charge that this approach explicitly or implicitly holds the victim responsible for the abuse. Program standards have been developed in many states that restrict the use of couples treatment and insight approaches, especially if they are used exclusively.

The dimensions listed above can be placed into three broad categories: (1) "therapeutic programs," which focus on the treatment of emotional pain and childhood traumas (see example 1 on the next page for an illustration of a process-psychodynamic group for the resolution of trauma); (2) "psycho-educational programs," which provide instruction in cognitive and social skills (see example 2, on page 166, for an illustration of cognitive restructuring); and (3) "didactic-confrontational" programs that provide consciousness raising about the consequences of and responsibility for abuse, such as the "Duluth model" described earlier. One study found that the most common type was psychoeducational.[4] One way these approaches can be integrated is over time, for example beginning with a didactic-confrontational approach and then leading into psychoeducation and then therapy phases.

EXAMPLE 1: EXCERPT FROM A PROCESS-PSYCHODYNAMIC GROUP

Female leader: I want to know not what you wrote in your autobiography, but how did you feel when you were writing it?

Group member: I try to live up to the standard that my father set. I have a mixture of emotions that I could not be as good as he was, but I am a better person.... Writing about my life reminded me of the past choices I made. I made the wrong choices, or the choices I made turned out the wrong way. It hurts to look at your bad choices.

Male leader: How does it feel being a victim of your father?

Group member: It is not a good feeling seeing your father kick you and your brother everyday. What I learned from it was nothing until I came here.... He hit me with his fist, kicked, (used a) stick.... As a child you do not learn anything, but as you grow up you learn. I always thought, when my father hit me and told me that it hurts him more, why are you doing it then? They feel guilty when they do it so that is why they say that.

In a later phase of the group, members integrate their individual socialization with gender role socialization:

Group member: I saw an ad in the newspaper that I liked a lot about a march about World Without Rape.

Female leader: I saw that ad too. Is there a part that had an impact on you?

Group member: Yeah, the part about the learned behaviors. Also when it said, "Free yourself from the prison of violence that you live in and inflict on other people," and that being a hardass does not mean shit. I see a lot of people thinking they are tough when they really are not.

Female leader: Thank you for that reaction. Does anyone else have anything to say about that?

Group member: Yeah. I was taught as I grew up that as a man you are not supposed to be hurt or feel hurt about anything. Then I believed it and it consumed me as I grew older. One time I sat and I cried because I needed it. It was there that I realized that I have feelings also and that I have a right to express them as anybody else. I cry harder when I realize all the time I wasted believing otherwise. Sometimes I feel alone. It took me time to realize that that macho attitude has not gotten me anywhere besides feeling frustrated and stressed.... Now that I can identify certain problems that I had in the past, I feel free. I can say to ____, "I like you," without fearing that he is going to think I am gay. I feel that I have spread my wings. (pp. 269–270)[5]

EXAMPLE 2: METHODS AND HANDOUT EXAMPLE FOR COGNITIVE RESTRUCTURING

Cognitive restructuring usually has the following elements:

- Recognizing physiological early warning signs of anger, like heart racing and adrenalin rush.
  - Recognizing common cognitive distortions about the event. It may also involve staying aware of early traumas, fears, and hurts and male socialization into entitlement norms.
- Cognitive rehearsal involves a cognitive reenactment of the event.
  - Thinking out loud.
  - Switching to positive self-talk.

A handout in group might help the men see how quickly they generate negative thoughts and emotions through self-talk like this:

"I see her talking with another man,
they are probably attracted toward each other,
I can't let her be tempted,
she is my wife,
she's done something bad,
I need to teach her a lesson,
I will hurt her as much as she's hurt me."

Examples of positive self-talk might include the following:

"She really does care about me. I trust we have a good relationship.
Relax, take a deep breath, and focus on caring for myself right now.
Love means not holding on tight. She can't love me if it's forced."

In a recent U.S. survey, 53 percent of the programs labeled themselves as a Duluth model (awareness of control tactics); 49 percent as cognitive-behavioral (skills training and cognitive restructuring); 26 percent as "therapeutic"; 14 percent as "EMERGE"; and 13 percent as "Other."[6] In an international survey, the topics covered the most in decreasing order of frequency (from 90 to 50 percent) were masculinity, healthy relationships, conflict resolution, cultural traditions, anger management, fatherhood skills, criminal sanctions, substance abuse, childhood trauma, and stress. A problem identified in many U.S. programs in the 1990s was that they made no special effort to understand the needs of minority communities. I describe below some promising developments in culturally sensitive approaches. Also described will be the way in which most programs are part of a community coordinated effort, working most closely with criminal justice and battered women's organizations. Most programs combine court-ordered and voluntary offenders in the same groups, with the majority being court ordered. Some programs accept only court-mandated clients. Programs tend to require that offenders have pled guilty or been found guilty (60 percent in one survey), as opposed to accepting offenders who are diverted from the court system. As described next, the commonly held assumption that criminal justice sanctions are the best way to motivate men for treatment does not always hold true.

MOTIVATORS FOR PROGRAM ATTENDANCE

A major barrier to ending violence is the low level of abusers' motivation for change. Dropout rates vary considerably across programs, from about 20 to 70 percent. One oft-noted rationale to use criminal justice sanctions is their potential to motivate the men to go to programs and stay in them. Survivors often want treatment for their partners rather than incarceration but feel powerless to get them into treatment. Unfortunately, much of the available evidence suggests that sanctions do not universally increase program attendance. Such sanctions seem to work best for younger, less educated men.

Close monitoring seems to have some positive effect on attendance, with the monitoring mechanism varying from "attendance checking" by partners, to "check-ins" by legal or social service personnel, to immediate court notification of missed sessions. Monthly court reviews have also been shown to have a positive impact on attendance. One method for improving retention is the use of "marathon" orientation groups. Orientation groups can be helpful in demystifying programs for potential clients and socializing them into the treatment process. The orientation normally lasts an hour or two and may be extended over several weeks. One marathon group was held over a day and a half. Participants were provided with an overview of upcoming treatment and taught some concrete skills. The men in this group had a much higher attendance rate than men in the normal orientation groups. Another innovation aims to develop compassionate feelings during the first group session in an attempt to block out aggressive feelings. A video called *Shadows of the Heart* is used. It portrays a very resistant offender followed by a scene of the man as a child helplessly watching his father abuse his mother. Abusers identify with both of these scenes and can learn to feel compassion for the child within themselves who never had a chance to heal from childhood traumas.

Men in groups with the video and related discussion were more likely to be active in group sessions, take extra homework, and stay in treatment. Other methods for improving attendance have relied on supportive phone calls and handwritten notes from group leaders after missed sessions. These methods seem to work regardless of race, class, and educational level.

Some studies show that men of color are more likely to leave treatment prematurely than white men and thus may benefit from more specialized orientation or treatment groups. Groups composed entirely of men from the same race seem to foster more cohesion than multirace groups. Because unemployment and low educational level may be crucial factors in explaining lower rates of attendance by many minority men, programs may need to help them meet basic needs and overcome discrimination. Culturally focused interventions for African Americans were the focus of one study and were compared with conventional groups composed of all African Americans and with conventional, racially mixed groups. There was a higher completion rate for men with high cultural identification who attended the culturally focused groups.

CULTURALLY SENSITIVE APPROACHES

Some experts distinguish programs based on the degree and type of cultural sensitivity they practice. For example, there can be color-blind programs that claim that "differences don't make a difference," culturally focused programs that pay attention to historical and contemporary experiences of particular cultural groups, and culturally centered programs that place a particular culture at the center of treatment and use culturally significant rituals. An example of a culturally focused method might be acknowledging historical traumas to one's cultural group and grieving the damages done, such as the forced relocation of Native Americans and the slavery and breakup of African American families. An example of a culturally specific ritual would be the burning of sage in a program for Native American men who batter. As programs become more culturally sensitive, they are offering specialized programs that give men the choice of same-race or mixed-race groups. Programs are now available for African American men, Southeast Asian men, Native American men, immigrant and nonimmigrant Latinos, and men from other ethnic and racial groups.

Programs seem to vary in how well they address the heightened resentment toward the criminal justice system and toward society as a whole for the historical and everyday oppression experienced by men of color. The EMERGE program in Boston has learned that a nonconfrontational approach seems to work best for clients from some cultures. This program also learned to appreciate the diversity within particular cultural groups. Beyond specific interventions, the entire organizational structure and climate of programs may need to change. Staff often need more training and information. Efforts need to be made to hire a diverse staff, network with the minority community, and seek consultation on culturally sensitive approaches.

ASSESSMENT AND INTAKE PROCEDURES

Programs vary greatly in the extent to which they assess potential barriers to treatment, such as illiteracy, suicide risk, mental illness, and substance abuse. Some conduct comprehensive assessment interviews over several individual sessions, while others may place offenders immediately into a group. Some programs provide individual counseling for men with severe psychological problems and others refer them to other agencies for these problems. Although there is not a higher than normal rate of severe mental disorders among men who batter, screening for these disorders is important. It is not clear what percentage of men might need treatment in addition to or in place of group counseling, but some evidence suggests that the percentage is small. By contrast, the overlap between substance abuse and domestic violence is high and there is increasing evidence that ongoing alcohol abuse is a risk factor for reassault after treatment. Practitioners seem increasingly comfortable with court-ordered or probation-ordered random urine screens during treatment. Some argue that alcohol treatment needs to be a standard feature of offender programs.

HOW TO JUDGE PROGRAM EFFECTIVENESS

Before turning to evidence of program effectiveness, I highlight the key criteria that distinguish the most rigorous outcome studies from others in the field. Readers can use these criteria to evaluate outcome research. Fortunately, as outcome studies have become more rigorous, there is growing consensus about the elements of good studies.

Outcome Measures

There is some consensus that total cessation of abuse needs to be the outcome criterion. However, reports of a reduction in the frequency and severity of violence can provide clues to promising treatments, even if the cessation rates do not change. Most evaluations today go beyond the measurement of physical abuse and typically measure threats, controlling behavior, sexual abuse, and emotional abuse.

Evaluations also may measure stalking, fear of abuse, relationship equality, parenting skills, safety of children, economic support by the offender, and other variables. Victim reports of any reabuse after treatment are a much more reliable source than reports from abusers and the use of arrest records. Arrest records are likely to show only the "tip of the iceberg" of actual reabuse. Victim reports a year or two after treatment will also be more telling than victim reports a few months after treatment.

Quality Control

We cannot automatically assume that a "treatment" described in the model was actually delivered as described. If it was not, then the claim that a given study measured the efficacy of the approach is invalid. One way to assess whether or not the intended treatment was actually delivered is through direct observations or by taping sessions. Attention should also be paid to the quality of the treatment, sometimes assessed through ratings of practitioner competence in delivering the service.

Dropouts from Treatment or Follow-Up

Even if treatment was delivered as promised, extremely high rates of treatment dropout may indicate that only the "cream of the crop" entered or completed treatment. If that is the case, not much can be said about treatment effectiveness. If only the most motivated men completed the program and these men stopped their abuse afterward, it is possible that they would have stopped under any circumstances (i.e., even without an intervention). Moreover, it is important to know whether certain types of abusive men complete treatment at higher rates. A program could be successful with one type of abuser but not another.

A related question involves the proportion of victims interviewed after treatment. Some studies now report interview completion rates with survivors of approximately 80 percent over periods as long as two years. We can naturally be much more confident in the results of such studies than in the results of studies that only followed up successfully with much lower percentages.

Comparison Groups

Firm conclusions are difficult to make if the study does not include an untreated comparison group. Experimental designs—the random assignment of men to different groups—are touted as the most rigorous, yet achieving this standard in real-world settings is extremely difficult. A case can be made for alternatives to experimental designs that consider contextual factors.

HOW EFFECTIVE ARE PROGRAMS?

Many studies of program effectiveness exist, but only a few have designs rigorous enough to produce firm conclusions. Fortunately, the rigor of studies is increasing due to a growing consensus that studies need to use broad definitions of abuse, victim reports as opposed to official reports, and follow-up interview rates over 80 percent.

Some early studies showed promise for changing attitudes about gender roles, reducing anger directed at the partner, and decreasing child abuse. These findings need to be regarded skeptically, however, because they were usually based on the men's self-reports. A number of studies compared treatment completers and noncompleters. Recidivism rates are generally higher for noncompleters. However, these findings are difficult to interpret because completers and noncompleters are likely to differ in their motivational levels and on important demographic characteristics. Several studies used arrest records to compare the outcomes of a treated group with various types of untreated comparison groups. Control groups used in this research included groups of men who: lived too far away, had the wrong schedule, were "unsuitable," were selected randomly from municipal court records; were referred to community corrections, and were on a "wait list" control group. While some positive results were noted, the studies were flawed because arrest reports, rather than victim reports, were used.

When victim reports and other measures are used in quasi-experimental designs, the results have generally been disappointing. In a large-scale, quasi-experimental comparison of programs in four different cities, no major differences were found across the four systems, despite differing program lengths and levels of additional services for men and women. The men reported that methods such as "time-out" (leaving the situation temporarily) and cognitive restructuring (positive self-talk) helped them the most to avoid being abusive. Interestingly, the perceived certainty and severity of sanctions were not related to dropout or reassault rates.

When true experimental studies have been used to compare different approaches, few significant findings emerge. Seven studies involved a variety of comparisons and yet did not find major differences between the approaches. The approaches compared were:

1. Semistructured self-help groups, a structured educational model, versus a combination of the two.

2. A feminist-cognitive-behavioral model versus a process-psychodynamic model (however, there were differences depending on the type of abuser).

3. Cognitive-behavioral group therapy versus supportive group therapy. The supportive group clients showed greater gains on negotiation skills and perceived ability to refrain from verbal aggression.

4. Court-mandated treatment versus a community service control condition (although a longer-term treatment showed better results).

5. Abuser program plus monthly judicial monitoring, versus abuser program plus court monitoring based on level of compliance, versus monthly court monitoring only, versus court monitoring based on level of compliance, versus condition consisting of abusers with neither monitoring nor treatment. The victim interview rate was low in this study. Younger men and those without a "stake in conformity" were more likely to be rearrested.

6. Six months of treatment and one year of probation compared with men on one year of probation only. This study also had a low victim interview rate. The number of sessions attended was associated with lower probation violation and arrest rates.

7. Culturally focused counseling in all–African American groups, versus conventional counseling in all–African American groups, versus conventional counseling in racially mixed groups.

Studies comparing couples groups and men's groups have also been conducted. These studies tend to include only intact couples and women who reported no injuries or fear of abuse. Two small sample studies showed no differences between the two approaches. In a large-scale study conducted in the U.S. Navy, an experimental comparison was made of four conditions: cognitive-behavioral men's groups, cognitive-behavioral "quasi-couples" groups (many wives did not attend), rigorous monitoring, and stabilization and safety. The men's groups and quasi-couples groups used similar content, but the couples groups placed more emphasis on communication training. The couples' condition is labeled "quasi-" because many of the men's partners did not attend the sessions or attended them sporadically. Rigorous monitoring involved regular safety checks with the men's partners and monthly meetings between the men and case managers. "Stabilization and safety" involved pretreatment screening, safety planning, and referrals for the women. This can be considered a no-treatment control condition, while the rigorous monitoring can be considered a minimal treatment control. No differences were found across the four conditions after treatment on measures such as physical and psychological abuse and fear of endangerment. There is speculation that a "surveillance effect" produced change across all conditions because the men were in the Navy and sanctions for reoffense could be severe. However, an analysis of the men's fears of sanctions did not support this contention.

When researchers attempt to combine the results of many studies, called "meta-analyses," the results do not reveal much additional information. Cognitive-behavioral and Duluth-style programs do not show different outcomes. Studies using arrest records show positive results, but the more stringent indicator, victim reports, shows very little effect from treatment. Overall, treated groups have about 5 percent lower recidivism rates than untreated groups. Although this difference may seem very small, it is not too surprising because clients are generally resistant to change and have chronic problems. Medical treatments, for example for cancer, are endorsed with equally small effect sizes. A promising avenue for further research is the matching of offender types to the type of treatment. In the study comparing feminist-cognitive-behavioral and process-psychodynamic treatments, those with antisocial personalities did best in the feminist-cognitive-behavioral groups and those with dependent personalities did best in the process-psychodynamic groups (see Table 8.1).

Another promising development is matching treatment to the motivational stage of the offender. This matching may be more important for treatment effectiveness than any particular theoretical approach. Evidence shows that abusers in the most advanced stage of change are most likely to use strategies to end the violence, and they blame their partners less.

Promising also is a focus on the therapeutic relationship and special motivational techniques, both for increasing attendance and for reducing abuse. A close therapist-client collaboration and group cohesion have been related to lower levels of psychological and physical abuse. Even one or two sessions of special motivational techniques at intake have shown positive results in promoting offenders' engagement in treatment and in offenders being less likely to blame their violence on external factors.

WHO IS MOST LIKELY TO SUCCEED IN PROGRAMS?

An important consideration in accepting men into programs or providing specialized services for them is knowing their likelihood of treatment failure. A fairly small percentage of abusers seem to account for a large percentage of severe and frequent violence after treatment. Factors consistently related to reassault are alcohol abuse and severe personality disorders. Not surprisingly, the chronicity and severity of prior assaults or arrests are good predictors of assault after treatment. One prognostic indicator scale showed that substance abuse and severity of domestic abuse predicted recidivism. Another analysis showed the following factors were associated with reassault: younger age, not having children, heavy drinking, emotional abuse or threats, low help seeking by women, and the women's use of a shelter.

COORDINATION WITH OTHER COMMUNITY SYSTEMS

Offender programs may hold the most promise when they are part of a coordinated, community-wide effort. Fortunately, many communities have implemented coordinated community response plans. There is growing evidence that combined intervention (arrest plus prosecution and/or treatment) is more effective than any one intervention. For

Table 8.1.
Three Types of Men Who Batter and Interventions to Match Them

Family Only—Suppressor Type—David. A police department receives a call from a woman who says that she is afraid of her estranged husband, David, who is outside her apartment door pleading to see her. She is referred to an agency that can help her file a restraining order. She is reluctant to do this, partly because it could affect his reputation. He is a 44-year-old, highly respected physician. She reports that he broke her wrist a few months earlier but she is now thinking of reuniting if he agrees to couple's counseling. Police records show a single arrest for a minor traffic accident while he was under the influence of alcohol.

This type of abuser is the least severely and least frequently violent. He has the least criminal record and not likely to abuse substances. He has the least hostility toward women and his communications skills are similar to men in unhappy marriages. He appears to be perfectionistic and over-inhibited – trying to "stuff" his emotions. He is likely to respond well to criminal justice interventions and to skills-based treatment. Of the three types he is the one who could be considered a candidate for couple's counseling.

Antisocial and Generally Violent—Jack. A police dispatcher receives a call from a hospital emergency room. A woman wants her boyfriend Jack arrested for severely bruising her about the face and neck. He previously assaulted her to the point of causing a miscarriage. He is the same man the police arrested a few months ago for a drunken brawl with three men in a bar. Jack is a seasonal construction worker in his mid 30s. He has a long history of alcohol-related crimes, including an assault on a police officer when he was in his early 20s. After serving time for that assault, he served two years in prison for drug dealing. As a youth he lived in foster homes and juvenile treatment centers.

The antisocial, generalized aggressor is violent inside and outside of the home and has the longest arrest record of the three types. He has the highest frequency and severity of violence, including sexual assault. He is likely to have a history of substance abuse and teen crimes. He probably experienced severe physical abuse as a child and as a result developed the motto: the best defense is a good offense. He is hostile and domineering in most of his communications and justifies violence more than other types. He is not overly attached to his partners and might say "good-bye, good riddance" when she wants to leave. Like most antisocial criminals, he is slow to learn and it may take multiple arrests and divorces for him to learn the impact of his actions. His childhood wounds may be difficult to treat because he tends to cover them with substance use and other means of repression. He seems to respond well to structured, skills-based programs. He probably needs long-term treatment and close probationary supervision.

Emotionally Violent/Abandonment Fears—Brian. A suicide hot-line worker calls the police for aid. She would like the police to check on a 23-year-old man, Brian, who has called them several times threatening suicide. He now says he has a gun and wants to "execute" himself. He is separated from his wife and young son and realizes how much he has hurt her through his abuse. He has slapped her and ridiculed her severely. In the last episode of violence she was holding their son. He has no criminal justice history. As a child he was affected by his mother's severe mental illness and abuse from his older brother. Especially painful was the way in which his mother humiliated him in front of his friends.

The emotionally volatile – borderline type fears abandonment and as a result is jealous and dependent. He is responsible for moderate levels of injury to his partner and has a history of some arrests and perhaps sexual assault. In childhood he was likely to have experienced rejection, humiliation, or the death or mental illness of a parent. His stance toward his partner is: "I hate you – don't leave me." He seem to be at highest risk of stalking, separation violence, and suicide-homicide. As a result, criminal justice sanctions may have little impact. Treatment aimed at resolving childhood traumas may be effective, along with methods for reducing physiological arousal.

---

example, more offender involvement with prosecution, probation, and counseling has been related to success. Information sharing among agencies regarding danger assessment also seems to be useful. As previously mentioned, court reviews seem to improve treatment compliance.

Gondolf describes several system changes likely to reduce reassault:

1. having three to four long sessions per week in the first few months, the period in which reassaults are most likely to occur
2. more continuous support for the men's partners from caseworkers and advocates, since only 8 percent of the partners in his study had contact with battered women's services three months after intake
3. moving the offenders more quickly into abuser programs
4. pretrial referral and "fast-track" prosecution, similar to drug courts.

INNOVATIONS AND UNANSWERED QUESTIONS

A number of innovations have been implemented but have yet to be evaluated. Some controversies have also arisen that might be resolved through research.

- *Prison programs*. Lengthy, prison-based programs are common for sex offenders but seldom used for domestic violence offenders, most likely because only a small percentage of men who batter are identified in prison populations. Some steps are being taken to develop and assess these programs.

- *Reduction of psychological abuse.* Rates of psychological abuse often remain high after treatment and can have severe impacts on survivors. In one large-scale study, 76 percent of the men were verbally abusive at least once and 52 percent used controlling behavior sometime during 15 months after treatment. An encouraging result was that those who used psychological abuse prior to treatment were significantly less likely to use it after treatment.

- *Integrated substance abuse and offender interventions.* Integration with substance abuse services is difficult, probably because some basic assumptions about the causes of problem behaviors differ so much across the two fields. The greatest promise might come from programs that use the same group leaders for both problem areas, such as the AMEND program in Denver.

- *Trauma-based interventions.* Increasing attention is being placed on resolving the childhood traumas of men who batter, but further development and evaluation are needed.

- *Leader gender.* Controversies exist over the use of male-female versus male-male co-therapy or co-leadership of groups, but as yet no outcome studies have been published.

- *Treatment length.* Evidence on the impact of treatment length or intensity is inconsistent and also requires further research.

- *Conjoint approaches integrated with gender-specific ones.* More work is needed to determine which couples might benefit from couples approaches. In addition, the screening mechanisms for this approach need further study. Initial results show that careful screening, for example including only women who are motivated for conjoint counseling, feel safe, and have not suffered severe violence, appear to protect women from reabuse.

- *Program standards and practice guidelines.* The primary policy enhancement in the abuser intervention field is the development of state and local standards. Controversy occurs in some cases because the standards may be highly specific, tied to government funding, and not evidence-based. Further research on many elements of standards, such as treatment length and theoretical orientation, will help to inform this controversy. In other fields, professional groups have developed "practice guidelines" that allow enough flexibility for clinical judgments to be made (e.g., the American Psychological Association and the International Society for Traumatic Stress Studies).

CONCLUSIONS

Programs for men who batter rely heavily on cognitive-behavioral and gender resocialization methods. Despite the existence of many outcome studies, very few are rigorous and solid answers about effectiveness remain elusive. A promising avenue for more research is matching the type of offender with the type of treatment. Eventually, the most dangerous offenders might be reliably identified and placed into intensive intervention "tracks." Fortunately, methods for reducing attrition are yielding promising results. Increased attention to cultural competence is another promising development. However, the integration of abuser, survivor, and criminal justice interventions within each community may lead to the greatest success in ending domestic abuse.

NOTES

1. S. Schechter, *Women and Male Violence: The Visions and Struggles of the Battered Women's Movement* (Boston: South End Press, 1982), p. 260.

2. B. Dalton, "What's Going On out There? A Survey of Batterer Intervention Programs," *Journal of Aggression, Maltreatment & Trauma* 15, no. 1 (2007): 59–74.

3. E. Pence and M. Paymar, *Education Groups for Men Who Batter: The Duluth Model* (New York: Springer, 1993).

4. E. W. Gondolf, "An Exploratory Survey of Court-Mandated Batterer Programs," *Response* 13, no. 3 (1990): 7–11.

5. K. O. Browne, D. G. Saunders, and K. M. Staecker, "Process-Psychodynamic Groups for Men Who Batter: A Brief Treatment Model." *Families in Society* 78, no. 3 (1997): 265–71.

6. B. Price and A. Rosenbaum, "National Survey of Perpetrator Intervention Program," paper presented at the International Family Violence and Child Victimization Research Conference, Portsmouth, New Hampshire, July 8–10, 2007.

RECOMMENDED READING

Aldarondo, E., and F. Mederos. *Programs for Men Who Batter: Intervention and Prevention Strategies in a Diverse Society*, ed. E. Aldarondo and F. Mederos. Kingston, NJ: Civic Research Institute, 2002.

Babcock, J. C., C. E. Green, and C. Robie. "Does Batterers' Treatment Work? A Meta-Analytic Review of Domestic Violence Treatment." *Clinical Psychology Review* 23, no. 8 (2004): 1023–53.

Bennett, L. W., and O. J. Williams. "Intervention Programs for Men Who Batter," in *Sourcebook on Violence against Women*, ed. C. M. Renzetti, J. L. Edleson, and R. Kennedy Bergen, 261–77. Thousand Oaks, CA: Sage, 2001.

Feder, L., and D. B. Wilson. "A Meta-Analytic Review of Court-Mandated Batterer Intervention Programs: Can Courts Affect Abusers' Behavior?" *Journal of Experimental Criminology* 1, no. 2 (2005): 239–62.

Gondolf, E. W. *Batterer Intervention Systems: Issues, Outcomes, and Recommendations*. Thousand Oaks, CA: Sage, 2002.

Jackson, S., L. Feder, D. R. Forde, R. C. Davis, C. D. Maxwell, and B. G. Taylor, *Batterer Intervention Programs: Where Do We Go from Here?* Washington, DC: Department of Justice, National Institution of Justice, 2003.

Murphy, C. M., and C. I. Eckhardt. *Treating the Abusive Partner: An Individualized Cognitive-Behavioral Approach*. New York: Guilford Press, 2005.

Rothman, E. F., A. Butchart, and M. Cerda. Intervening with Perpetrators of Intimate Partner Violence: A Global Perspective. Geneva, Switzerland: World Health Organization, 2003.

Saunders, D. G. "Group Interventions for Men Who Batter: A Summary of Program Descriptions and Research." *Violence & Victims* 23 (2008): 156–72.

Shepard, M. F., D. R. Falk, and B. A. Elliott. "Enhancing Coordinated Community Responses to Reduce Recidivism in Cases of Domestic Violence." *Journal of Interpersonal Violence* 17, no. 5 (2002): 551–69.

Chapter 9

Batterer Programs and Beyond

Michael Rempel

The past three decades have seen a dramatic surge in the number of domestic violence cases handled by criminal courts nationwide. Driven initially by the feminist and battered women's movements of the 1970s, police and prosecutors are now far more likely to bring domestic violence cases to court. Similarly, new federal and state laws encouraged police officers to arrest the perpetrator. New funding streams encouraged prosecutors to pursue these incidents more vigorously, even when the victim was reluctant to file charges. As a result, one study reports a 178 percent increase in criminal domestic violence caseloads over a single decade, 1989 to 1999, a period that already followed the initial policy ferment and caseload expansions of the late 1970s and 1980s.[1]

This massive influx of domestic violence cases placed enormous pressure on criminal courts to develop innovative responses. A high proportion of these cases involved misdemeanor offenses (e.g., harassment or simple assaults), which were legally insufficient to merit a jail sentence. As a result, the emerging response of choice with cases ending in a conviction was to order attendance at a batterer program, typically involving weekly classes running anywhere from 26 to 52 weeks.

A 2007 study identified 2,265 batterer programs nationwide, a number that almost certainly underestimates the true figure.[2] Although some programs allow persons to enroll voluntarily, approximately 80 percent of the nation's batterer program participants are ordered to attend by a court. In some states, including California, Florida, Oregon, and Rhode Island, court orders to batterer programs are not merely a preferred practice but also required by law. California imposes perhaps the most stringent set of requirements, mandating that all domestic violence offenders attend a 52-week batterer program, supervised by the local probation department.

Despite the widespread use of batterer programs, controversy continues to surround their purpose, effectiveness, and long-term impact. Such controversy has only escalated as the result of several recent studies questioning whether batterer programs prevent, or even reduce, future violence. Despite these studies, some practitioners remain hopeful that batterer programs will eventually be shown to have positive effects on at least some categories of offenders—perhaps those with a less serious criminal history or general propensity for violence. Others, who have long doubted the ability of batterer programs to change the behavior of individual men, oppose any further research, viewing it as a drain on resources that might otherwise aid the victims of domestic violence. Underlying this debate is the reality that batterer programs are unlikely to disappear any time soon because as courts often lack legally and practically feasible alternatives.

To help make sense of this state of affairs, this chapter will review what we know about the effects of batterer programs, and will provide a tentative roadmap for the future. One particularly critical direction, implemented by itself or in conjunction with court orders to a batterer program, would involve the use of more rigorous approaches to monitor offenders. Intensive monitoring may deter future offending; at the least, monitoring can guarantee that offenders are held more fully accountable for their violent behavior.

THE GOALS OF COURT ORDERS TO BATTERER PROGRAMS

Before the advent of batterer programs, police officers generally did not make arrests when responding to domestic violence incidents and prosecutors generally did not prosecute the cases even when arrests were made. Thus, courts had little incentive to devise appropriate sentencing strategies. When domestic violence cases began to flood the courts in the late 1970s, particularly in cases unable to justify a jail sentence, the advocacy community pressured courts nationwide to develop new responses. Court orders to batterer programs filled this void by making demands on offenders in place of the preexisting alternatives of doing nothing, levying a small fine, or giving offenders a conditional discharge sentence with few, if any, real conditions attached.

When these programs first arose, their supporters did not generally assume those attending would change offenders' behavior. They saw these programs as one prong in a more comprehensive community response that had the overall goal of decreasing society's tolerance for domestic violence. A related advantage of batterer programs is that they effectively place the offenders under court oversight for an extended period, even after a conviction. Participants are required to attend the program, and the court can verify if they actually fulfilled all of their responsibilities. In response to program absences, other violations of program rules, or additional misbehavior that comes to the court's attention, the court can impose additional sanctions, up to and including jail time.

By comparison, traditional sentences such as a fine, or even community service, tend to be completed shortly after sentencing and deprive the court of any long-term opportunity to watch over these offenders and so perhaps prevent further misconduct. Emphasizing the monitoring function, the founders of the first batterer programs understood the significance for including tracking systems as an integral component of their program and recommended that courts establish systems for tracking offender behavior and responding to noncompliance before ordering offenders to programs. Some advocates flatly stipulated that, in the absence of workable tracking systems, batterer program orders should not be used. As the founders saw it, the Duluth model was not merely a batterer program curriculum. Instead, it was a comprehensive intervention, which involved program orders, follow-up tracking and accountability mechanisms, and cooperation among a broad array of agencies both within and outside the criminal justice system. The intent was to emphasize the message that domestic violence is unacceptable.

Despite the remarkably broad goals held by those who established the initial batterer programs, the emphasis quickly shifted to much narrower rehabilitative outcomes. The shift from comprehensive accountability to violence reduction and rehabilitation was not surprising. If these programs were going to be widely used and paid for in part at public expense, there needed to be clearly defined and measurable behavioral or attitudinal outcomes. Furthermore, specialized programs were already used by the courts for other types of offenders, including those with substance abuse issues and/or mental health problems, and those in need of specific vocational or employment services. These programs were all predicated on the expectation of rehabilitative results, so it was logical to expect similar results from batterer programs. Moreover, changing individual behavior is intuitively much easier and shorter term compared to the broader societal changes sought through application of the Duluth model. For all of the above reasons, court administrators and judges were ultimately drawn to the reduction of reoffending as a primary goal for ordering offenders to attend batterer programs. Following their implementation in the late 1970s, there have been more than 65 studies examining their effects on recidivism.

Many practitioners continued to focus on the idea of batterer programs as a strategy for ensuring accountability rather than as a step toward rehabilitation. For example, while accepting the premise that individual offenders can change, the "New York model of batterer programs" maintains that such programs cannot be relied upon to produce that change. Instead, the model views batterer programs "as a service to the courts"—an appropriate punitive sanction that criminal courts can impose in cases unable to elicit a jail sentence. Driven by a focus on accountability, one of the model's core tenets is that referrals should only be accepted from courts that are prepared to impose further consequences in the event of noncompliance with program policies (echoing a similar expectation originally linked to the Duluth model). In a sense, the New York model holds the court, not the programs themselves, responsible for accomplishing the main purpose of batterer programs, since only the court has the legal authority to enforce noncompliance by imposing additional sanctions.[3]

Implicitly embracing this focus on accountability, California law details an extensive array of reporting and supervision requirements that are enforced by probation whenever a court orders an offender to a program. These requirements include the rereferral of a noncompliant offender back to court for additional sanctions by charging the offender with violation of probation. Yet, as will be seen below, California appears to have achieved greater success in its commitment to an accountability model in theory than in the execution. The California story raises the question of whether the goal of rehabilitation continues to drive everyday practice, even in places where accountability appears prominently in official policies and rhetoric.

The following two sections examine how successful court orders to batterer programs have been in achieving either of their main postulated goals: rehabilitation and accountability.

BATTERER PROGRAMS AS A TOOL FOR REHABILITATION

Even though batterer programs have been extensively researched, high-quality empirical evidence is in short supply. Most studies published prior to the 2000s failed to compare offenders attending these programs with offenders who did not. Instead, most researchers simply compared the rearrest rates of batterer program completers and dropouts. From the court's perspective, these comparisons are unhelpful because the court has no way to know beforehand who will complete the program and who will not. Hence, the relevant policy question is not whether completers outperform dropouts but whether *all* of those ordered to a program perform better, on average, than those not so ordered; in other words, does a systematic policy of sentencing offenders to batterer programs achieve better results, on net, than the opposite policy of not doing so? As a further consideration, those who dutifully attend all of the sessions of an assigned program are likely to be inherently more prone to compliance and less prone to recidivism than those who drop out, what is termed "selection bias" by researchers.

Thus, finding that completers outperform dropouts, by itself, signals little except that those who are compliant in one way (completing an assigned program) are particularly prone to be compliant in another way (avoiding future violence). This led those types of studies to find relatively high success rates. Such studies do suggest, though they do not prove, that practices that would increase the proportion of completers might produce better outcomes.

Recent debates have focused on a small group of five randomized experiments, four of which were completed in the last decade. In these experiments, domestic violence offenders were assigned through a random lottery mechanism either to a batterer program or not. Since the only distinguishing characteristic between those assigned and not assigned to the program was the luck of the draw, they represent the "gold standard" in social science research.

The first experiment was conducted in Hamilton, Ontario, in 1992. It reported significantly lower rearrest rates among those assigned to a batterer program.[4] However, all four subsequent experiments failed to detect any difference in recidivism rates between those assigned and not assigned to a program. The locations for these four recent experiments were San Diego, California; Broward County, Florida; and Brooklyn and the Bronx, New York.[5] Two measures of outcome are commonly used: rearrest and assessments based on victim reports of violence. Two reviews of all but the more recent Bronx study concluded that, on net, court orders to batterer programs appear to have very small but positive effects.[6] However, a third review points out that, whereas the average effect size is slightly positive when relying on police arrests for new offenses, it is zero when relying on victim reports of reabuse.[7] This distinction is significant since many domestic violence incidents go unreported. Indeed, when the available Bronx results are factored in, the average difference in rearrest rates would also be close to zero. In short, the sum of what we know is discouraging.

Another question of practical significance to the court is whether some program types work better than others. Unfortunately, the results are similarly discouraging when we consider the specifics of the batterer program curricula under examination. Each of the five randomized experiments involved batterer programs for groups of men operating according to variants of what are known as the cognitive-behavioral, educational, or psychoeducational curricular models. A cognitive-behavioral approach seeks to identify the specific thoughts or "triggers" that lead participants to become violent, and to introduce alternative, nonviolent responses for participants to draw upon when those triggers arise. Considering that cognitive-behavioral therapy has been highly successful with other types of offenders, it is a reasonable model for batterer programs to adopt. Explaining the lack of positive results, it is possible that attempts to foster productive group

discussions among men who are particularly prone to anger and violence and who lack internal motivation to change are uniquely ineffective, or even counterproductive. It is also possible, as some have
suggested, that today's batterer programs are routinely plagued by
high staff turnover, poor supervision of group leaders, and imperfect
model implementation, whereas a perfectly executed cognitive-behavioral
approach might elicit more favorable results. Finally, it is plausible that certain categories of offenders would be responsive to a cognitive-behavioral
approach, but that the group sessions appear unsuccessful when they indis-
criminately bring in everyone, including extremely violent men, with little
potential for change.

The second widely adopted approach, the educational, seeks to impart
information rather than provide therapy. Batterers would be instructed on
topics such as the history and roots of domestic violence, different forms
of violence (e.g., ranging from the purely physical to more emotional
forms of abuse), and the need for them to take responsibility for their violence as a choice they do not have to make. Few programs are exclusively
educational. More often, as is meant by the "psychoeducational" terminology, cognitive-behavioral content (psycho) alternates with didactic content
(educational).

The preceding models have dominated the field since batterer programs first arose in the late 1970s. Although in the minority, several
other models have also been developed. They include psychodynamic
approaches (emphasizing the roots of domestic violence in damaging
childhood experiences), the compassion model (emphasizing the need
to show empathy to the participants themselves and for them to show
greater empathy for themselves and others), couples counseling, and
unstructured self-help groups (akin to Alcoholics Anonymous/Nar-
cotics Anonymous groups for substance abusers). To date, there is no
clear evidence supporting the effectiveness of any of these models despite their widely varied program requirements and curricula.

Considering all that we now know, it might seem fair to conclude
that court orders to batterer programs are a failed intervention. However, returning to the five major randomized experiments, each carries
important methodological limitations calling into question whether the
results would apply in other settings. The most serious problems
include: unusually small sample size (Hamilton, which studied only 59
men); unrepresentative social context (San Diego, which exclusively
studied offenders employed by the U.S. Navy); serious deviations from
the intended random assignment procedures (Brooklyn); low response
rates on victim interviews (all studies except San Diego); and weak levels of judicial coercion designed to pressure participants to complete
their programs as ordered (all studies except Broward).

Another problem, the possible imperfect execution by the batterer
programs themselves of their formally promulgated models, may be

endemic as well. The idea that the batterer programs included in the major studies may not have been effectively implementing their formal curricula raises an important distinction between studies of efficacy and effectiveness. An "efficacy test" evaluates an intervention that is implemented exactly as designed, thereby testing whether that design yields positive results. An "effectiveness test" evaluates an intervention that is implemented as it exists in the "real world," without attempting to correct or perfect the execution. Most of the completed batterer program studies are effectiveness tests. Researchers did not explicitly select courts that refer offenders to batterer programs known for perfectly implementing their model and following the expected curriculum. Such a qualification does not necessarily make these results less valuable for policy makers, as it is arguably more important to know what to expect in the real world (effectiveness) than under ideal laboratory conditions (efficacy). Nonetheless, the efficacy-effectiveness distinction is important to recognize. Perhaps if a true efficacy test yielded more positive results, courts might be inclined to issue stronger demands, including better staff supervision, more rigorous adherence to official curricula, written lesson plans, and other steps to improve their performance.

In sum, it may be premature to dismiss the rehabilitative potential of batterer programs. At the same time, it would be equally unwise to view the preceding limitations as evidence that batterer programs probably do work or that courts should blithely continue what they are doing now. It remains noteworthy that the strongest empirical research studies agree in their primary findings. Therefore, a prudent general position would be to advise policy makers and practitioners not to expect batterer programs to keep victims safe; nor should safety be the primary reason for their use.

BATTERER PROGRAMS AS A TOOL FOR ACCOUNTABILITY

When we turn from rehabilitation to accountability, the research is even more limited. Here, the greatest difficulty is properly conceptualizing the outcome measure or "definition of success." That is, how would we know if a court was successful in using batterer programs to advance accountability? What would our evidence look like?

Phyllis Frank, founder of the New York model for batterer programs, points to the court's response when an offender fails to comply with the order to attend the program. Her argument is that if the court does not respond by imposing further consequences, up to and including jail time, the court effectively sends a message that the batterer program order was not serious and, hence, that the violence that gave rise to the order must also not have been serious. In this scenario, the court allows the offender to flaunt the court's mandate, thereby failing to convey a message that domestic violence is unacceptable. Conversely, where the court imposes a swift and certain response to noncompliance, the court effectively promotes accountability by affirming that the batterer program is indeed an important penalty that must truly be served.

Unfortunately, it appears that most courts nationwide do *not* enforce their orders to batterer programs as prescribed. Two comprehensive investigations, one in California and the other a national study, support earlier reports that courts rarely penalize domestic violence offenders for noncompliance. In the first of these studies, a 2006 report by the California State Auditor, reviewed the performance of 58 county probation departments in enforcing California's law that domestic violence offenders complete a 52-week batterer program. Implicitly embracing a focus on accountability, California law details an extensive array of reporting and supervision requirements that are to be enforced by probation whenever a court orders an offender to a program. The auditor's review found, however, that only half of a random sample of 125 cases completed their assigned program. Most of the offenders violated program rules or other probation requirements, some multiple times. However, local probation departments routinely failed to notify the court when such violations took place and, of those courts that were notified, many sent the offenders back to their programs without imposing additional sanctions. The report's cover letter to the governor observed that, in these situations, the court thereby "unintentionally sends the message that program violations are not serious and therefore will be tolerated."[8] The California story raises the question of whether the goal of accountability is difficult to achieve in practice, even in places where accountability appears to be advanced by official laws, policies, and rhetoric.

In a second study, local criminal courts, batterer programs, and victim assistance agencies were surveyed in 262 jurisdictions nationwide.[9] Findings indicated strong support for accountability, in principle, as a valid goal of court orders to batterer programs (cited by over three-quarters of courts, batterer programs, and victim agencies). The findings also demonstrated that virtually all courts surpass the minimum threshold for holding the offenders accountable in practice by having their local batterer programs submit compliance reports to the court, probation, or both under at least some circumstances.

However, a less sanguine portrait emerged from survey questions tapping actual responses to noncompliance. Even though approximately three-fourths of responding courts perceived that they "always" or "often" impose a sanction in response to a report of program noncompliance, only half of the batterer programs agreed with this assessment. Also, both types of respondents agreed that the more severe the sanction, the less likely the court was to impose it. Sanctions such as verbal admonishment or bringing the offender back to court were typical, whereas only a little over a quarter of courts and 16 percent of batterer programs believed that the court often or always responds by imposing jail time.

The California and national studies suggest that most criminal courts have implemented the basic mechanisms for using batterer programs to promote accountability—that is, compliance tracking and reporting protocols. However, while some courts routinely respond to a report of noncompliance by imposing sanctions, a large proportion of the courts do not.

Since there is considerable national variation, it is helpful to understand under what conditions courts become more or less likely to enforce noncompliance. Are there policies or specific conditions that seem to increase the probability of a forceful response?

One potentially promising condition is the presence of a specialized domestic violence court.[10] Such a court brings all or most of a jurisdiction's domestic violence cases together to be heard on the same, specialized court calendar. Most domestic violence courts also feature one or more dedicated judges who hear the cases and thereby gain expertise in the substantive and legal issues related to domestic violence. The first domestic violence courts were implemented in the early 1990s, and there are currently more than 250 in existence nationwide. However, there is substantial diversity in the goals and practices of these courts. This is not surprising considering that domestic violence courts currently lack a national information clearinghouse or training institute that might move the field toward a more universal approach.

Despite this diversity, domestic violence courts share several practices that promise to increase offender accountability. Domestic violence courts make frequent use of program mandates, including both batterer programs and substance abuse treatment.[11] These courts frequently employ extra staff, such as case managers or dedicated probation officers, to monitor compliance and report noncompliance to the court. Finally, domestic violence courts generally bring offenders back to court for postconviction judicial status hearings. During these hearings, a judge or judicial officer can review compliance information, admonish the offender, or impose additional sanctions.[12] Perhaps stemming from these practices, domestic violence courts are very likely to impose additional consequences when offenders are noncompliant with court orders.[13]

In San Diego, batterer program compliance was often assumed unless the court was informed otherwise, typically by accident. Even when the court then learned of noncompliance, further sanctions were rarely imposed.[14] However, after the city instituted domestic violence courts, regular judicial status hearings were held, and a revised set of reporting and sanctioning policies was implemented. In Milwaukee, probation played a critical role. After the establishment of Milwaukee's domestic violence court, probation monitoring intensified, and the offenders were more likely to have their probation revoked and be resentenced to jail in response to noncompliance.

In addition to the growing use of domestic violence courts, two more specific practices may become increasingly widespread—intensive probation monitoring and judicial monitoring through postconviction judicial status hearings. Even without an umbrella domestic violence court initiative, these practices might enhance offender accountability in themselves. However, it remains unclear whether the encouraging results just summarized are truly representative of the country.

NEW DIRECTIONS

Responding to evidence that batterer programs may not reduce future violence, in 2006 the Center for Court Innovation held a round-table conversation in New York City among eight researchers and 11 practitioners and policy makers to identify new directions. Proposals fell into one of three general areas:

1. alternative program mandates
2. greater use of offender supervision in addition to or in lieu of program mandates
3. other types of penalties

The discussion of program mandates drew attention to the possible role of substance abuse or mental health treatment for certain types of domestic violence offenders. Attention was also paid to using batterer programs to promote the potentially achievable goal of accountability rather than the more elusive goal of rehabilitation.

Proposals for supervision strategies focused primarily on the two practices cited above: probation monitoring and judicial monitoring. Apart from their potential effects in holding offenders more accountable, roundtable participants also considered whether intensive monitoring might proactively deter future violence. Although most research on this issue involves offenders in areas other than domestic violence, previous studies of probation monitoring indicate that it is usually ineffective as a deterrence strategy. Nevertheless, it works best when supervision officer contacts are more frequent, the imposition of sanctions for noncompliance is swift and certain, and offenders are engaged in an individualized "process of change."[15] It has also been found that offenders with a less serious criminal background were significantly less likely to be rearrested if assigned to an intensive probation monitoring regimen as opposed to regular probation.[16]

Judicial monitoring has proven to be an extraordinarily effective practice with drug offenders,[17] but the few studies conducted with a domestic violence population have had mixed results. A recent study completed in the Bronx found that judicial monitoring failed to deter reoffending. However, the Bronx site was described as having implemented an extremely weak form of monitoring—featuring brief and perfunctory exchanges between the offenders and the judicial officer, the frequent use of legal jargon that the offenders probably did not understand, a failure to reiterate the consequences that would follow from future noncompliance, and the inconsistent use of sanctions for noncompliance. This suggests that a weak judicial monitoring regimen is ineffective, leaving open the possibility that a true "best practice" model would produce more favorable results.[18]

Many observers believe that community service and steep financial penalties are potentially effective sanctions that are currently underutilized. Community service sentences pose a number of clear advantages. First, such sentences could symbolize direct remuneration to the community for the harm inflicted by the offender's violence. Second, community service could easily work in tandem with a judicial monitoring requirement. If the community service sentence was spaced over a significant period of time, the judge could verify recent compliance at each judicial monitoring appearance and impose sanctions in response to noncompliance. A final advantage is that, by definition, community service is not "treatment," and therefore its use would carry little risk of perpetuating the potential misunderstanding implied by court orders to batterer programs that the sentence will "cure" offenders of their violent tendencies. Facilitating implementation, most jurisdictions already have an infrastructure in place for mandating offenders to community service. However, such sentences are rarely tied to the kinds of rigorous tracking and reporting requirements that would be needed if, for example, the offenders were required to return to court multiple times to verify whether each one in a series of community service appointments had been completed. Therefore, important implementation challenges would remain.

While imposing steep financial penalties—fines, garnishment of wages, or restitution to the victim—is appealing in theory, it poses practical problems due to the endemic difficulties presented by nonpayment. The large numbers of offenders who fail to pay court-imposed fines typically have a summary judgment rendered against them that adversely affects their future credit rating. Since such judgments often fail to extract an immediate penalty, they may not be perceived by many offenders as terribly deleterious. Of course, those jurisdictions that are already succeeding in the collection of fines and court costs would not incur this problem. A final concern with the use of fines is its impact on victims who may depend on the offender for child support or other financial assistance.

THE CHALLENGE OF BATTERER PROGRAM PREDOMINANCE

Based on the evidence accumulated to date, it appears logical for criminal courts to continue exploring new sentencing strategies. However, since batterer programs are currently the predominant sentence of choice nationwide, efforts to develop alternatives may encounter legal and practical obstacles. In states with laws requiring the use of batterer programs, this would necessitate legislative revisions, not simply shifts in judicial preferences. Elsewhere, courts and prosecutors have relied upon court orders to batterer programs for many years, and there are strong institutional interests in favor of the status quo.

In response to the recent research questioning the impact of batterer programs on future acts of violence, some courts have decreased their reliance on such programs. However, many other jurisdictions continue their commitment to batterer programs. Therefore, there is an urgent need for reflection on how batterer program orders can become more effective. This was the intent articulated by Phyllis Frank and others who sought a transition away from the idea that batterer programs can rehabilitate and toward a focus on their utility at maintaining offender accountability. Clearly, this type of court control can make a difference by improved tracking and the enforcement of noncompliance.

The final sections of this chapter address what courts can change *without* abandoning their reliance on orders to batterer programs. It is important to reiterate the key assumptions underlying this discussion—that any new practices should promote accountability without foreclosing the pursuit of recidivism reductions. Such a position is relatively uncontroversial. There is widespread nationwide support for the goal of accountability in principle, even where its practical achievement may be called into question. In addition, a recent national survey found that 90 percent of criminal courts and 85 percent of batterer programs considered "treatment/rehabilitation" to be an important function of batterer programs.[19] To engage this view, it would be helpful to make strategies available that do not appear to preclude rehabilitation, even while experimenting with more profound alternatives, such as the use of community service, fines, or program models that explicitly eschew rehabilitation, in those places where doing so is practically feasible.

LESSONS LEARNED FROM DRUG COURTS

What is remarkable about the expectations that policies related to batterer program orders should allow for both accountability and the reduction of reoffending is that one can envision a strikingly similar approach providing the best chance to achieve both purposes at once. This point is developed by introducing lessons learned from drug courts, a highly effective intervention now in use across the country with substance-abusing criminal offenders. As early as 2002, professor of social work Edward Gondolf recommended the application of select drug court practices to domestic violence offenders. The authors of the randomized batterer program experiment in the Bronx (including myself) expanded on this suggestion in the conclusion to their 2005 report. Specific proposals for exactly how this should be done remain undeveloped.[20]

Drug courts seek to promote rehabilitation through court orders to substance abuse treatment coupled with intensive judicial oversight. Their judicial oversight components lead drug courts to provide an instructive model for how to exact greater accountability from an offender population. Participating drug court defendants must make frequent court appearances, usually weekly or biweekly at the outset of participation and declining in frequency to once every three or four weeks later on. At these hearings, the judge directly interacts with the defendants by discussing compliance reports from the treatment program, asking questions about progress in treatment, and offering encouraging or admonishing feedback. The judge also administers a system of tangible incentives and sanctions in response to progress or setbacks. Typical sanctions include a range of options such as short-essay assignments, community service, and several days in jail.

Participating defendants are subject to frequent drug testing, and many drug courts employ court-based case managers who provide additional supervision. Persistent noncompliance results in the imposition of a final jail or prison sentence; however, through the use of intermediate sanctions, drug courts attempt on one hand to penalize noncompliance whenever it occurs while on the other hand affording participants multiple chances before failing them out entirely.

Research has reported that drug courts have had considerable success in reducing recidivism.[21] Furthermore, some studies have found that their judicial oversight components may be at least as critical as, if not more critical than, the use of community-based treatment in producing these positive outcomes.[22] For example, results from an ongoing nationwide drug court evaluation indicate that the frequency of judicial status hearings, frequency of contacts with a case manager, frequency of drug tests, and extent to which participants believe that their interactions with the court in general and the judge in particular have been fair all contribute more to reduced drug use and reduced criminal activity than the number of days spent at a treatment program.[23]

What is particularly striking is that substance abuse treatment programs have been the subject of decades of research reporting their effectiveness, whereas batterer programs have not reported similar success. However, when compared, it appears that even substance abuse treatment programs may play a less critical role in producing positive behavioral changes than proactive judicial involvement. If the non-treatment-based components of drug courts are critical to their success, then it would appear all the more important to ensure such components exist with domestic violence offenders, for whom a known and proven effective treatment intervention does not exist.

Qualifications

What works with one group of offenders may not work with others. Indeed, drug and domestic violence offenders have several important differences that limit the ability for comparison. First, one can use a urine or blood sample to test for drug use, whereas there is no equivalent monitoring tool that can be used to test for ongoing domestic violence. Second, substance abuse treatment is predicated on a medical model that sees a substance addiction as a disease that often involves permanent physiological changes not under the voluntary control of the addicted individual. A medical model, however, has long been considered inappropriate for domestic violence offenders. Violence is seen as a behavior that offenders choose to use against their partners, for which they are therefore fully accountable. This second distinction has additional policy implications. Whereas a best practice approach with substance-addicted offenders would afford them multiple "second chances" in response to initial relapses, because domestic violence is not seen as a disease that requires time to control, affording repeated chances would be considered highly inappropriate. For similar reasons, positive incentives that are commonplace in today's drug courts, including praise from the judge for compliance, courtroom applause, or tangible rewards like journals or movie tickets, would send a wrong message in cases of domestic violence.

A final barrier to the comparison with drug courts concerns the duration of the intervention; court-ordered substance abuse treatment generally involves significantly more time than attempts at intervention through batterer programs. The reason is that many drug court participants face significant incarceration time if they refuse participation in treatment. Therefore, drug courts generally possess sufficient legal leverage to require treatment attendance of several days per week over an extended period of usually one year or longer. In contrast, most domestic violence offenders ordered to batterer programs do not receive that sentence as an alternative to incarceration, as incarceration is not initially considered a viable sentencing option for their (largely misdemeanor) offenses. Thus, for reasons of proportionality, courts are unable to require domestic violence offenders to complete an intervention that is as lengthy and time-intensive as that required of many drug offenders. As a practical matter, if courts attempted to impose such requirements, defense attorneys would balk at agreeing to plea bargains that they currently accept.

Applications

The preceding differences notwithstanding, the drug court model still offers pertinent lessons. Practices such as frequent judicial monitoring, direct judicial interaction, routine reminders to the offenders of their responsibilities, use of clear nonlegal language, and consistent use of sanctions are all easily transferable. With respect to sanctions, the key lessons from drug courts are:

1. to use sanctions in response to each and every infraction (certainty)
2. to impose sanctions soon after the underlying infraction occurs (celerity)
3. to ensure that sanctions are of sufficient seriousness to serve as a meaningful deterrent and statement of the court's displeasure (severity)
4. to use the same sanctions in response to the same misconduct from different offenders (consistency)

In a domestic violence context, one necessary adaptation would involve a more rapid escalation in the severity of sanctions. Drug courts generally build up the severity of their responses as more infractions accumulate (dubbed a "graduated sanctions model"). On the other hand, given the seriousness of domestic violence and the rejection of a medical model, a lower threshold would be appropriate before, for example, revoking probation or imposing a final jail alternative. Indeed, proponents of an accountability-based approach routinely advocate the swift imposition of jail time in response to termination from an assigned batterer program or other forms of serious noncompliance. They argue that most courts fail to provide this type of surveillance. Yet, even in cases where the legal merits of the case may make an initial jail sentence inappropriate, the subsequent imposition of jail time in response to noncompliance with a noncustodial sentence would be a standard and acceptable court practice.

Another adaptation is that, in a domestic violence context, many jurisdictions would require a slower process than is common in drug courts to uphold the due process rights of the offenders—for example, sanctions in many places could not be administered "swiftly"—without a probation violation hearing and unbiased judicial ruling based on the presentation of adversarial positions.

A final adaptation would be to expand the role of probation officers to implement a rigorous monitoring regimen as well. In many jurisdictions, courts depend on probation to track and report domestic offender noncompliance. In such places, the establishment of rigorous compliance tracking and reporting systems would be essential to facilitate communication both between community-based programs and probation, and between probation and the court. This would make probation officers a critical agent, in addition to the judge, as they would be responsible for reminding the offenders of their responsibilities and of the likely consequences of noncompliance.

Specific factors have been identified that lead drug offenders assigned to a substance abuse treatment program to perceive greater levels of legal pressure and, in turn, to be more likely to comply with court orders.[24] These factors include:

1. the number of criminal justice agents who explain the program's rules
2. the number of agents who explain the consequences of noncompliance
3. the number of times the offender promises to complete the assigned program
4. the time it would take for the identification of noncompliance
5. the perceived severity of the consequences for program failure

In addition to instructions that offenders receive, the number of times and the number of criminal justice personnel who inform offenders are significant as well. Compliance tends to increase with the frequency with which expectations are conveyed to offenders and the more frequency with which the offenders themselves are required to mirror back their understanding of these obligations.

If such practices were institutionalized, it would represent a dramatic change from the current judicial response to domestic violence. In the recent national survey, only 11 percent of responding courts reported bringing the offender back to court for a compliance check within two weeks of a conviction, and only 25 percent reported doing so within three or four weeks. This contrasts with the weekly or biweekly judicial monitoring that is typical for at least over the first several months in the vast majority of today's drug courts. Even upon receiving a specific report of batterer program noncompliance, only 26 percent of courts reported bringing the offender back to court within two weeks, and only 37 percent reported within three or four weeks. Finally, only 12 percent of responding courts reported having a written protocol delineating the use of sanctions in response to noncompliance with an order to a batterer program. Without the necessary groundwork established through formal protocols, it is no wonder that the national survey found that large numbers of courts do not consistently impose sanctions, and that only a quarter of the responding courts (27 percent) reported always or often imposing jail time.

Currently, most (not all) courts fail to respond swiftly and consistently with severe sanctions to batterer program noncompliance. They have not established the necessary monitoring mechanisms needed to ensure compliance (e.g., through the kinds of reminders and warnings that were shown to be effective with drug offenders). However, this is a fundamentally optimistic perspective, as it proposes that judicial intervention might actually work, if only it was rigorously applied. The drug court example then demonstrates the practical feasibility of such applications in courts across the country. There are currently more than a thousand drug courts nationwide serving adult criminal defendants, as well as another thousand similarly modeled programs serving DWI defendants, juvenile delinquents, or respondents in family abuse and neglect cases.

Implications

The establishment of comprehensive monitoring and sanctioning protocols would immediately enhance offender accountability. Domestic violence offenders would receive complete and accurate information concerning their obligation to complete their court-ordered programs. Offenders would be reminded of these obligations through intensive monitoring protocols involving the court, as well as probation where applicable. Probation officers and judges would demonstrate that the court's orders need to be taken seriously by imposing swift, certain, and consistent sanctions on noncompliant offenders, including probation revocations and imposition of alternative jail sentences. As the theory of accountability would propose, through these actions, the court would convey to offenders, and perhaps to the larger community as well, that domestic violence is a serious offense.

Of equal interest is the significance of lessons learned from drug courts regarding how to change individual offender behavior. Independent of the impact of the actual batterer program, a rigorous monitoring regimen might *in itself* induce greater compliance and deter future violence. In the drug court example, although it is widely recognized that substance abuse treatment can have positive effects, several studies found that judicial oversight was at least as important as, if not more important than, treatment in eliciting positive behavioral changes from the defendants. The evidence with domestic violence offenders is not yet clear or extensive enough to anticipate such outcomes, but they are certainly plausible.

In addition, it is possible that the use of intensive monitoring and sanctioning protocols might lay the groundwork for batterer programs themselves to be more effective. As some have proposed, batterer programs may be understood as part of a larger "intervention system," in which case they are less likely to reduce recidivism by themselves unless that larger system is also functioning. The ideal components of such a system include regular judicial status hearings; swift and certain responses to noncompliance; the use of case managers or court liaisons to link offenders to services and to coordinate compliance reporting back to the court; the availability of a continuum of program modalities, including substance abuse treatment and mental health treatment for suitable offenders; pretrial referral to programs so that the offenders are already engaged by the time of sentencing; and support groups or services for victims and their children.[25] According to this argument, before dismissing the rehabilitative potential of batterer programs, it is first necessary to evaluate them in the context of an overall strong and comprehensive intervention system.

Of course, as a practical matter, most criminal courts lack the necessary resources or staffing to implement this kind of comprehensive system, particularly the use of offender assessments, intensive case management, and court-initiated support groups for victims. Yet the most salient argument ultimately has less to do with these features than with the need for components that enhance judicial coercion. As noted earlier, courts typically lack swift and certain responses to noncompliance; without this legal pressure, batterer programs can be expected to suffer from high failure rates. Therefore, a logical step would be to focus on the judicial component rather than the entire intervention—on precisely the kinds of monitoring and sanctioning practices that could be directly adapted from drug courts. The questions would then become as follows: where such components are strong, do more offenders complete the full dosage of the program, and, ultimately, do those higher completion rates actually lead recidivism to decline or not?

The idea that batterer programs might successfully rehabilitate offenders with sufficient levels of judicial coercion is appealing, but we still lack the empirical evidence needed to support such a position. Most of the previous studies already detect reasonable batterer program completion rates in excess of 50 percent. The recent Bronx experiment reported a completion rate of 61 percent; yet batterer program assignment did not lead to a reduction in official rearrests or victim reports of reabuse. Moreover, as discussed earlier in this article, it is possible that completion by itself merely signals compliance with court orders, not the internalization of program content. Therefore, it appears more plausible that intensive monitoring would deter future violence directly than by creating conditions for the batterer program curricula to have a more positive impact. Of further note, it is conceivable that, by holding more offenders accountable through a rigorous monitoring and sanctioning regimen, completion rates might actually decline— more offenders might be sent to jail and fewer back to the program in response to initial noncompliance.

Therefore, the central conclusion to be drawn is not that the adaptation of key components of the drug court model is likely to achieve all of the goals that have been ascribed to court-ordered participation in batterer programs. Instead, the conclusion is that many of the same types of reforms would provide the greatest *potential* for achieving multiple goals simultaneously. Consequently, where unfeasible, it may not be necessary to pressure resistant court administrators and practitioners to abandon their use of batterer programs or their hopes that batterer programs can rehabilitate. If courts take aggressive steps to strengthen their approach to monitoring and sanctioning, there is no reason for them not to pursue rehabilitation, as long as they simultaneously pursue more immediate benefits as well—increasing accountability and, quite possibly, using intensive monitoring as a mechanism to deter recidivism. A truly rigorous system of accountability would serve not only as an appropriate response to individual offenders but also as a means of conveying the unacceptability of domestic violence to all members of society.

CONCLUSION

Since the 1970s, courts have increasingly relied upon batterer programs as their sentence of choice with domestic violence offenders. With research now calling into question the ability of these programs to change the behavior of individual offenders, there is a need to examine alternatives. The prospects for court intervention in general may not be as bleak as the specific literature on batterer programs implies. Recent studies suggest that specialized domestic violence courts, intensive probation monitoring, and judicial monitoring offer the possibilities of holding offenders more accountable for their violence as well as deterring future violence. Policy makers and practitioners can continue to debate whether and how their use of batterer programs rehabilitates offenders and increases victim safety. But as part of this process, there is a unique opportunity to apply practices that are successful in other contexts in order to make dramatic improvements in our current court response to domestic violence. Despite the lack of research with a domestic violence population, the positive experience of drug courts with judicial oversight is promising. If courts resolve to experiment and change, the years ahead are sure to see dramatic new shifts in domestic violence sentencing strategy. If we are fortunate, this will greatly expand the contribution that courts can make to combat domestic violence.

NOTES

1. B. Ostrom and N. Kauder, *Examining the Work of State Courts* (Williamsburg, VA: National Center for State Courts, 1999).

2. M. Labriola, M. Rempel, C. S. O'Sullivan, P. Frank, J. McDowell, and R. Finkelstein, *Court Responses to Batterer Program Noncompliance: A National Perspective* (New York: Center for Court Innovation, 2007).

3. See P. Frank, "New York Model for Batterer Programs," http://www.nymbp.org/home.htm.

4. S. Palmer, R. Brown, and M. Barerra, "Group Treatment Program for Abusive Husbands," *American Journal of Orthopsychiatry* 62, no. 2 (1992): 276–383.

5. R. C. Davis, B. G. Taylor, and C. D. Maxwell, *Does Batterer Treatment Reduce Violence: A Randomized Experiment in Brooklyn*, final report to the National Institute of Justice (New York: Victim Services, now Safe Horizon, 2000); F. W. Dunford, "The San Diego Navy Experiment: An Assessment of Interventions for Men Who Assault Their Wives," *Journal of Consulting and Clinical Psychology* 68 (2000): 468–76; L. R. Feder and L. Dugan, "A Test of the Efficacy of Court-Mandated Counseling for Domestic Violence Offenders: The Broward County Experiment," *Justice Quarterly* 19, no. 2 (2002): 343–75; and M. Labriola, M. Rempel, and R. C. Davis, "Do Batterer Programs Reduce Recidivism? Results from a Randomized Trial in the Bronx," *Justice Quarterly* 25, no. 2 (2008). Of note, the results of the Brooklyn experiment were ambiguous. The offenders who were randomly assigned to the batterer program were, overall, less likely to reoffend than those not assigned. However, closer inspection of the data led the study's authors to conclude that the batterer program was not in itself responsible for this effect. Instead, it appeared that those whose mandate placed them under court control for a longer period of time (those required to attend a 26-week batterer program as opposed to either an eight-week program or the control group) were less likely to reoffend, but batterer program participation itself was not relevant. That is, reoffending rates did not differ between those who completed the batterer program, those who attended some but not all of the sessions, and those who showed up for none of the scheduled sessions. Also, based on follow-up defendant interviews, those who were assigned to a batterer program did not show any evidence of changed beliefs or attitudes. The authors concluded that rather than through batterer program participation per se, it might be possible to reduce future violence by extending the period of time during which the court retains authority over the case.

6. See J. Babcock, C. Green, and C. Robie, "Does Batterers' Treatment Work? A Meta-Analytical Review of Domestic Violence Treatment," *Clinical Psychology Review* 23 (2004): 1023–53; and L. Bennett and O. Williams, "Controversies and Recent Studies of Batterer Intervention Program Effectiveness," University of Minnesota, Applied Research Forum, 2004, http://www.vaw.umn.edu/documents/vawnet/ar_bip/ar_bip.html.

7. L. Feder and D. B. Wilson, "A Meta-Analytic Review of Court-Mandated Batterer Intervention Programs: Can Courts Affect Abusers' Behavior?" *Journal of Experimental Criminology* 1 (2005): 239–62.

8. E. M. Howle, *Batterer Intervention Programs: County Probation Departments Could Improve Their Compliance with State Law, but Progress in Batterer Accountability Also Depends on the Courts* (Sacramento: California State Auditor, 2006).

9. Labriola et al., *Court Responses.*

10. For an overview of domestic violence court principles and practices, see R. Mazur and L. Aldrich, "What Makes a Domestic Violence Court Work? Lessons from New York," *Judges Journal* 2, no. 42 (2003): 5; and E. Sack, *Creating a*

Domestic Violence Court: Guidelines and Best Practices (San Francisco: Family Violence Prevention Fund, 2002).

11. A. Harrell, J. Castro, L. Newmark, and C. Visher, *Final Report on the Evaluation of the Judicial Oversight Demonstration*, final report submitted to the National Institute of Justice (Washington, D.C.: Urban Institute, 2007); K. Henning and L. Klesges, *Evaluation of the Shelby County Domestic Violence Court: Final Report* (Shelby County, TN, 1999); J. Goldkamp, *The Role of Drug and Alcohol Abuse in Domestic Violence and Its Treatment: Dade County's Domestic Violence Court Experiment* (Washington, D.C.: National Institute of Justice, 1996); and E. Gondolf, *The Impact of Mandatory Court Review on Batterer Program Compliance: An Evaluation of the Pittsburgh Municipal Courts and Domestic Violence Abuse Counseling Center (DACC)* (Indiana, PA: Mid-Atlantic Training Institute, 1998).

12. Gondolf, *The Impact of Mandatory Court Review*; L. Newmark, M. Rempel, K. Diffily, and K. M. Kane, *Specialized Felony Domestic Violence Courts: Lessons on Implementation and Impacts*, final report submitted to the National Institute of Justice (Washington, D.C.: Urban Institute, 2001); and San Diego Superior Court, *Evaluation Report for the San Diego County Domestic Violence Courts* (San Diego, CA: State Justice Institute, 2000).

13. A. Harrell, M. Schaffer, C. DeStefano, and J. Castro, *Evaluation of Milwaukee's Judicial Oversight Demonstration* (Washington, D.C.: Urban Institute, 2006); Newmark et al., *Specialized Felony Domestic Violence Courts*; and San Diego Superior Court, *Evaluation Report*.

14. San Diego Superior Court, *Evaluation Report*.

15. For example, see J. Petersilia, "A Decade of Experimenting with Intermediate Sanctions: What Have We Learned?" *Perspectives* 23 (1999): 39–44; and F. Taxman, "Supervision: Exploring the Dimensions of Effectiveness," *Federal Probation* 66 (2002): 14–27.

16. A. R. Klein, D. Wilson, A. Crowe, and M. T. DeMichele, *Evaluation of the Rhode Island Probation Specialized Domestic Violence Supervision Unit*, final report submitted to the National Institute of Justice (American Probation and Parole Association and BOTEC Analysis Corporation, 2005).

17. D. B. Marlowe, D. S. Festinger, P. A. Lee, M. M. Schepise, J. E. R. Hazzard, J. C. Merrill, F. D. Mulvaney, and A. T. McLellan, "Are Judicial Status Hearings a Key Component of Drug Court? During-Treatment Data from a Randomized Trial," *Criminal Justice and Behavior* 30 (2003): 141–62.

18. M. Rempel, M. Labriola, and R. C. Davis, "Does Judicial Monitoring Deter Domestic Violence Recidivism? Results of a Quasi-Experimental Comparison in the Bronx," *Violence Against Women* 14, no. 2 (2008): 185–207.

19. Labriola et al., *Court Responses*, 35–36.

20. Gondolf, *Batterer Intervention Systems*, 215; and Labriola et al., *Testing the Effectiveness of Batterer Programs and Judicial Monitoring*, 66–67.

21. For example, see S. Aos, P. Phipps, R. Barnoski, and R. Lieb, *The Comparative Costs and Benefits of Programs to Reduce Crime Version 4.0* (Olympia: Washington State Institute for Public Policy, 2001); Government Accountability Office, *Evidence Indicates Recidivism Reductions and Mixed Results for Other Outcomes*, report to Congressional Committees, February (Washington, D.C.: Government Accountability Office, 2005); and D. Wilson, O. Mitchell, and D. L. MacKenzie, "A Systematic Review of Drug Court Effects on Recidivism," *Journal of Experimental Criminology* 2 (2006): 459–87.

22. See A. Harrell and J. Roman, *Findings from the Evaluation of the D.C. Superior Court Drug Intervention Program: Final Report* (Washington, D.C.: Urban Institute, 1998); and Marlowe et al., "Are Judicial Status Hearings a Key Component of Drug Court?"

23. S. Rossman and M. Rempel, "Preliminary Results from the Multi-Site Adult Drug Court Evaluation," paper presented at the Annual Conference of the New York State Association of Drug Court Professionals, Buffalo, NY, 2008.

24. D. Young and S. Belenko, "Program Retention and Perceived Coercion in Three Models of Mandatory Drug Treatment," *Journal of Drug Issues* 22:2 (2002): 297–328.

25. E. W. Gondolf, *Batterer Intervention Systems: Issues, Outcomes, and Recommendations* (London: Sage, 2002); and E. W. Gondolf, "Evaluating Batterer Counseling Programs: A Difficult Task Showing Some Effects and Implications," *Aggression and Violent Behavior* 9 (2004): 605–31.

Chapter 10

Why Sex and Gender Matter in Domestic Violence Research and Advocacy

Molly Dragiewicz

Support for efforts to assist battered women increased and spread alongside the growth of the battered women's movement in the 1970s. Institutionalization of this support culminated in the United States with the passage of the Violence Against Women Act (VAWA) in 1994. Although awareness of domestic violence as a social problem has increased exponentially over the last 30 years, there continues to be confusion about some of the key terms and concepts related to the problem. The lack of clarity in the language and definitions used in discussions about domestic violence can sometimes make it difficult for people to understand the research on the issue. In this chapter, I describe the difference between sex and gender and explain why this distinction is important to understanding domestic violence.

I use the term "domestic violence" to refer to what Evan Stark has called coercive control, "a course of calculated malevolent conduct employed almost exclusively by men to dominate individual women by interweaving repeated physical abuse with three equally important tactics: intimidation, isolation, and control."[1] This is the specific kind of violence and abuse that led to the passage of VAWA and the establishment of an array of services tailored to battered women. The initial provision of emergency shelter services for battered women was informed by women's disproportionate risk of death and injury at the hands of abusive male partners, even after separation. These services also reflect pervasive cultural norms and economic realities that present barriers to women when they try to leave an abusive relationship. In order to fully understand the nature of domestic violence and identify the factors that contribute to it, prevent it, and enable survivors to leave safely, it is necessary to consider the multiple social and structural factors that influence women and men's experiences of domestic violence.

While many scholars recognize the contribution of gender to human violence, others would like to frame domestic violence as "gender neutral." Questions frequently raised by these people include "How can domestic violence be a gender issue if women and men are both sometimes violent?" and "How can domestic violence be a gender issue if it happens in same-sex couples?" These questions are based on the incorrect conflation of the concepts of sex and gender. This is not simply a semantic concern.

Proponents of a "gender-neutral" approach assert that the omission of gender is a panacea that will make domestic violence discourse and services gender inclusive, and therefore welcoming and appropriate for male victims and lesbian victims of partner abuse. Proponents of this approach suggest that, by eliminating the discussion and consideration of gender, barriers to seeking services are eliminated for these groups. However, the failure to consider gender does not address the social realities that shape violence against intimate partners or the barriers to help-seeking that these groups report. The omission of gender makes discussions of domestic violence more imprecise and less accurate, but not more inclusive. Domestic violence discourses and services that acknowledge the pervasive influence of gender norms on human experience, rather than seeking to avoid consideration of these factors, would more accurately be termed "gender inclusive"—they include gender. Widespread confusion about what we mean when we talk about violence and gender results from a lack of clarity about the terms sex and gender in scholarly and popular discussions of domestic violence.

SEX AND GENDER

An elementary discussion of sex and gender might seem unnecessary in a book on domestic violence. However, many scholars and others continue to use the terms interchangeably, often conflating the concepts. This contributes to confusion about the content of the research on domestic violence. Even some experienced scholars continue to make claims about violence and gender based on research that only includes sex variables. For example, John Archer's 2000 meta-analysis of research on sex differences in partner aggression did not include studies on gender (or much of the research on sex differences), but Archer contends that his findings support "gender-free explanations emphasizing individual differences and relationship problems" for aggression rather than social and cultural factors.[2] Some people rely on this kind of slippage to advance their argument that domestic violence is not a gender issue.

So what are sex and gender? "Sex" refers to the biologically based categories "female" and "male." Although a significant minority of babies are born intersex, babies are typically placed in the category female or male at birth based on biological differences like chromosomes and genitalia. The sex categories female and male are consistent over time and across cultures. Researchers in the social sciences often use the categories female and male as variables in their studies. This allows scholars to compare and contrast the experiences of women and men. When scholars use the variables male or female, they can comment on sex differences, or differences between women and men. This does not mean these differences are biologically determined, only that participants in a given study identify as one sex or the other. In order to make comments about the role of gender in human experience, you need to ask about more than just sex.

Although the terms are often used interchangeably, "gender" is a distinct concept from sex. Gender includes the categories "feminine" and "masculine." Femininity describes the traits stereotypically associated with women, like being caring or emotional. Masculinity refers to the characteristics typically associated with men, such as being tough or stoic. Unlike sex differences, which are stable across cultures and historical periods, gender differs according to time and context. For example, women are currently much more likely than men to wear makeup and high heels. This is not a permanent or universal state of affairs. At other times in history and in other countries, men have also worn high heels or makeup without being considered effeminate.

The distinction between sex and gender is widely recognized in the social sciences, where it has been taught in introductory courses for more than 40 years. However, awareness of the distinction does not always translate into clear and accurate use of the terms in research or writing. The sex-gender distinction was explicitly articulated in 1972 by Ann Oakley, who distinguished sex, the biological categories female and male, from gender, the socially imposed characteristics associated with the sexes and labeled femininity and masculinity. More recent formulations of gender reflect a growing awareness of the ways that gender is context specific, changes over time, and is created in the performance of everyday actions from what we wear to how we walk.

Contemporary understandings of gender also make the connection between cultural pressures around gender and sexuality, noting that social pressure to conform to gender norms is often tied to heterosexuality. In other words, women who are not considered feminine enough are taunted with homophobic slurs like "dyke." Men who are not considered to be masculine enough are mocked with anti-gay slurs like "fag." Both of these examples show how women and men who are judged by others to be inadequately enthusiastic or successful at conforming to dominant gender norms have their sexuality called into question. This brings with it the threat of more than just verbal abuse and insults. Hate crimes show how violence is used to enforce gender and sexual norms. Matthew Shepard was killed because he was gay. Brandon Teena (whose story was the subject of the film *Boys Don't Cry*) was killed because he lived life as a man despite being biologically female.

The sex-gender distinction is conceptually important because it challenges the biological determinism that pervades popular notions about human violence. If differences in rates of violence between the sexes are significantly rooted in culture and socialization rather than biology, they are changeable. Prevention and intervention would target those changeable factors contributing to the etiology and persistence of violence. If the causes of violence are "essential," or biologically determined, on the other hand, cultural and structural changes are ill advised as useless or even harmful. Individual treatment or avoidance strategies would be more helpful. The sex-gender distinction is therefore at the crux of debates about how (and whether) to prevent and respond to domestic violence.

PATRIARCHY

It is impossible to have an adequate discussion of sex, gender, and violence without also talking about patriarchy. Gender is not only socially constructed but also imbued with hierarchical power relations that are relevant at the individual, interpersonal, and cultural levels. Allan Johnson describes societies as patriarchal to the extent that they constitute male privilege "by being male dominated, male identified, and male centered."[3] Johnson argues that, although maleness is the "taken-for-granted" normative category against which women are judged, white men "are often made invisible when their behavior is socially undesirable and might raise questions about the appropriateness of male privilege."[4] Sylvia Walby writes, "Patriarchy is not a historical constant."[5] It changes form over time, and different components of it become more or less important in different contexts. As explanations of patriarchal peer support for violence assert, the unevenness of patriarchal values and realities across time and context contributes to variation in violent behavior among men.[6]

Contemporary understandings of patriarchy do not suggest that every man has power over every woman in every context, or that all women and all men share the same status. However, they do imply that being biologically male conveys historically specific advantages (i.e., different advantages in different societies) to men relative to women. Although these advantages are independent of race and class, they interact with race and class systems as well as other sources of social advantage that may reinforce or diminish privileges based on "simply being men." Patriarchy is explicitly *not* a single factor, although that is sometimes claimed by those antagonistic to feminism. It is instead the intersection of numerous factors relevant at multiple levels of the social ecology.

The authorization, in policy and practice, of putatively "gender-specific" approaches to violence that recognize the experiences of women versus ostensibly gender-neutral perspectives implicitly based on the experiences and authority of men poses a multivalent threat to existing gendered, patriarchal power relations. Anti-feminist men's reactions to perceptions of the institutionalization of women's authority (as when a judge believes a woman's report of violence and issues a restraining order, or police believe a woman's account of her injuries and arrest her male partner) indicate that this threat may be heightened where the state is called upon to enforce the "female" perspective, as in the following example.

> Men risk jail, legal bills, and the loss of family, house, and job if they so much as argue with a woman. This is the result of the widespread "zero tolerance" policy which defines domestic assault as any physical contact, no matter how innocuous. The charge is laid by the state even if no harm has been done. Ostensibly this policy protects women but its real purpose is to emasculate men and persecute heterosexuals. It's another front in the Rockefeller-based elite's campaign to degrade society, destroy family, and decrease population by making heterosexuality unworkable.[7]

This kind of overwrought response to the enforcement of assault laws despite the relationship of the abuser to the victim points to the symbolic importance of men's jurisdiction over the definition of violence in heterosexual relationships. This particular example also links the male prerogative to violence against women with heterosexuality. Like this objection to the enforcement of domestic violence laws, calls for gender neutrality are not really neutral. They seek to reassert patriarchal gender relations by returning things to the way they were before women's reports of domestic violence were taken seriously. While the loss of the prerogative to define what counts as violence in heterosexual relationships certainly constitutes a loss of privilege for men, this does not mean men are being discriminated against. The objection here is to women's authority, not men's subordination.

THE CONTEXT AND COST OF GENDER BLINDNESS

The demand for formal equality is one tactic that has been appropriated by those who oppose feminism and other movements for social justice. Formal equality is a legal concept that says all people should be treated the same, according to the same laws and rules. In the past, some feminists used calls for formal equality to attack laws that explicitly discriminated against women. The idea was that by removing legal barriers to women's participation in the workplace, for example, women would be able to attain equal status to men. While this approach may sound appealing on the surface, formal equality has been criticized as exacerbating inequality in practice. While laws may ignore sex or gender, they are applied in a world where these categories continue to be important organizing principles of social life. In other words, rules that ignore gender can have very different outcomes for women and men because of the context in which they are applied.

The best way to understand the problem with demands for formal equality is to look at an example. Contemporary laws against assault ostensibly apply equally to women and men. However, prior to VAWA and state laws targeting domestic violence, police officers routinely declined to enforce laws against assault when the perpetrator was a husband and the victim was his wife. Most police precincts had explicit or implicit policies favoring nonintervention in these cases. The law was blind to the sex of the perpetrator and victim. However, dominant ways of thinking about the family defined it as a private sphere beyond the reach of the law, with men as head of household. Because men are most often assaulted by male acquaintances, and women are most often assaulted by their male partners, this pattern of nonintervention disproportionately affected female victims. This example shows how laws and policies that ignore sex and gender can still have highly gendered outcomes in the real world.

Efforts to oppose the acknowledgment of gender have perhaps focused on violence because this is one of the areas where women's perspectives have arguably had the largest impact on law and policy, with significant implications for both women and men. Although anti-feminism is alive and well, opposition to men's violence against women has expanded, and many popular approaches to the problem carry the implicit threat of validating feminism's complaints about ongoing and institutionalized patriarchy and sexism. As a result, anti-feminist commentators regard VAWA and other efforts to address violence against women as key targets in the battle against feminism.

Demands for gender neutrality in scholarly and popular commentary on domestic violence run counter to the competing trend toward the recognition of the difference between sex and gender, the socially constructed and context-specific nature of gender, and their significant implications for scholarship on public health and social justice. For example, medical research is moving toward a distinction between sex and gender and recognition of the gendered aspects of human experience that contribute to differences in women's and men's health. A

Canadian report on health research argues, "The inclusion of sex and gender as variables in health research is now recognized as good science, and the omission of these variables leads to problems of validity and generalizability, weaker clinical practice and less appropriate health care delivery."[8] Another article observes,

> Unfortunately, the language of difference in the biomedical literature is often imprecise, conflating the two terms [sex and gender] and treating them as virtual synonyms. This imprecise use is not only linguistically problematic but has serious implications for future research, clinical practice and treatment, as well as our very understanding of the nature of the health outcomes and status differences that we are studying. Without a strong conceptual and theoretical understanding of the distinction originally intended by those who clarified the difference between sex and gender, confusions are replicated.[9]

The medical writing on the sex-gender distinction makes clear that human behavior is gendered in significant ways that have serious implications for health and well-being. Rather than improving medical practice and research, ignoring the distinction between sex and gender has resulted in the production of flawed data that impair our understanding of the factors contributing to health and disease. Medical examples can perhaps help those interested in violence to understand why it is important to include gender in order to improve health and well-being.

Gender has an impact on health in a variety of ways. Powerlessness and lack of control underlie much of the exposure to HIV/AIDS amongst women in Africa. Disproportionate barriers (that is, relative to men) in access to resources such as food, education, and medical care disadvantage women throughout the developing world. Risk-taking behavior is the norm amongst males throughout the world. Socially defined traits often stereotype men and women as having fixed and opposite characteristics such as active (male) and passive (female), and rational (male) and emotional (female). The language of medicine and its underlying philosophy have equated, and may still equate, male with normal, leaving female to be considered as "other" or, perhaps, abnormal. Both women's and men's occupational and behavioral roles, constrained by social norms, can result in hazardous, though different, exposures to dangers and illness. Any of these aspects of gender may intercede in the pathway from an individual to his or her health.[10]

In other words, leaving gender out has not made health research more inclusive or more effective. Instead, it has hindered our ability to understand the nature of health problems and what is required for prevention. Medical researchers seeking a fuller understanding of health have not set out to limit the factors considered in order to develop a more generic understanding; they have moved toward specificity in

the interest of improving the accuracy of their research and its effectiveness in real-life applications. Scholars of violence would be well
advised to take a similar tack, seeking to understand and address the
contributing factors specific to violence in different contexts in order to
increase, not decrease, our focus and capacity for understanding.

Antifeminists appear to be particularly opposed to the recognition of
gender as a relevant factor in domestic violence. Antifeminists display
a range of inaccurate interpretations of the word gender in their objections to it. One activist criticizes a book for "misusing gender as if the
term were a polite reference to sex," suggesting that the term was created by feminists because they are antisex: "Having reduced it to [sic]
a dirty biological act, feminists dare not speak of sex, so they pervert
grammar, which is only the beginning of their assault against our civi-
lization."[11] Regardless of the reasons for the inaccurate use of the terms
sex and gender, the point is that it creates problems for understanding
domestic violence.

WHY IS GENDER ESSENTIAL TO UNDERSTANDING
DOMESTIC VIOLENCE?

Gender matters because domestic violence, like other forms of
human violence, exhibits both sex and gender differences. These differences are important because they help to tell us how and why domestic violence happens. Sex and gender differences are relevant to
decisions about where and how to expend scarce resources for domestic violence prevention, intervention, and treatment.

Despite frequently repeated claims to the contrary, the research continues to document significant sex differences in domestic violence.
Men are far more likely to kill their intimate partners than women are.
Men are also more likely than women to injure their partners and to
assault them frequently. They are many times more likely than women
to sexually assault their partners. Men are more likely than women to
continue abusing their partner after they leave the relationship, for
example by stalking, raping, or killing them after separation. These sex
differences are not questioned by the vast majority of those who assert
that domestic violence is "sex symmetrical." Rather, proponents of sex
symmetry tend to dismiss these forms of violence, claiming that women
are just as violent to their spouses as men, or reducing these sex differences to asides such as "Men are just as likely as women to be victims of
domestic violence (though women are more likely to be injured)." I argue
that the omission and marginalization of these forms and consequences of
violence, all of which are integral to domestic violence, render claims of
sex symmetry profoundly inaccurate and misleading.

A small number of commentators do explicitly dispute the research
on sex differences in domestic violence. Some antifeminists even

dispute the homicide statistics, attributing unsolved homicides to angry wives: "[N]o one knows for sure which sex kills the other more. In a second, we'll see why it's likely that more wives kill husbands, but until the government is willing to collect data about the three female methods of killing, we can only do an educated guess."[12] Others claim that evidence of women's greater injury is suspect because they believe that women's injuries are self-inflicted and arrests of men are based on false allegations.

Sex differences in homicide and injury rates relate in fairly obvious ways to the prioritization of emergency services for female victims of domestic violence. Male victims are at much less risk of harm or death during and after domestic violence and on average have greater resources with which to avoid entrapment in an abusive relationship. Many additional factors also point to the sex asymmetry of domestic homicide. Dobash, Dobash, Wilson, and Daly argue,

> Studies of actual cases lend no support to the facile claim that homicidal husbands and wives "initiate similar acts of violence." Men often kill wives after lengthy periods of prolonged physical violence accompanied by other forms of abuse and coercion; the roles in such cases are seldom if ever reversed. Men perpetrate familicidal massacres, killing spouse and children together; women do not. Men commonly hunt down and kill wives who have left them; women hardly ever behave similarly. Men kill wives as part of planned murder-suicides; analogous acts by women are almost unheard of. Men kill in response to revelations of wifely infidelity; women almost never respond similarly, though their mates are more often adulterous. The evidence is overwhelming that a large proportion of the spouse-killings perpetrated by wives, but almost none of those perpetrated by husbands, are acts of self-defense. Unlike men, women kill male partners after years of suffering physical violence, after they have exhausted all available sources of assistance, when they feel trapped, and because they fear for their own lives.[13] (Internal citations omitted)

This passage illustrates the extent to which the meaning of "symmetry" must be distorted in order to suggest that women's and men's violence against partners is similar in its etiology or dynamics, or that sex and gender are irrelevant to it. Symmetry means that the sides of something are reciprocal, proportionate, and balanced. As a whole, the body of research on domestic violence does not indicate that it fits that definition.

Although the above quotation refers to consistently documented *sex* differences in domestic homicide, virtually all of these sex differences are likely contributed to by dominant *gender* norms. For example, there is a special word for men whose wives are unfaithful, "cuckold," and no parallel term for a woman whose husband has been unfaithful. Men whose wives cheat on them find their masculinity challenged, while women's femininity is not called into question by men's cheating. Men's homicide of women in response to suspicions of infidelity is based in part on the different social expectations for women's and men's sexuality and how it reflects on their spouses.

These examples show how the interaction of gendered patriarchal cultural expectations and interpersonal stress is one of the key components of patriarchal peer support for domestic violence. Theories about violence that discuss stress without paying attention to the gendered nature of those stresses are likely to miss an important part of the big picture. For example, research pointing to unemployment as a stress contributing to domestic violence needs to take into account that being a breadwinner is central to most men's masculine identity. Not only is being unemployed stressful because it means less income, but it is also an assault on men's identity *as men*. Research on violent men consistently indicates that the need to defend their "manhood" plays a key role in their violence against men and women. Women do not report similarly gendered motives for violence.

Beyond contributing to motives for lethal and sublethal violence, gender shapes domestic violence in myriad other ways. Looking at abused mothers can help to illustrate the impact of gender. Women continue to be responsible for the majority of child care. The expectation that women take on this primary responsibility means that women are more likely than men to take on employment that is flexible or limited in order to accommodate child care. Some women leave the workforce altogether to care for children. Being away from work, or taking on limited employment to facilitate child care, has permanent implications for women's earning power.

In the event of domestic violence, a stay-at-home mom will probably have a very difficult time securing a job that will support her and her children. The lack of affordable child care will further harm her ability to attain economic self-sufficiency. Meanwhile, men's relative freedom from child care responsibilities during the relationship, including housework, grocery shopping, and other personal services still mostly performed by women, permanently enhances fathers' earning power. When a battered woman goes to court to try to get sole custody of her children to protect them from further exposure to abuse, the judge may well count her low income against her, ruling that the father can provide a better home for the child because he has more money. In addition, the judge may assume that the father will soon enter another relationship with another woman who will provide surrogate care for the children, while the newly divorced mom will likely be working full-time to make ends meet, and is less likely to remarry. As a result, women's disproportionate child care during the marriage can actually harm their chances at getting custody when they leave an abusive husband.

Abusive fathers often take advantage of the closeness that comes from mothers' disproportionate caregiving role. Many abusers threaten to harm or kill the children to keep the mother from leaving, or get her to bargain away child support in return for more time with the kids. Many abusers also use the expectation that mothers care for their children as a tool in emotional abuse, criticizing their partner's parenting skills and accusing them of being bad mothers. Others make false claims of child abuse to Child Protective Services in order to punish women for reporting the violence they have experienced or for seeking a divorce. In turn, child protection workers often hold mothers responsible for exposing children to men's violence rather than holding the violent man himself accountable for his behavior. All of these examples show how gendered social expectations contribute to the dynamics of violence and abuse as well as having an impact on the ability to leave an abuser safely. I am sure that readers can think of many other ways that gender norms can shape abusive behavior and its implications.

Ironically, the difficulties that men have when their interpersonal relationships do not match community expectations for male domination are a recurrent theme in antifeminist objections to recognizing the contributions of patriarchy and gender to domestic violence. Antifeminist writers claim that men report domestic violence much less often than women and use this claim to explain why there are so few reports of women battering men and so few men seeking services as victims of domestic violence. Consider the following examples:

- "Men who are abused by their wives are fodder for jokes."[14]

- "The one defining characteristic of most abused men is that they are extremely embarrassed by their predicament. Most men who have reached out for help have been laughed at or scorned. They are often portrayed as weak and cowardly."[15]

- "Men are also less likely to call the police, even when there is injury, because, like women, they feel shame about disclosing family violence. But for many men, the shame is compounded by the shame of not being able to keep their wives under control. Among this group, a 'real man' would be able to keep her under control. Moreover, the police tend to share these same traditional gender role expectations."[16]

- "In 18th- and 19th-century France, a husband who had been pushed around by his wife would be forced by the community to wear women's clothing and to ride through the village, sitting backwards on a donkey, holding its tail. . . . This humiliating practice, called the charivari, was also common in other parts of Europe. . . . Modern versions of the charivari persist today. Take Skip W., who participated in a program on domestic violence aired on the short-lived Jesse Jackson Show in 1991. Skip related how his wife repeatedly hit him and attacked him with knives and scissors. The audience's reaction was exactly what male victims who go public fear most: laughter, and constant, derisive snickering."[17]

These same commentators insist that a sex- and gender-blind approach to domestic violence is the answer to these men's problems. They argue that taking a formal equality tack and talking about domestic violence as if it were sex symmetrical would make men more comfortable in asking for help. This logic is fatally flawed, however. As these quotations illustrate, patriarchal gender norms are a primary reason that violence against men is not taken seriously. The quotations above all point to the threat of feminization, made menacing by the low status accorded to women in patriarchal societies, as a shaming tactic used to punish men who fail to dominate their wives or partners. This enforcement of patriarchal gender norms is precisely what feminists talk about in their references to domestic violence as shaped by gender and patriarchy. Patriarchal gender norms have negative implications for men as well as women, but ignoring sex and gender does nothing to loosen their grip.

Domestic violence varies according to the relative status of both partners, and there is still much to learn about these variations. However, if we accept the antifeminists' own claims about why men allegedly don't report victimization by women (which as of yet are based on speculation, not research), neither leaving gender out nor talking more about male victims will solve the problem. In order to decrease the shame of being dominated by a woman, it would be necessary to challenge the patriarchal gender norms for dominance, invulnerability, and male supremacy that are the source of that shame. After all, the existing vocabulary for men who do not dominate "their" women is already rich, frequently used, and highly gendered: hen pecked, pussy whipped, browbeaten, fag, pussy, queer, and so on. The solution would appear to be in addressing the source of shame for each of these terms—challenges to male supremacy and heteronormativity.

WHAT ABOUT SAME-SEX DOMESTIC VIOLENCE?

Some commentaries point to violence in gay and lesbian relationships as evidence that domestic violence is not gendered. Although explicit discussion of domestic violence against gay men is notably absent from the antifeminist analysis of domestic violence against men, the assertion that same-sex couples experience domestic violence, too, is used to challenge both the existence of patriarchy and the relevance of gender to domestic violence. Antifeminist commentators suggest that feminist analyses of domestic violence as gendered and gender roles as tied to patriarchy are invalidated by the existence of women who are abusers and victims who are men. This claim is also based on a misunderstanding of the concept of gender, which is about socially prescribed roles rather than biological sex or sexuality.

Claims that domestic violence in same-sex relationships proves that gender is irrelevant also ignore the influence of homophobia on violence against gay and lesbian people. As we saw above, homophobia is linked to rigid patriarchal gender roles. Hatred of gays and lesbians is based on naturalized ideas about sexuality, which prescribe heterosexual relationships and stigmatize homosexual ones, in part because they contradict cultural ideals for gender-polarized heterosexual couples. Rather than refuting the influence of gender, domestic violence in gay and lesbian relationships demonstrates how gender norms shape violence and the likelihood it will be reported. Domestic violence in gay and lesbian relationships, by highlighting the specific needs of the community, reveals the need to respond to different forms of domestic violence in ways that consider their social context. The fact that women can abuse women and men can abuse men does not cancel out the importance of gender to violence and abuse. We need to create services that are explicitly designed for gay and lesbian victims of violence and can address the additional barriers that homophobia creates alongside gender.

Writing about gay men and domestic violence also sometimes denies that gender has anything to do with abuse; for example, Patrick Island and David Letellier state, "Domestic violence is not a gender issue, since both men and women can be either batterer or victim."[18] However, later in their book there is a section entitled "Batterers Are Unclear on the Concept of Masculinity." In this section, rigid gender roles are named as a fundamental contributing factor to abuse: "All violent men who batter and abuse their partners are obviously confused about the concept of masculinity."[19] Like the antifeminist discussion of battering, this is clearly a question of vocabulary. Although Island and Letellier describe their desire to expand the work of the battered women's movement, they are not aware of the sex-gender distinction and so misunderstand feminist claims about gender to the extent that they claim to reject them while their writings actually reinforce many feminist claims about gender and domestic violence.

WHAT DOES THIS MEAN FOR VIOLENCE PREVENTION AND INTERVENTION?

Although much media attention has been devoted to the debate over whether sex differences are relevant to domestic violence, sex differences are of limited interest to those who are primarily concerned with understanding violence in order to prevent it, decrease it, and effectively intervene in it. There is no question that the research on domestic violence shows marked sex differences in the dynamics, frequency, and outcomes of domestic violence, especially when domestic violence–related sexual assault, separation assault, stalking, and homicide are included. The domestic violence research has not focused on assessing whether or not sex differences exist in domestic violence, but rather on the dynamics of the violence. These dynamics show that gender matters considerably to victims and perpetrators.

I argue that those who would enhance our collective understanding of domestic violence need to be familiar with the research on the causes and character of domestic violence, including the copious body of research produced by feminist scholars and others who recognize gender and sex differences in domestic violence. At the very least, those presuming to critique feminist perspectives on domestic violence must understand the basic terms and concepts of this research. In addition, researchers and commentators should work to articulate the different dynamics and outcomes of domestic violence based on gender, sexuality, power, and other salient factors, rather than blurring these important distinctions by making claims about symmetry.

Efforts to maintain the invisibility of socially constructed patriarchal gender norms pose significant problems for work to prevent and intervene in domestic violence. Antifeminist authors are so concerned with keeping gender out of the discussion about domestic violence that they fail to take seriously even the incontrovertible sex differences in domestic violence dynamics, outcomes, and fatalities. This requires silencing survivors of violence, those who work with them, and the parts of batterer narratives that implicate patriarchal gender roles in the violence. It also requires dismissing much of the research on domestic violence in favor of a narrow focus on survey research emphasizing self-reported counts of a limited number of aggressive acts taken out of context. In silencing many of those who are most familiar with domestic violence, antifeminist approaches impede the dissemination of accurate information and obstruct efforts to prevent this violence and intervene effectively on behalf of survivors. In ignoring the dynamics, outcomes, and causes of violence, gender-blind approaches render prevention unlikely or impossible in favor of interventions after abuse has occurred.

Proponents of a "gender-free" perspective on domestic violence claim they are protecting men from women's rhetorical and physical violence by refuting explanations of domestic violence that take gender into account. They claim that research that acknowledges the role that gender plays in domestic violence intentionally obscures the fact that men are also victims, and women are also perpetrators, in order to shore up bogus claims about the relevance of gender and the patriarchal culture that shapes it. Those who insist upon excluding gender from discourse on, and consideration of, domestic violence often claim that such an omission is the only way to *really* know about domestic violence.

Contrary to antifeminist claims, however, the lack of comprehension of feminist research demonstrated by the conflation of sex and gender demands a more careful consideration of feminist writing about domestic violence, not its dismissal. Not only is domestic violence a gendered phenomenon, but the failure to distinguish between sex and gender impedes accurate and adequate understandings of the problem. In order to be truly inclusive, those concerned with domestic violence need to listen carefully to batterers, survivors, advocates, and researchers in order to better understand the multiple, context-specific causes of human violence and potential avenues for prevention.

NOTES

1. E. Stark, *Coercive Control: How Men Entrap Women in Personal Life* (New York: Oxford University Press, 2007), 5.

2. J. Archer, "Sex Differences in Aggression between Heterosexual Partners: A Meta-analytic Review," *Psychological Bulletin* 126, no. 5 (2000): 668.

3. A. G. Johnson, *The Gender Knot: Unraveling Our Patriarchal Legacy* (Philadelphia: Temple University Press, 2005), 5.

4. Johnson, *The Gender Knot*, 155.

5. S. Walby, *Theorizing Patriarchy* (Oxford: Basil Blackwell, 1990), 173.

6. M. D. Schwartz and W. S. DeKeseredy, *Sexual Assault on the College Campus: The Role of Male Peer Support*. (Thousand Oaks: Sage, 1997), 42–49.

7. H. Makow, "The Dawn of the Feminist Police State," http://www.save-themales.ca/000202.html (accessed February 16, 2008).

8. L. Greaves et al., *CIHR 2000: Sex, Gender and Women's Health*, Vancouver, British Columbia: Centre of Excellence for Women's Health, British Columbia Women's Hospital and Health Centre, http://www.cwhn.ca/resources/cihr2000/cihr2000.pdf (accessed March 1, 2008).

9. J. R. Fishman, J. G. Wick, and B. A. Koenig, "The Use of 'Sex' and 'Gender' to Define and Characterize Meaningful Differences between Men and Women," *Agenda for Research on Women's Health for the 21st Century* 2 (2008): 15–20, 5.

10. S. P. Phillips, "Defining and Measuring Gender: A Social Determinant of Health Whose Time Has Come," *International Journal for Equity in Health* 4, no. 11 (2005), 1–4, http://bmc.ub.uni-potsdam.de/1475-9276-4-11/1475-9276-4-11.pdf (accessed April 2, 2008).

11. J. R. Graham, "Save the Males: A Review," 2006, http://www.california-menscenters.org/files/Transitions_2006.5b.pdf (accessed March 1, 2008).

12. W. Farrell, "If Your Man Knew You Feared His Potential for Violence," 1999, http://www.ejfi.org/DV/dv-6.htm (accessed January 3, 2008).

13. R. P. Dobash, R. E. Dobash, M. Wilson, and M. Daly, "The Myth of Sexual Symmetry in Marital Violence," *Social Problems* 39, no. 1 (1992): 71–91, 81.

14. K. Dunn, "Truth Abuse: The Media's Wife Beating Hype," *New Republic* 211, no. 5 (1994): 16–18.

15. C. Hoff Sommers, "Figuring Out Feminism: How Feminists Abuse Statistical Information to Serve Their Political Agenda," *National Review* 46, no. 12 (1994): 30–34.

16. Hoff Sommers, "Figuring Out Feminism."

17. A. Brott, "Battered Men: The Full Story," 1994, http://www.vix.com/men/battery/commentary/brott-hidden.html (accessed November 23, 2000).

18. D. Island and P. Letellier, *Men Who Beat the Men Who Love Them: Battered Gay Men and Domestic Violence* (New York: Haworth, 1991), 16.

19. Island and Letellier, *Men Who Beat*, 49.

Index

abandonment fears, 175*t*

abuse denial, 143

abusers: domestic violence sentences, 106–7, 108; use of alcohol/drug, 119–20. *See also* batterers; offenders

abusers, following arrest and prosecution, 137, 155–59; change in, 149–55; on courts, 141, 157–58; criminal history, 125, 143; experience, 140–43; on gender bias, 141–42; loss, 150–52; money matters, 142–43; narratives, 137, 143–49; overview, 137–40; on police, 140–41, 142, 156; on race, 142; religiosity, 149–50; stigmatized identity, 152–55

abusive fathers, 211

abusive men programs, 161, 176–77; assessment and intake procedures, 169; cognitive restructuring, methods and handout example, 166–67; comparison groups, 170; completers, 182–83; coordination with other community systems, 173–75; culturally sensitive approaches, 168–69; didactic-confrontational, 165; dropouts, 170, 182; effectiveness, 171–73; formats and methods, 162–65; history, 161–62; innovations and unanswered questions, 175–76; motivators for program

attendance, 167–68; outcome measures, 169–70; process-psychodynamic group, excerpt, 165–66, 174–75*t*; prognostic indicator, 173; psycho-educational programs, 165; quality control, 170; quasi-experimental comparison of programs, 171; standards and practice guidelines, 176; studies comparisons, 171–73; therapeutic programs, 164–65. *See also* batterer programs; prison programs

access to resources/services, 31–33, 207; for African American women, 32; for battered lesbians, 32–33

accountability, 182, 185–88, 195

active motives, for women's violence: control, 60–61; retribution, 61–62

advocates, 5, 23, 35–36, 130; and abuser programs, 162; and client collaboration, 42–43; editing battered women's stories, 39–40, 41; making counterstories, 42; silencing client voices, 40; and victims, relationships, 102

African American women, 27–28, 29–30, 31–33; access to resources and services, 32; fighting back against abusers, 38; legal system confrontation, 33–34

age factor and reabuse, 125–27

alcohol/drug abuse, 119–20. *See also* drug court; substance abuse
AMEND, 176
Anglo-American common law, 5
anti-social and generally violent batterers, 174*t*
antifeminism, 206, 208, 211, 212, 214
antistalking law, 14
anxiety, 63
arrest decisions, 94–95, 96, 118–19; callers, 83–84, 117; of children, 81; differential impact, 81; increased role of, 80–81; normative ambiguities in family and relationship, 86–87; offender absent upon police arrival, 83; offender behavior and demeanor, 86; offender's criminal history, 84–85, 107, 117–19; offense seriousness, 82–83; power restriction, 71, 94; protocols for domestic violence, 48–49; role of race, 82; use of weapons by offenders, 84; victim demeanor, 85–86; victim preferences, 87; of women, 81–82
assaults, 121

battered lesbians. *See* lesbians
battered women, fighting back against abusers, 23; access to shelters/services, 31–33; African American women, 38; characteristics, 24–27; community and societal constraints, 27–29; credibility, 30–31, 37–39; legal system confrontation, 33–35; lesbians, 28–31; owning narratives, importance of, 35–41; self-image, 29–30; stereotyping, 30–31; victim narrative, rewriting, 41–43
battered women's movement, 40
batterer programs, court's intervention, 130–31, 179–80, 197; challenge of predominance, 190; cognitive-behavioral approach, 183–84; comparison of programs, 183–84; compassion model, 184; couples counseling, 184; court orders to, 180–82; debate, 180, 183; drug courts, lessons learned from, 190–97; effectiveness, 183; efficacy-effectiveness distinction, 185; new directions, 188–90; problems, 184–85; psycho-educational approach, 184; psychodynamic approaches, 184; rigorous compliance tracking and reporting systems establishment, 193–94; as a tool for accountability, 185–88; as a tool for rehabilitation, 182–85; unstructured self-help groups, 184. *See also* abusive men programs; prison programs
batterers, 11; abuse denial, 143; abuse excuse, 144; abuse justifications, 144–45; abuse minimizations, 143–44; anti-social and generally violent, 174*t*; categorization, 120–21; cheating partner, 148–49; emotionally violent/abandonment fears, 175*t*; gender and violence, 146–48; harm inflicted by, 115–17; perception of victimization, 137–38, 142, 155; self-defense story, 144, 145–46; stopping, 129–31; suppressor type, 174*t*; typical batterers identified, 117–21. *See also* abusers; offenders
battering, 1, 2, 7, 14; as a course of conduct, 15–16; decontextualization of, 4, 7, 11, 12; power and control (*see* power and control manifestations). *See also* domestic violence
blaming, 146

California law, 182
chain of dominance, 3
child, as a tool to emotional violence, 211
childhood trauma/abuse, influence on women's violence, 62
Children's Court of Conciliation, 92–93
coercive control, women's abusive behavior, 55–56, 58, 201. *See also* power and control manifestations
cognitive restructuring, 163; methods and handout example, 166–67

cognitive-behavioral approach, 183–84. *See also* cognitive restructuring; skills training

community service sentences, 189

community and societal constraints, for women who fight back, 27–29

compassion model, 184

Conflict Tactics Scale, 50

conflicts and violence, 147–48

conjoint approaches and gender-specific ones, integrated, 176

connection between incarceration and religiosity, 159n.4

control, women's motive for violence, 60–61. *See also* power and control manifestation

control tactics awareness, 163

counseling, 162; couples counseling, 184

counterstories, 42. *See also* narratives

course of conduct, battering as, 15–17, 21n.46

court orders to batterer programs, 180–82

Crawford v. Washington (2004), 99

credibility, 9–10, 30–31, 37–39

crime, transactional model of, 6

criminal careers, 127–28

criminal history of abusers/offenders, 84–85, 107, 117–19, 125, 143

criminal justice system, 1–2, 4, 5, 50; case example, 7–9; domestic violence cases, 9; evolution, 15–17; new sentencing strategies, 190; and offenders (*see* offenders and criminal justice system); transaction-bound nature, 6

criminal law paradigms, 6–7; problem of injury, 6–7, 16; problem of time, 6, 16

criminalization of domestic violence, 1–2, 4–5, 6, 48; criminal justice evolution, 15–17; effects of incompleteness, 12–13; in historical context, 4–5; progression, 13–15; as a course of conduct, model statute, 21n.46

Crown Prosecution Service (CPS), 97

culturally sensitive approaches, 168–69

defendant motive, in domestic violence trial, 11

defense of children, women's motive for violence, 60

defensive motives, for women's violence: defense of children, 60; fear, 60; self-defense, 59

depression, 63

didactic-confrontational programs, 165

domestic violence: courts for, 188; criminalization of (*see* criminalization of domestic violence); as pattern of behavior, 2; perpetrator treatment program, 49 (*see also* *specific programs*). *See also* battering

domestic violence cases/trials. *See also* prosecution of domestic violence

domination, 3–4, 7. *See also* coercive control; power and control manifestations

drug courts: applications, 193–95; compliance check, 193–94; components, 195–96; duration of intervention, 192–93; implications, 195–97; lessons learned from, 190–97; qualifications, 192–93

Duluth model, 49, 164, 181. *See also* control tactics awareness

economic self-sufficiency, of women, 210

EMERGE, 162, 164, 169

emotionally violent batterers, 175t

English Common Law, 71

equality, formal, 205–6

evidence, 19n.23, 20n.29, 20n.44, 99

family agencies, referrals to, 93. *See also* shelter services

family and intimate relationships loss, 151

family court, 92

family disputes intervention, police attitudes toward, 71–73

family/household member, defined,
    21
family systems approaches, 163, 164,
    174*t*
fear: women's motive for violence, 60;
    of abandonment, 175*t*
federal criminal law, 15
federal laws, 129
felony, 126, 130
femininity, 203
financial loss, 151
financial penalties, 189–90
firearms, 129
first offenders, 129–30
formal equality, 205–6
formal services to survivors of
    domestic violence, 23

gay, 212
gender, defined, 203
gender bias, 115, 141–42; in prosecu-
    tion, 109
gender blindness, context and cost of,
    205–8, 212, 214
gender difference, 63
gender inclusive approach, 202
gender-free approach, 214
gender-neutral approach, 202
gender-sex distinction, 203–4, 207

hate crimes, 203
heterosexual relationships, violence
    in, 205
homicide, 116, 128; sex differences in,
    209
homophobia, 28–29, 34, 213

incarceration, 107–9. *See also* arrests
incident-based criminal statutes, 6,
    8–9, 13–14
independent domestic violence
    advisors. *See* advocates
injury, due to domestic violence, 56,
    58
injury rates, sex differences in,
    209
intimate partners violence/homicides,
    115–16, 128–29; gender symmetry
    in, 50; male and female differences,

128; women's violence (*see*
    women's violence)
intimate terrorism, 56
isolating and atomizing violence, 6–7
isolation, 10, 29, 55

judges, skeptic view on battered
    women's claims, 37
judicial monitoring, 188, 189
juror apathy, in domestic violence
    trial, 11–12

leader gender, 176
learned helplessness, 23
legal consciousness, 159n.1
legal paradigms. *See* criminal law
    paradigms
legal system, women's confrontation,
    33–35; African American women,
    33–34; lesbians, 34–35
lesbians, 28–29, 30–31; access to
    resources and services, 32–33; and
    homophobia, 28–29, 34; legal
    system confrontation, 34–35
lethal reabuse, 128–31; abusers'
    characteristics, 128–29; intimate
    homicide, 128
loss, following encounters with police
    and courts, 150–52

male, source of shame, 212
male intimate partners, women's
    violence with, 47
marital rape, 19n.21
masculinity, and violence, 203, 146–48
metal illness. *See* psychological
    disorder
Metropolitan Police, 87
misdemeanor assaults, 71, 78, 93, 96,
    100, 108
Misdemeanor Complaint Bureau,
    93–94
misdemeanor domestic assaults, 119,
    126, 121, 179
monitoring system, 180, 181, 188–89,
    193–95
motivations for women's violence,
    59–62; active motives, control,
    60–61, retribution, 61–62; defensive

motives, defense of children, 60, fear, 60, self-defense, 59
motive of defendant, in domestic violence trial, 11
mutually violent relationship, 58–59

narratives, of abusers. *See* abusers, following arrest and prosecution
narratives, of women who fight back: importance of owning, 35–41; rewriting, 41–43
National Probation Association, 92
New Haven study, on women's violence and victimization, 51; coercive control, 47, 55–56; focus group, 51–52; injury, 56, 58; physical aggression, 52–53, 57–58; psychological aggression, 55, 57; sexual coercion, 53, 58; stalking, 53–55
New York model of batterer programs, 181–82
no-drop policies, 5, 97, 100, 138
nonintimate family abuse, 118
nonphysical abuse, 4, 6
nontransactional realities, 19n.23
North Carolina law, 92

offenders, and criminal justice system, 115; assaults, 121; criminal history, 84–85, 107, 117–19; first offenders, 129–30; harm inflicted by batterers, 115–17; lethal reabuse, 128–31; reabuse, basic factors, 125–28, likelihood, 122–25, 128; stopping repeat batterers, 129–31; systemic abuse, 121–22; typical batterers identified, 117–21
orientation groups, 167
owning narratives, importance of, 35–41

patriarchy, 204–5, 210, 212
perpetrators, 3; age factor, 118; mental illness, 120
physical abuse, beyond the, 2–4
physical abuse/violence, 4, 122
physical aggression, women's abusive behavior, 52–53, 57–58

police: actual behavior, 75–76; arrests (*see* arrest decisions); attitudes toward intervention in family disputes, 71–73; batterers on, 140–41; best practice implications, 87–88; as crime fighter, 72, 74; current practice, 80; during the Great Depression, 70; fears, 73–74; marinating public order, 70; practices change, reasons for, 77–80; response by victims, 73–74; response to domestic violence, 69; role in private disputes, 70, 72; screening and downgrading of domestic violence calls, 76–77; statutory limits, 71; traditional response, 69–87; training, 74–75; whipping, 72
policing, 157. *See also* monitoring; tracking
political gag order, 28
posttraumatic stress disorder, 63
power and control manifestations, 2, 3, 4, 6, 16, 49
presumptive arrest policies, 137–38, 155, 156–57
prison programs, 175; abusive men programs; batterer programs
pro-prosecution policies, movement toward, 95–104
probation monitoring, 188, 193–94
problem of injury, 6–7, 16
problem of time, 6, 16
process-psychodynamic group, excerpt, 165–66, 174–75t
proportionality, 38
prosecution of domestic violence, 9, 91, 179; conviction, 107–8; defendant motive, 11; difficulties in tracking, 97–98; future directions, 109–11; historical perspective, 91–95; impacts, 104–9; juror apathy, 11–12; newspapers review, 100; post-1970s, 95–104; prosecutor-victim contact, 101–2; prosecutors, commitment and determination, 99–101; reforms, reasons for slowness in, 96–99; reoffending, 107–9; sentencing convicted abusers,

106–7; specialized courts, 92–93, 101, 102, 103; victim participation, 99, 103; victim retraction, 103–4; victim credibility, 9–10; victim safety, 104–5; victim satisfaction, 105–6
prosecution policies, 137–38, 155
protective/restraining order, 125
psychiatric disorder intervention, 64
psycho-educational programs, 165, 184
psychodynamic approaches, 184
psychological abuse, reduction of, 176
psychological aggression, women's abusive behavior, 55, 57
psychological disorder, 120
psychological functioning, influence on women's violence, 62–63

race, 38, 142
racism, 33
Racketeer Influenced and Corrupt Organizations Act (RICO), 20n.43
RAVEN, 162
reabuse, 173; abuse careers, 127–28; age factor, 125–27; factors, 125–28; lethal, 128–31; likelihood, 122–25, 128; stopping repeat batterers, 129–31; during trial period, 123–24
recidivism, reduction, 121
rehabilitative programs. See batterer programs
relationship, 7
religiosity, effect of incarceration, 149–50
remedial steps, informal, 94
reoffending, 107–9
restorative justice, 109, 110
retribution, women's motive for violence, 61–62

same-sex violence, 212–13. See also gay; lesbians
selection bias, 182
self-defense, 24, 47; batterers' narratives, 144, 145–46; women's motive for violence, 59
self-image, of women who fight back, 29–30
self-talk, 166

sentences: community service sentences, 189; for convicted abusers, 106–7, 108
separation assault, 14
serial abusers, 122–25
sex, defined, 203
sex and gender in domestic violence, 201, 202–4; gender blindness, context and cost of, 205–8, 212; importance, 208–12; medical examples, 207; patriarchy, 204–5, 210, 212; same-sex, 212–13; for violence prevention and intervention, 213–15
sex asymmetry approach, 209
sex equity in abuse, 115. See also women's violence
sex role resocialization, 163
sex symmetry approach, 208, 209
sex-gender distinction, 203–4, 207
sexual coercion, women's abusive behavior, 53, 58
Shadows of the Heart (video), 168
shared gender, 33
shelter services, 162, 201–2
silencing survivors of violence, 40, 214
situational couple violence, 56
skills training, 163
stalking, 14, 116–17; law against, 14–15; women's abusive behavior, 53–55
stereotyping and credibility, women who fight back, 30–31
stigmatized identity, 152–55
substance abuse, 63, 119–20; and offender interventions, integrated, 176; treatment programs (see drug courts)
suffering, 2–3. See also beyond physical abuse
suppressor type batterers, 174t
Supreme Court, 10, 12, 99
systemic abuse, 121–22

therapeutic jurisprudence, 109–10
therapeutic programs, 164–65
Thurman v. City of Torrington (1984), 48
tracking system, 181
trauma-based interventions, 164, 176

treatment length, 176
treatment program, 49
trust, loss of, 151–52

unemployment, as a factor of violence, 210
unstructured self-help groups, 184

victim, 24, 117; credibility, in domestic violence trial, 9–10; empowerment, 110; narrative, rewriting, 41–43; participation, in prosecution of domestic violence, 99; retraction from cases, 103–4; safety, 104–5; satisfaction, 105–6
victim-friendly proceedings, 101
victimization, 31, 57
violence: prevention and intervention, 213–15; to defend, 24, 25; to express identities, 24
Violence Against Women Act (VAWA), 201, 206

violent resistance, 25
weapons, 129
wife beating, 5
women battering men, 211–12. *See also* sex and gender
women's violence, in intimate relationship, 47; background, 48–51; characteristics, 62–63, childhood trauma/abuse, 62, psychological conditions, 62–63; court-mandated treatment program, 49; due to violence from male partner, 56–57; impacts, 58–59; implications, 63–64; and men's violence, difference between, 57–58; motivations (*see* motivations for women's violence); and victimization, a study (*see* New Haven study)

younger abusers, likelihood of reabuse, 125

About the Editors and Contributors

Evan Stark is a professor at the Rutgers School of Public Affairs and Administration, Rutgers University–Newark; the Department of Women and Gender Studies, Rutgers University-New Brunswick; and the University of Medicine and Dentistry School of Public Health, where he chairs the Department of Urban Health Administration. His most recent book is *Coercive Control: How Men Entrap Women in Personal Life* (Oxford University Press, 2007).

Eve S. Buzawa is a professor and the chairperson of the Department of Criminal Justice at the University of Massachusetts–Lowell. She is the co-author of the best-selling *Domestic Violence: The Criminal Justice Response* (Sage, 2003) among other works.

Jennifer E. Caldwell is currently attending the University of South Carolina, where she is pursuing her PhD in clinical-community psychology. Her research interests include motives for men and women perpetrating intimate partner violence, its physical and psychological health consequences for male and female victims, and partner violence prevention.

Molly Dragiewicz is Assistant Professor in the Department of Criminology, Justice, and Policy Studies at the University of Ontario, Institute of Technology, Canada. She received her PhD in cultural studies from George Mason University. Her research interests include violence and gender, human rights, and the antifeminist fathers' rights movement. She teaches courses on human trafficking, public policy, violence and gender, and qualitative methods.

Leigh Goodmark is an associate professor of law and Director of the Family Law Clinic at the University of Baltimore School of Law. Prior to joining the School of Law, Professor Goodmark directed the Children and Domestic Violence Project at the American Bar Association Center on Children and the Law. Professor Goodmark has represented hundreds of women who have experienced domestic violence in protective order, custody, visitation, and divorce proceedings.

Keith Guzik is an assistant professor in the Department of Sociology at Bloomfield College. His research on mandatory arrest and no-drop prosecution policies has previously appeared in *Law and Social Inquiry* and *Law and Society Review*. This research is also the basis for a forthcoming book, *Arresting Abuse: Mandatory Legal Interventions, Power, and Intimate Abusers*, which will appear in Summer 2009.

David Hirschel is professor of criminal justice at the University of Massachusetts–Lowell and professor emeritus of criminal justice at the University of North Carolina at Charlotte. Before entering academics, he worked in the juvenile justice systems in both England and the United States, and served as criminal justice coordinator for the Erie County, New York, Department of Anti-Rape and Sexual Assault. Dr. Hirschel's primary research and teaching interests are in victims of crime, particularly spouse abuse; international criminal justice; and legal issues in criminal justice. He has been involved in many funded research projects, both as a principal investigator and as a consultant, and has provided assistance to a wide variety of criminal justice agencies and social service organizations.

Andrew R. Klein served as chief probation officer of the Quincy District Court for more than two decades before retiring in 1997. As chief, he helped develop the first domestic violence court in the country as well as the first specialized domestic violence supervision program. Since retirement, he has served as a principal investigator on numerous research and evaluation grants for multiple federal, state, and county government and nonprofit agencies covering a diverse range of areas including family and domestic violence, Temporary Assistance for Needy Families (TANF), victim rights, batterer intervention, faith-based rural domestic violence programming, and residential prison substance abuse treatment. He is editor and columnist of Thomson-West's *National Bulletin on Domestic Violence Prevention*, a monthly publication, and author of two text- and trade books, *Alternative Sentencing, Intermediate Sanctions and Probation* and *The Criminal Justice Response to Domestic Violence*, as well as numerous journal articles.

Christopher D. Maxwell is Associate Dean for Research and Associate Professor in criminology at Michigan State University, and he is Associate Research Scientist in the Institute for Social Research at the University of Michigan. He earned a PhD in criminal justice from Rutgers University. Dr. Maxwell's research largely focuses on understanding the causes, prevention, control, and consequences of intimate partner violence. He has served as the principal investigator on many major research projects funded by a variety of government agencies and private foundations.

Michael Rempel is the Research Director for the Center for Court Innovation in New York City. He has been actively involved in projects concerning drug courts, domestic violence, and applications of problem-solving principles in traditional court settings. He recently directed a statewide evaluation of New York's adult drug courts; a randomized experiment testing the impact of batterer programs; and a national survey examining how courts respond to the noncompliance of domestic violence offenders with judicial orders. Currently, he is principal investigator of a national study of specialized domestic violence courts and co-principal investigator of a multi-site evaluation of adult drug courts across the country. He is co-editor of *Documenting Results: Research on Problem-Solving Justice* (2007).

Amanda L. Robinson is senior lecturer in criminology at Cardiff University, Wales, United Kingdom. She earned her PhD in interdisciplinary social science at Michigan State University. Dr. Robinson conducts empirical research in the American and British criminal justice systems. Specifically, her research interests include police discretion and decision making, community policing, domestic and sexual violence against women, hate crime, sentencing policy and practice, and specialist courts.

Daniel G. Saunders is Professor of Social Work and Co-Director of the Interdisciplinary Research Program on Violence across the Lifespan at the University of Michigan. He established one of the nation's first intervention programs for men who batter and helped to establish crisis and advocacy programs for battered women in the 1970s. His research, teaching, and service center on the problems of dating and domestic violence. His specific studies focus on offender and supervised visitation program evaluations, the traumatic effects of victimization, and the responses of professionals and the public to dating and domestic violence.

David L. Snow, is a professor of psychology in psychiatry, Yale Child Study Center, and epidemiology and public health at Yale University

School of Medicine, and is Director of the Consultation Center and Division of Prevention and Community Research, Department of Psychiatry. Dr. Snow has extensive experience in the design and evaluation of preventive interventions in community settings and in research aimed at identifying key risk and protective factors predictive of psychological symptoms, substance use, and family violence.

Tami P. Sullivan, is Assistant Professor and Director of Family Violence Research and Programs in the Division of Prevention and Community Research, Department of Psychiatry, Yale University School of Medicine. Dr. Sullivan's research focuses on understanding the relationships among intimate partner violence, posttraumatic stress, and co-occurring substance use. She is particularly interested in risk and protective factor research in an effort to develop preventive interventions. Dr. Sullivan directs programs for domestic violence offenders, as well as training and consultation to domestic violence and substance use programs in the community.

Suzanne C. Swan is an assistant professor in the Department of Psychology and the Women's and Gender Studies Program at the University of South Carolina. Dr. Swan conducts research in the area of intimate partner violence, with particular interests in women who use violence in intimate relationships. She is also working to develop preventive interventions to engage male college students in becoming involved in preventing violence against women. Dr. Swan teaches courses on the Psychology of Women, Women's Health, Social Psychology, and Relationship Violence.

Deborah Tuerkheimer is a professor of law at the University of Maine where she teaches courses on Criminal Law, Criminal Procedure, Evidence and Domestic Violence. She formerly prosecuted domestic violence in the New York County District Attorney's Office. Professor Tuerkheimer focuses her scholarship and has published extensively on the role of criminal law in the lives of women and children. Effective July 1, 2009, she will be a professor of law at DePaul University College of Law.